Global Governance in the New Era

Institute of Russian, Eastern European and Central Asian Studies, CASS · Russian International Affairs Council
Editors

Global Governance in the New Era

Concepts and Approaches

Editors
Institute of Russian, Eastern European and
Central Asian Studies, CASS
Beijing, China

Russian International Affairs Council
Moscow, Russia

ISBN 978-981-19-4331-7   ISBN 978-981-19-4332-4   (eBook)
https://doi.org/10.1007/978-981-19-4332-4

Jointly published with China Social Sciences Press
The print edition is not for sale in China (Mainland). Customers from China (Mainland) please order the print book from: China Social Sciences Press.

This book is the joint research result of Institute of Russian, Eastern European and Central Asian Studies at the Chinese Academy of Social Sciences and the Russian International Affairs Council (SEP. 2021– MAR. 2022)
Translation from the Chinese language edition: "新时代全球治理: 理念与路径" by Fuzhan Xie et al., © China Social Sciences Press 2022. Published by China Social Sciences Press. All Rights Reserved.
© China Social Sciences Press 2023
This work is subject to copyright. All rights are solely and exclusively licensed by the Publisher, whether the whole or part of the material is concerned, specifically the rights of translation, reprinting, reuse of illustrations, recitation, broadcasting, reproduction on microfilms or in any other physical way, and transmission or information storage and retrieval, electronic adaptation, computer software, or by similar or dissimilar methodology now known or hereafter developed.
The use of general descriptive names, registered names, trademarks, service marks, etc. in this publication does not imply, even in the absence of a specific statement, that such names are exempt from the relevant protective laws and regulations and therefore free for general use.
The publishers, the authors, and the editors are safe to assume that the advice and information in this book are believed to be true and accurate at the date of publication. Neither the publishers nor the authors or the editors give a warranty, expressed or implied, with respect to the material contained herein or for any errors or omissions that may have been made. The publishers remain neutral with regard to jurisdictional claims in published maps and institutional affiliations.

This Springer imprint is published by the registered company Springer Nature Singapore Pte Ltd.
The registered company address is: 152 Beach Road, #21-01/04 Gateway East, Singapore 189721, Singapore

Preface I

China's Insight and Endeavor to Address the Deficit of Global Governance

At this critical moment featuring intertwined challenges from unprecedented shifts in the global landscape and the centennially rare COVID-19 pandemic, continued changes in cooperative and confrontational relations among major powers as well as complicated spillover effects by a new round of scientific and technological revolution, the world now faces rising instabilities and growing uncertainties, putting human beings at a historical crossroads that would determine the future direction of global governance.

First of all, the COVID-19 pandemic has exacerbated the dilemma for global governance. Bearing the brunt of the sudden and strong pandemic, the global economy suffered its worst recession since the Great Depression in the 1930s. As the virus spreads all over the world and the combat against this enemy becomes a long-term reality, the global economic and political order has undergone profound and complex changes. The most noticeable result is that the pandemic has accelerated the decoupling of the global economy in both objective and subjective dimensions. In the objective dimension, the pandemic has disrupted global production and hindered logistical connection: The global supply chain is now in stagnation while the industrial chain and value chain have been forced to change. In the subjective dimension, the virus has triggered the resurgence of economic nationalism, as more and more countries are now increasingly inward-looking, which has accelerated the localization and regionalization of the supply chain, the industrial chain, and the value chain. In addition, to deal with the impact of such decoupling, some countries, despite their true intention to advocate openness, have adopted policy measures that actually promote the decoupling of this kind into a reality, resulting in a *decoupling paradox*, i.e., efforts against something ultimately result in it.

What's more, the ongoing COVID-19 pandemic has increased political instability at both international and domestic levels. At the international level, the virus has highlighted the differences among a variety of cultures and the corresponding models of their social governance, giving some countries the chance to ignite hostility and confrontation among different ideologies and values. At the domestic level, the pandemic has accelerated the accumulation of social malcontent, which puts racial conflicts, religious disputes, refugee crises, and other issues on the rise, triggering political turmoil in some countries. Global governance in the post-pandemic era, therefore, faces more complex problems and complicated challenges.

Secondly, the game among great powers intensifies the competition for superiority in global governance. Over the past few decades, emerging markets and developing economies have maintained a "two-speed growth" trend with weak recovery in developed countries, vibrant growth in many developing countries, and a more balanced landscape of the world economy. However, in order to suppress the developmental momentum of other countries and to unilaterally maximize their own interests, a few major powers still stick to Cold War mentalities and believe in the logic of a zero-sum game, so they pursue the law of the jungle and want the survival of the fittest. Therefore, these countries try to organize small blocs or groups in the international community, recklessly wielding the stick of sanctions as well as continuously creating contradictions and differences everywhere in the world, which pushes global affairs into disorder, division, and even confrontation.

In this context, the competition and cooperation among great powers or major groups in the world have been deeply adjusted, while the severity of battling in and the usage of weapons for global governance have become increasingly prominent. When it comes to many global challenges, some major powers use global governance as an instrument to seek their own interests and force other countries to undertake more obligations, making global governance increasingly deviate from its original intention of international coordination and worldwide cooperation. As for the progress to modernize the World Trade Organization, to restructure the governance of the International Monetary Fund and to optimize the running mechanism of the World Bank, differences and contradictions among relevant parties have been on the rise due to the obstruction and interference by a few great powers who, further, try to turn climate change, cybersecurity, artificial intelligence and other fields into battlegrounds in international games.

Last but not least, a new round of technological revolution has generated new challenges for global governance. Such round of scientific and technological revolution is a process for the coordinated transformation of technological and economic paradigms. It is, by all means, an important driving force for the structural development of global governance, while it is also without doubt a double-edged sword with high complexity and uncertainty. It is true that scientific and technological advancement promotes economic growth, boosts industrial innovation, and improves social welfare; it also exerts many spillover effects on the global political and economic order, therefore causing new problems for global governance.

Preface I

At present, the science and technology have become strategic fields for the competition among major powers: For example, technological innovation in the energy sector is triggering a deep round of adjustment for the worldwide geopolitical landscape, while the IT industry and the cyberspace have gradually become new grounds for both shared interests and source of conflicts. At the same time, scientific and technological progress will change the form of warfare and bring unprecedented challenges to world peace. The widespread use of digital technologies in the military field has opened up a new front parallel to the conventional one while, in particular, the fast development and wide deployment of artificial intelligence systems such as lethal autonomous weapons (LAWS) will make it possible that a war might be waged without any prior human decision. However, incompatible with the rapid advancement of scientific and technological innovation is the corresponding governance, with a multitude of problems such as outdated mechanisms, imperfect rules, and imbalanced sectorial development. In conclusion, the international community still fails to respond to these problems and challenges in global governance, in a systematic and effective way.

Together we live in such a small metaphorical world village, where countries across the globe are highly interdependent and the international community has a shared future with overlapping interests and common grounds. In the face of increasingly severe global challenges and unabated global governance deficits, all countries in the world, including China and Russia, must be the advocates for and contributors to global governance, particularly by providing brain and brawn for building a better world for mankind.

In this regard, the **priority** is to practice genuine multilateralism. The response to global challenges requires strong global efforts, which is the primary consensus held by the international community. In the face of increasingly prominent global problems, no country can stand atop or be immune to external threats, nor can it maintain its own security or guarantee its interests alone. All countries in this world need to work together with coordinate actions in a responsible manner. Multilateralism, therefore, is the major direction and dominant logic that must be adhered to when dealing with global governance deficits and promoting the corresponding reform. When it comes to the new round of industrial revolution driven by cutting-edge IT advancement, the significance of multilateralism has become even more prominent. Multilateral cooperation is not only an institutional paradigm for a country to share the dividends of industrial revolution to a greater extent, but also a fundamental way-out to effectively cope with the challenges in this context. To make multilateralism a powerful tool for addressing global challenges, it is highly necessary to firmly uphold genuine multilateralism and make real practice correspondingly, instead of exercising hegemonism and unilateralism in the name of multilateralism. The concept of *Genuine Multilateralism* means to adhere to openness and inclusiveness instead of closeness and exclusiveness; to stay committed to international law and international rules instead of seeking one's own supremacy; to stick to consultation and cooperation instead of conflict and confrontation, as well as to stay committed to keeping up with the times instead of rejecting change. In order to embrace and practice genuine multilateralism, we must uphold the basic norms of international relations based on the purposes and principles of the UN Charter, champion the multilateral trading system based on the World Trade Organization, and promote the establishment of a more open, dynamic, inclusive, and sustainable world economy.

The **second** task is to promote common development across the globe. There are many problems around the world being our headaches today, while development is one and the only *master key* to solve many of these thorny issues. Only by adhering to worldwide common development can we find a chance to resolve the root causes of conflicts. At this moment, there are more than 200 countries and regions in this world with more than 2500 ethnic groups and over 7 billion people. On this blue planet, we live together and should therefore conduct equal dialogue and cooperation, share the outcomes of economic globalization and global economic growth, and thus achieve common development, progress, and prosperity. To this end, all countries in this world should work together to promote the liberalization and facilitation of trade and investment, and promote the development of economic globalization in a more open, inclusive, mutually beneficial, balanced, and win-win manner. Across civilizational boundaries, we must talk to each other instead of building estrangement, learn from each other instead of launching conflicts, and achieve coexistence among all instead of seeking superiority over others. As the world's largest developing country, China has made great contributions to the common development of the world while achieving its own advancement. China's contribution rate to world economic growth has ranked indisputably the first for many years in a roll and has become a key driver of global growth. On September 21, 2021, President Xi Jinping proposed a global development initiative during the general debate of the 76th United Nations General Assembly, systematically expounding the policy and action framework for achieving inclusive development. This is another important public good and cooperative platform that China has provided to the international community in addition to the Belt and Road Initiative, which has helped to bring global development to a new stage featuring balance, coordination, and inclusiveness.

The **third** mission is to perfect the global governance system. For quite a long time, many global challenges have not been effectively solved, with the substantial deficit still in place. As the existing system of global governance cannot adapt to the newly emerged trends, the necessity and urgency of reforming the current global governance system are all the more increasing. The future development of the global governance system means so much for every individual country, for the prosperity and stability of the world, and for the common destiny of mankind. It is therefore the responsibility and obligation of every one of us to perfect the global governance system. In this process, all countries in the world must adhere to the idea of *Collaboration, Coordination, and Cooperation*, advocate extensive consultation and joint contribution, as well as give full play to each country's advantages, so that outcomes and benefits are shared by all. We must say no to the philosophy of zero-sum games or the idea of winner-takes-all. Differences should be resolved through dialogue and consultation, instead of by the arbitrary decision from a single country or the one-sided ruling from a particular bloc. We must adhere to fairness, justice, equality, openness, transparency, and inclusiveness, yet never put our own interests above that of the whole mankind or coerce other countries into following our own ideas. We must stand firm to support a rule-oriented system of international rules that is to be both formed and obeyed jointly by all countries with no exceptions, let alone taking advantage of it in favorable situations and discarding it while self-interests cannot be achieved. In addition, we must adhere to the spirit of *Common but Differentiated Responsibilities*, i.e., making contributions and undertaking responsibilities that are commensurate with a country's strengths and rights. As a participant, constructor, and contributor to the current global governance system, China has always been committed to exploring both ideas and models for cooperation with other countries, so as to promote the development of the global governance system in a just and reasonable manner.

Forth, it is also essential to promote theoretical innovation regarding global governance. In global governance, correct theoretical thinking can enhance people's ability to know and follow the laws in which things develop, while erroneous ideas will lead the world into astray or even abyss. With the in-depth development of globalization and the increasing number of global challenges, theoretical guidance tends to be more and more important for the practice in this aspect. At present, global governance challenges and global governance deficits are prominent; yet, the Western-centric global governance theoretical paradigm fails to function and even comes to a deadlock, making it even more urgent to construct a louder voice for developing countries in global governance and to promote the innovation of global governance theories. Both China and Russia have long history and excellent cultural tradition, with large numbers of theorists and thinkers who have promoted the progress of human civilization. As China and Russia participate in the construction and restructuring of global governance, they also show great motivation and potential for theoretical innovation. Being the highest academic institution of Chinese philosophical studies and social sciences, the Chinese Academy of Social Sciences is willing to work with academic circles of various countries, including Russian colleagues of course, to focus on the research in theoretical questions and practical issues of global governance, and particularly summarize both positive and negative results by past and present mechanisms of global governance, so as to constantly promote the innovation of global governance concepts, viewpoints and academic ideas, as well as to provide theoretical and intellectual support for addressing the deficit in global governance.

At this moment, human civilization has come to a historical period of extraordinary significance. Faced with the ultimate questions in this era of *what happened to the world and what should we correspondingly do*, President Xi Jinping made a loud and powerful voice in his speech at the UN headquarters in Geneva, calling for joint efforts to build *a community with a shared future for mankind* as China's response to current challenges shared by the whole world. Further, China will continue its commitment to promoting the global consensus of peace, development, fairness, justice, democracy, and freedom for all mankind, double its effort in practicing genuine multilateralism and advancing shared growth for the globe, as well as take initiatives to participate in the construction and reformation of the global governance system, therefore providing both insights and endeavor for addressing the deficit of global governance and usher in a better future for all.

Beijing, China

Fuzhan Xie
Former President of the Chinese
Academy of Social Sciences

Preface II[1]

International Relations Amid the Pandemic

We could rest assured that COVID-19 will be defeated, sooner rather than later. The excessive angst and fear we currently feel will gradually subside, while our science will find effective antidotes so that people can look back on the pandemic years as a ghastly dream.

At the same time, it is also clear that a post-pandemic world will be quite different from the world we knew before. The argument that the world needs a massive shake-up to move to the next stage of its development has been quite popular ever since the end of the Cold War. Some prophesied that this would come as a result of a profound economic crisis, while others argued that a large-scale war may well be on the cards. As often happens, however, what turned the world on its head came as if out of nowhere. Within a short span of just a few months, the COVID-19 pandemic sheds light on all the many contradictions and setbacks of our age. It went on to outline the trajectory for economic prosperity, scientific breakthroughs, and technological advancements going forward, opening up new opportunities for self-realization and fulfillment. The question pertinent today is: Who will be able to best exploit the new reality and take advantage of the opportunities that are opening up? And how?

COVID-19 has also left its mark on the current architecture of international relations.

At the turn of the century, it was mired in crisis. The end of the Cold War toward the late twentieth century effectively signaled the beginning of the transition from the bipolar world order established in the wake of the Second World War to a model that had yet to be created. A bitter struggle would unfold as to what the new world order had to be, with the issue still unsettled today. A number of states, as well as

---

[1] The article was originally published in "Rossiyskaya Gazeta" on September 13, 2021, https://rg.ru/2021/09/13/igor-ivanov-mezhdunarodnaia-sistema-v-celom-vyderzhala-pervyj-udar-pandemii.html.

non-state actors, willing to take advantage of this uncertainty in global affairs and redistribute the spheres of influence in the world are what it ultimately boils down to. In a sense, such a scenario should have come as no surprise since the contradictions between the profound changes encompassing the public domain and the rigid model of international relations established in the mid-twentieth century by the powers victorious in the Second World War have continued to grow in recent decades.

The COVID-19 pandemic has proven to be a stern and unprecedented test of strength that has revealed the limits of the current architecture of international relations. Previous crises—be they financial turmoil, struggle against terrorism, regional conflicts, or something else—were, in fact, temporary and rather limited in their implications; however, they were severe. The COVID-19 pandemic has affected every country in the world, regardless of their political regimes and social conventions, economic prosperity, and military might. The pandemic has exposed the fragility of the modern world as well as the growing risks and challenges, and if ignored, they could plunge the world into a descending spiral of self-destruction.

The pandemic continues, which means we have yet to draw a final conclusion on its consequences for the system of international relations. That being said, a number of tentative conclusions are already taking shape.

Point 1. Globalization, despite its obvious side effects, has already changed the face of our world, irreversibly making it truly interdependent. This has been said before; however, the opponents of globalization have tried—and continue to try—to downplay its consequences for modern society. As it happens, they would like to think of globalization as little more than an episode in international life. Although it has been going on for quite some time now, it is nevertheless incapable of changing the familiar landscape of the world. The pandemic has raised the curtain on what the modern world truly looks like. Here, state borders are nothing more than an administrative and bureaucratic construct, as they are powerless to prevent active communication among people, whether spiritual, scientific, informational, or of any other kind. Likewise, official borders are not an obstacle to the modern security threats proliferating among states. The waves of COVID-19 have wreaked havoc on all countries. No nation has been able to escape this fate. The same will also happen time and again with other challenges unless we recognize this obvious reality to start thinking about how states should act amid the new circumstances.

Point 2. The international system withstood the initial onslaught despite the incessant fearmongers prophesying its impending collapse. Following a rather brief period of confusion and helplessness, the United Nations, the World Health Organization, the World Bank, G20, and other global and regional organizations got their act together (albeit some better than others), taking urgent action to contain the pandemic. This proves that the system of international relations that was constructed after the Second World War still functions, although it is far from perfect or devoid of shortcomings.

In a similar vein, the fight against the pandemic has demonstrated that many international structures are increasingly out of step with modern reality, proving incapable of mobilizing quickly enough to make a difference in our ever-changing world. This, once again, pushes to the fore the issue of a reformed United Nations system (and other international institutions), while the issue is progressively getting even more urgent. Moving forward, the international community will likely have to face challenges no less dangerous than the current pandemic. We have to be prepared for this.

Point 3. As the role of international institutions in global affairs weakens, centrifugal tendencies gain momentum, with countries—for the most part, global leaders—starting to put their national interests first. The global information war surrounding various anti-COVID-19 vaccines is a prime example of this. Not only has it seriously upset successes in the fight against the pandemic, but it has also added a new dimension to mutual distrust and rivalry. The world has effectively fallen back to the "rules" of the Cold War era, when countries with different sociopolitical systems were desperate to prove their superiority, with little regard for common interests such as security and development.

Pursuing such a policy today is fraught with grave consequences for every nation, since new security threats care little for borders. The events in Afghanistan should serve as a lesson for us all, showing that any serious regional crisis, even in a most remote corner of the world, will inevitably have global implications. Therefore, we are all facing a stark choice: either unite against these new challenges or become hostage to the various extremists and adventurers.

Point 4. Some political leaders have been quick to use the challenges of the pandemic as a pretext to strengthen the role of the state at the expense of fundamental democratic principles and binding international obligations. This may be justified or even necessitated at a time of the most acute phases of a severe crisis, when all available resources need to be mobilized to repel the threat.

However, one gets the impression that some politicians are increasingly in the groove for these extended powers and would very much like to hold onto them, using the likelihood of new crises as a justification. This line of thinking could prove to be an insurmountable obstacle to a new model of international relations to be established in accordance with modern reality, where states would be expected to pool their efforts in the interests of global security and development.

Point 5. As always happens in times of profound crises, the international community is looking to major powers and their leadership for guidance. The future course of history in all realms of life, naturally including international relations, will hinge on what these countries choose to do, deciding whether solidarity prevails over national egoism. President Putin's initiative to hold a meeting of the heads of state of the permanent UN Security Council members could be a good starting point to foster understanding and seek new ways of moving forward. We cannot keep putting off a frank and thorough conversation about the future world order, as the costs of new delays could be too grave for everyone to handle.

Moscow, Russia

Igor Ivanov
President of the Russian International
Affairs Council, Minister of Foreign
Affairs of the Russian Federation
(1998–2004), Russian President
of CASS-RIAC China–Russia Think
Tank Exchange Mechanism Program

Contents

The World: New Global Governance Needed

What Should We Expect of "Globalization 2.0"? 3
Andrey Kortunov

Global Governance: History, Logic, and Trend 15
Zhang Yuyan

"Black Swans" of Globalization 27
Alexey Fenenko

A World on the Verge of Total Chaos 39
Nikolay Plotnikov

Open Multilateralism: Evolutionary Results of the International Institutions

Idea and Act: Multilateralism in the Governance of Eurasia 51
Zhuangzhi Sun

International Institutions in Contemporary Global Politics 65
Irina L. Prokhorenko

Reshaping Global Governance with Genuine Multilateralism 71
Zhongping Feng and Zhigao He

UN Security Council Reform: Pro et Contra 87
Dmitriy Kiku

Non-neutral Global Governance and BRICS Cooperation 91
Xiujun Xu

Balance of Power Versus Balance of Interest: Great Powers in Globalization

Illusions of a New Bipolarity 111
Alexey Gromyko

China–Russia–US Trilateral Relations Amid Global Governance in the New Era 117
Dapeng Pang

China–Russia–India Cooperation in an Era of Global Transformation 131
Yi Jiang

Transport Corridors, Belt and Road Initiative, Eurasian Economic Union, and Economic Prosperity Across the Eurasian Continent 145
Evgeny Vinokurov

China–Russia–Europe Relations in a New Era of Global Governance 153
Yonghui Li

Global Governance: Solutions for the Future

Environmental Governance: A Perspective from Industrial Civilization to Ecological Civilization 167
Yongsheng Zhang

Challenges for the Environmental Restructuring of the Global Economy 185
Natalia Piskulova

Role, Competition and Cooperation: China, Russia and the United States in Global Climate Governance and Low-Carbon Green Growth 193
Hongfeng Xu

Outlook: An Era of Eurasia for Global Economic Governance 223
Zhonghai Li

Post-COVID-19 Sanction Policies 237
Ivan Timofeev

A World Crowned with "Corona": Path to Increased Cooperation or Isolation? 255
Natalia Romashkina

The World: New Global Governance Needed

What Should We Expect of "Globalization 2.0"?

Andrey Kortunov

Currently, humankind goes through a protracted and painful process of deglobalization. It remains to be seen whether this process was historically predetermined and unavoidable; if this is not the case, one can speculate about who should be held responsible for such a turn of events. In any case, the global financial crisis of 2008–2009 and the post-crisis recovery of 2010–2013 sent a clear signal that globalization would hardly be a linear—let alone exponential—process. In the aftermath of the crisis, some of the key dimensions of global connectedness (international trade, foreign direct investments) returned to their pre-crisis levels only by the mid-2010s, only plummeting once again by the end of the decade. Centrifugal trends, both of political and economic dimensions, have already accumulated a powerful momentum in the modern world; it would be rather naïve to expect that a single—however significant—international event such as the 2020 victory of Joe Biden at the U.S. Presidential election could reverse or stop them. The immediate task of the international community for the next couple of years seems to be cutting the costs and reducing the risks associated with economic and political deglobalization.

This formidable task notwithstanding, one should not dismiss longer-term global trends. There is little doubt about globalization coming back in one form or another. Two major factors push the world in this direction, with both of them getting stronger over time, no matter what anti-globalists have to say today.

First, humankind feels a constantly increasing pressure of common problems and challenges, ranging from accelerating climate change to the threats of new pandemics to the coming global resource crunch. For the sake of our survival, these issues call for joint action in some form or fashion. The instinct of self-preservation of the human species should eventually embrace the form of "globalization 2.0".

Second, the ongoing deglobalization has not hindered technical progress. In contrast, technical progress goes faster than ever, and it continues to provide new

---

A. Kortunov (✉)
Russian International Affairs Council, Moscow, Russia

© China Social Sciences Press 2023
Institute of Russian, Eastern European and Central Asian Studies, CASS and Russian
International Affairs Council, *Global Governance in the New Era*,
https://doi.org/10.1007/978-981-19-4332-4_1

opportunities for remote communications of various kinds. The global physical space and the global resource pool are shrinking, while feasible models of geographically disbursed work, education, entertainment, and social and political activities are multiplying. Napoleon's old saw that "geography is destiny" is losing its former axiomaticity. In a sense, given its boost for online activities, the COVID pandemic turned out to be a Great Equalizer eroding many of the traditional hierarchies and international barriers.

Eventually, we will herald the dawn of a new globalization cycle. This "globalization 2.0" will be markedly different from what we lived through earlier this century, but it will evolve in a mostly similar direction, retaining some of the essential characteristics of the previous cycle. If we take the global 2008–2009 crisis as the starting point and assume that today's world is already at or near the lowest level of ongoing deglobalization, we can rather reliably predict the next U-turn in global connectedness to take place in the mid-2020s. Should we make allowances for the more complex and comprehensive nature of the 2020–2021 crisis compared to that of 2008–2009, we would have to move the U-turn moment further forward by two, three, or even five years—somewhat closer to the end of our century's still young third decade.

After all, predicting the exact timing of the U-turn and the arrival of "globalization 2.0" is not that important. What is of true importance is to try and foresee the fundamental parameters of the new cycle of globalization, which will make this cycle quite different from what humankind experienced at the beginning of this century.

Globalization with No Hegemon

Globalization of the late twentieth–early twenty-first century coincided with the historical peak of the U.S. international power and influence. Indeed, U.S. Presidents—from Bill Clinton to Barack Obama—were the ones who defined basic rules of the game in the emerging globalized world. U.S. hegemony extended both to international development and to international security. All major multilateral institutions—be it the United Nations, NATO, G8 and later G20 or the IBRD and the IMF, the WTO and even the OECD—reflected the U.S. global agenda and camouflaged the commitment to preserve Pax Americana for as long as possible. In rare cases, when the United States would fail to channel its decisions through appropriate multilateral organizations, Washington did not hesitate to bypass them with very limited, if any, resistance from the international community (e.g., the U.S.-led "coalition of the willing" military intervention in Iraq back in 2003).

The new cycle of globalization will be entirely different from this model. The United States is unlikely to remain the indispensable driver of "globalization 2.0". Moreover, it is far from evident that the world will need a committed and highly motivated global hegemon to launch a globalization reset. We are more likely to see the horizontal model of globalization, truly based on genuine multilateralism, making headway. Examples of this model are already there. For instance, late in 2020, fifteen

Asian Pacific nations signed an agreement to form the Regional Comprehensive Economic Partnership (RCEP). The agreement formally launched the world's largest free trade zone, with a total population of 2.2 billion people and the GNP of $28 trillion, or approximately one-third of the global GNP. Interestingly, both friends and adversaries of the United States in the region joined the agreement. Contrary to what one could have imagined, it was not China that played the central role in getting the RCEP off the ground; the true drivers behind the agreements were the ASEAN nations that had been working on this ambitious project for approximately twenty years.

For the United States, the U.S. leadership will have to accept that Washington will not always be in a position to act as the indisputable leader of the new cycle of globalization or as the indispensable actor in setting the rules of the game. Like any other country in the world, the United States will have to take the position of a yet another participant and sometimes that of an observer to the changing rules. In some areas, the United States will continue to be the rule-maker, while it will have to be a rule-taker in others. Such a shift will inevitably turn out to be very painful for the numerous factions in the U.S. political establishment who appeared on the political scene and matured there in times of the bipolar and the unipolar international systems. It is yet to be seen how the U.S. leadership will cope with this challenge.

Globalization with No Center and No Periphery

At the dawn of the previous cycle of globalization, the common vision was that its "waves" would spread primarily from the economic, technological, and political core of the modern world, which is to say from the "Grand West", to its periphery. Large semiperipheral countries, such as China, Russia, India, and Brazil, were supposed to serve as transmission gear in this process. Early prophets of globalization also assumed that as we move away from the core toward the periphery, the resistance to globalization will increase, giving rise to conflicts and trade wars as well as sowing isolationism and nationalism. These "counter waves" would slow the overall globalization process down, but they would not profoundly affect the global core, being gradually weakened in the course of their proliferation from the periphery. While the periphery had to stay fragmented for some time, the core would continue to consolidate.

However, for "globalization 2.0", the terms of engagement will be very different from this pattern. "Waves" of globalization are likely to go in the opposite direction, from the global periphery to the global core. The "Grand West" is already trying to isolate or—at least—protect itself from the Global South although capping international migration, reinstalling protectionism, repatriating industries from overseas, and demonstrating growing vulnerabilities to nationalism and xenophobia. Such a shift reflects a continuous fundamental change in the balance of economic power between the global core and the periphery. In 1995, on the eve of "globalization 1.0", the GNP (PPP) of the seven top emerging economies—China, India, Russia, Brazil,

Indonesia, Turkey, and Mexico—amounted to about one half of the G7's GNP, which includes the United States, the United Kingdom, France, Germany, Japan, Canada, and Italy. In 2015, the GNPs (PPP) of the two groups were roughly the same. By 2040, the "emerging seven" will be twice as powerful in economic terms as the "developed seven".

The global core still enjoys a major advantage over the global periphery—should we rather say the former global periphery?—in terms of their respective levels of engagement in major globalization processes. Nevertheless, this advantage is rapidly shrinking. For instance, China surpassed the United States in 2020 as the global leader in receiving foreign direct investments. The question about who is to lead "globalization 2.0" remains open. One can even question whether "globalization 2.0" might have a single geographical center or whether it should be associated with a particular region or a group of nations. The next cycle of globalization is more likely to evolve as a network process without a clearly defined geographical hierarchy. The whole distinction between the global core and the global periphery might completely lose its meaning since virtually every country in the world features elements both of the former and of the latter.

Sustainable Development Rather Than Linear Economic Growth

The previous cycle of globalization was about the acceleration of economic growth and increases in private and public consumption. Notably, "globalization 1.0" contributed quite a lot to overcoming global poverty and to expanding the middle class globally, especially in Asia. Flourishing international trade, augmenting foreign direct investments, and emerging sustainable transnational economic and technological chains—all these factors contributed to the success of many ambitious projects of national modernization. Because of these positive changes, many in the world came to be convinced that "the rising tide would lift all boats", meaning that the benefits of globalization will eventually become available to everybody on the planet.

To a certain extent, this assumption turned out to be valid. The average inhabitant of Earth lives a better, brighter, and longer life than his or her parents thirty years ago. Nevertheless, globalization failed to distribute its benefits among the global population in an unquestionably fair manner; in contrast, "globalization 1.0" divided the world into new winners and new losers. Apparently, the borderline between the former and the latter does not always separate "successful" states from "unsuccessful" countries. More often, we observe deepening divisions within states—between certain demographic and professional groups, between metropolitan and rural areas, between wealthy and poor regions, and so on. In short, the new divisions emerge between those who were able to fit into the new way of life and those who were not. For example, the median incomes of the poorer half of the U.S. households experienced no increase over the last forty years but only a steady decline. It goes without saying that such a situation serves as fertile soil for various forms of social unrest and political populism.

"Globalization 2.0" is likely to change the criteria of success. High rates of economic growth will still be important, but meeting sustainable development goals will become even more important than returning economic growth per se. This shift means that much more attention has to be drawn in the future to issues of social equity, life quality, environmental and climate agendas, community building, personal and public security, etc. The linear increase in private and public consumption is not sustainable; it will give way to the much more nuanced indicators of "smart consumption". Moreover, the whole concept of the "consumption society" will undergo quite radical changes. Countries will increasingly compete with each other in terms of the overall opportunities for self-fulfillment that they can offer to their citizens rather than in simple GNP per capita terms.

Social Drivers Rather Than Financial Drivers

Transnational financial businesses were in the vanguard of "globalization 1.0". Internationalizing financial markets, interstate competition for access to foreign investments, growing geographical and sectorial capital mobility, the emerging transborder community of financial managers aligned by their professional skills, and a shared culture—all these trends have had a profound impact on production, politics, and even on mass culture and lifestyles. The cosmopolitan technocratic professional has come to be a role model and symbol of change.

However, the 2008–2009 financial crisis exposed serious limitations of this model of globalization. Transnational capital has moved too fast ahead and too far away from the national production base as well as the domestic social environment. Cosmopolitan technocratic professionals have become a symbol of greed, moral relativism, and social irresponsibility. Because of the permeating disappointment, the formerly limitless expansion of capital was contained by highly nationalistic economic and financial strategies, with the economic and financial priorities of the Trump administration being a graphic illustration of the defeat suffered by international bankers. Hopes and expectations of the self-confident economists of the early twenty-first century did not come true, as the economy never managed to defeat politics, turning it into an obedient servant. The opposite happened. Politics started overshadowing the economy and dictating decisions that were quite different from the narrative of economic feasibility. Paradoxically, "globalization 1.0" fostered a whole spectrum of new opportunities for anti-globalists to build their transnational alliances. Currently, anti-globalists have arguably mustered globalization-related opportunities much better than their opponents.

There are reasons to believe that "globalization 2.0" will primarily have social rather than financial drivers. Even today, with international trade and foreign direct investments plummeting, it is worth mentioning that trans-border information flows continue to grow at a very high speed. The COVID-19 pandemic has become a powerful factor causing humankind to disunite; however, this is only its immediate impact. The long-term impact may well be the opposite, since the pandemic turned out to be an extraordinary accelerator of new information and communication technologies, and it would not be an exaggeration to argue that one of the most remarkable features of the post-pandemic world is the emergence of the first truly global civil society. Trans-border NGOs, professional communities, public movements, and advocacy coalitions are likely to play a more active role in "globalization 2.0" than the old financial elites of nation states. If so, we can conclude that "globalization 2.0" will have a much broader and more robust social base than the previous cycle of globalization. Therefore, future resistance to anti-globalist trends might also grow stronger.

Social Justice Rather Than Individual Freedoms

The previous cycle of globalization reflected the public demands for individual freedoms that were dominant in the global community since the 1980s or even earlier. The impulse of globalization had its roots in economic and political programs of such leaders as Margaret Thatcher in the United Kingdom and Ronald Reagan in the United States; it gained momentum amid leftist egalitarian ideologies being in a crippling crisis caused by the failure of the communist experiment in the Soviet Union and Central European states. Visionaries of "globalization 1.0"—from Jacques Attali to George Soros to Thomas L. Friedman—dreamed of the future society populated by completely atomized "citizens of the world" with unlimited freedom of choice and very few, if any, constraints imposed by archaic group identities and related commitments.

The global political pendulum reached its extreme point in the very beginning of the century, and in the 2010s, it started moving in the opposite direction. It is very likely that we will see much more articulated and persistent public demand for social and political justice in the second quarter of the century. This implies a renaissance of leftist ideologies and an advance of left political movements and parties. There are already many indicators that societies in various parts of the world are more inclined to sacrifice some of their economic and political freedoms for the sake of what they consider to be the guarantees of social justice and fairness. We can envision an increase in the tax burden on the private sector and wealthier social groups as well as new egalitarianism, politically motivated censorship and self-censorship, proliferation of political correctness practices, the emergence of new restrictive approaches to information management, and restrictions of privacy justified by security considerations. Neither of the above-mentioned trends implies a total defeat of liberal democracies by authoritarian political models, although liberal democracies will have to put more emphasis on social justice to survive and compete with the alternative forms of social organization (as it was the case between the two world wars).

Globalization based on the priority of social justice must be quite different from globalization based on the priority of individual freedoms. Modern society has yet to produce universal and legitimate standards of justice—both to be applied domestically and in managing relations between states. This suggests that the world in throes of "globalization 2.0" will not necessarily become a fair and just world—it will remain unfair and unjust for many social, political, ethnic, religious, and other groups as well as for many nations. However, we can predict a much more consistent emphasis on national and international affirmative actions, non-market mechanisms of massive redistribution of material wealth on the national and international levels, and more persistent efforts to bridge the gap between the "haves" and the "have-nots". The art of successful global and national governance under these circumstances has to include the ability to balance diverging understandings of justice that exist in the world at large or within a given country.

Multitude of Actors Instead of Nation States

The retreat of "globalization 1.0" was largely accelerated, if not caused, by the demise of non-state actors in international relations. Notions of national sovereignty and the supremacy of nation states and concerns about the interference of foreign nations into domestic political affairs have become quite popular in many societies and, especially, within traditional state-oriented national elites. These elites now have their revenge: Almost everywhere in the world, we stand to witness the rise of social and political status enjoyed by state bureaucrats, the military, the defense sector, special services, and law enforcement agencies. To some extent, the traditional (i.e., linked to the industrial sector of economy) middle class also experiences upward social mobility. At the same time, many role models of the early twenty-first century are losing their former lure and influence; the new creative class, private financial sector, cosmopolitan factions of national elites, liberal media, comprador intellectuals— all of these have to fight truly hard to avoid complete marginalization. The world is getting back from the post-modern paradigm to the neo-modern one, while in a number of dimensions, the world is even falling into the archaic. The former non-state drivers of globalization—such as universities, independent think tanks, professional networks, transnational NGOs, and foundations as well as a globally oriented private sector—are pushed to the sidelines of the international system.

Nevertheless, the subsequent period of deglobalization demonstrated that such reinvigoration of nation states has its own limitations. The nearly universal emphasis on national sovereignty has prevented neither the COVID-19 pandemic, the implosion of global oil prices, nor the increase in the volatility of currency exchange rates. Stricter national fiscal regulations failed to eliminate global offshores, much as tighter border controls, and visa regimes did not prevent millions of illegal migrants from getting to Europe. Despite their frantic efforts, nation states thus far have achieved only limited success in reinstalling their control over trans-border flows of money, goods and services, information, and people. It is hard to believe that the "final victory" is just around the corner.

"Globalization 2.0" is likely to offer a different model of interaction between state and non-state actors in international relations. Although states will undoubtedly remain the main building blocks of the global system, an increasing number of international problems might find their solutions only in the format of broad partnerships (PPP). For instance, to block the most dangerous and destabilizing avenues of the arms race, active engagement by private companies from the defense sector and research universities appears to be indispensable. The advancement of the "green agenda" is impossible without involving multiple civil society institutions and local communities all around the globe. Successful development projects in the poorest countries in the world are doomed to fail if the private sector does not shoulder the efforts of national or international technical assistance agencies. It is important to mention that non-state actors in such PPPs are unlikely to limit their role to that of state subcontractors; they will come to partnerships with their own interests and priorities, sometimes very different from the interests and priorities of states. The ability to build efficient PPPs will be critical for state leaders of the future.

Plurality Instead of Universality

The previous cycle of globalization coincided with the global spread of political and economic liberalism. Many politicians and scholars regarded the notions of "liberal globalization" and "global liberalism" as almost synonymous terms or, at least, as terms that are inextricably linked with each other. A predicted final and global victory of liberal economic and political models should have become both a key accelerator of globalization and one of its most significant accomplishments. In this context, any non-liberal or illiberal developmental models appeared to be manifestations of archaism, symptoms of inconsistent and incomplete modernization, preventing their bearers from fitting into the new global world. One could have argued about what the most efficient modernization trajectories were when it came to one society or the other, but the view that the West stood as the symbol and the incarnation of modernity itself looked axiomatic.

Today, a direct causal link between globalization and political/economic liberalism is less evident than it was three decades ago. Political and economic liberalism is under pressure. Even in the "historical West", they now question some of the liberal centerpieces, whereas alternative social, economic, and political models demonstrate their sustainability and resilience, often coupled with high efficiency. One of the most emblematic illustrations of this new situation is the comparative experience of the United States and China in fighting the COVID-19 pandemic. The West has already lost its former monopoly on how to define modernity, having itself turned into a target for condescending statements about archaism and obsolescence.

This new dynamic of global development suggests that "globalization 2.0" should find a way to combine the needed degree of global universality and pluralism of national trajectories for economic, social, and political development. The rules of the game in the emerging international system have to be balanced in such a way that they become equally comfortable for a large variety of participants who go through different stages of their social and political maturation. It is not realistic to expect that only an adherence to political liberalism can grant nations free and unrestricted access to the global world; this world should be open to all—whether liberal democracies or illiberal autocracies, theocratic republics, or absolute monarchies. Multilateral global projects should emerge around common interests rather than around common values. One can assume that "globalization 2.0" (or a later "globalization 3.0") should—at the end of the day—lead to a global convergence of values. The assumption is debatable, but it is clear that such a convergence can only follow globalization in some rather distant future, while it cannot serve as a precondition for "globalization 2.0".

Asynchrony in Lieu of Synchronization

Though "globalization 1.0" studies initially focused primarily on its financial and economic dimensions, it was more than apparent that globalization was a complex process with a profound impact on all aspects of human existence. They assumed that financial and economic globalization would inevitably pull behind itself—just as a locomotive pulls cars behind itself along the railway—other dimensions, such as social, cultural, political, and so on. Furthermore, they expected globalization to somehow synchronize its advances in various areas. By interacting with each other, the various dimensions of globalization accelerated each other, resulting in a cumulative impact on the international system at large. Such a reductionist vision of the future of globalization can be partially explained if we recall that most of those who originally analyzed this phenomenon were scholars majoring in macroeconomic and financial matters; therefore, their economic and technocratic determinism should not look too surprising. The idea of synchronization looked nice—for some time, it seemed that global developments proved it right.

Over time, however, it turned out that 'globalization resistance' in certain dimensions of human life is visibly stronger than in others. Furthermore, it became clear that there is no direct causal relationship between integration and unification. The famous Aristotle's quote about the polis as a "unity of dissimilar" can be applied to the globalized world just as well. It turned out to be impossible to synchronize, shall we say, the economic and the political facets of globalization. The growing gap between its economic and political dimensions turned out to be the most formidable challenge to "globalization 1.0", as economic imperatives called for strategic, system-driven, global, continental, proactive, and multilateral solutions, while political needs pushed tactical, opportunistic, local, reactionist, and unilateral moves to the forefront. As was previously argued, economic rationality failed to prevail over political considerations, which makes a globalization setback practically unavoidable.

It is clear that "globalization 2.0" will have to be asynchronous, which is to say that it will imply diverging speeds of globalization in various domains of human life. For instance, the resilience of national cultural patterns to the global advance of mass culture should not become a formidable obstacle to the economic dimension of globalization. Commitments of societies to their historied traditions and unique identities should not pose a challenge to the growing unity of humankind—on the contrary, they should serve as a national contribution to global diversity. Global diversity, in turn, should enhance the overall stability of the global social system. Amid a profoundly asynchronous "globalization 2.0", harmonizing the multiple elements of universalism and particularism transnationally as well as within the boundaries of nations will be an immense political challenge, as it will require extremely delicate and highly professional political fine-tuning. Today, we can only guess about how future politicians will muster the skills needed.

Situational Coalitions Rather Than Rigid Alliances

"Globalization 1.0" made full use of the Western security and development institutions that remained essentially intact since the end of the Cold War. The common expectation was that the continuous geographical and functional expansion of these institutions would ultimately facilitate the unification of humankind under a common umbrella, which would solve most of the pressing global problems. In reality, most of these institutions, including NATO and the European Union, too soon manifested their limitations, even bordering organic deficiencies in some of the cases. At the same time, most attempts at launching new institutions as alternatives to the old West-led organizations were freighted with a chronic institutional fatigue that often prevented these initiatives from going much beyond a club format of their activities. Global politics polarizing even further over the second decade of the century contributed to incapacitating many multilateral institutions, including the United Nations framework.

It is difficult to imagine the emerging world order with no institutional backbones inherited from the previous period. Nevertheless, the odds are that most of the international activity will revolve around specific political, social, environmental, and other problems rather than within rigid bureaucratic organizations inherited from the twentieth century. The remaining international hierarchies will gradually lose their former omnipotence; the notions of "superpower" or "great power" will look archaic and contain little, if any, explanatory power. At the same time, no "global government" endowed with extensive powers and universal legitimacy is looming on the horizon.

Seeking to approach specific problems, nations will likely form flexible situational coalitions of the willing, which will include not only committed nation states but also various actors from the private sector, civil society, and other players involved in international affairs. Such coalitions will assemble, disassemble, and reassemble with relative ease. There will be no place for complex and resource-consuming bureaucracies or excessively complicated decision-making procedures. Such a problem-based approach to international cooperation is not ideal, though; it has its own limitations and liabilities. Nevertheless, it may well turn out to be more meaningful and, therefore, in greater demand by the international community than the old institutional approach.

North–South Divide Replacing East–West Divide

Conventional wisdom suggests that "globalization 1.0" has tripped over the confrontation between the United States and China. The 2020–2021 economic and epidemiological crisis is believed to accelerate the drift of the global economy and politics toward a U.S.–Chinese bipolarity. This logic implies that the main issue of our time is how rigid or flexible this bipolarity may come to be. Rigid bipolarity will literally divide the world into two opposing systems, as it was during the most part of the second half of the twentieth century. A flexible bipolarity will allow most international actors to preserve some freedom of maneuver and a degree of autonomy in their respective foreign policies. This logic looks compelling, but only if one looks at the immediate future of the next couple of years. However, keeping "globalization 2.0" in a longer-term perspective, it seems highly likely that political and economic bipolarity will increasingly shift from the "East–West" axis, typical of the twentieth century, to that of "North–South".

Surely, the current divisions between the East and the West will not disappear for a long time. For at least a couple of decades, China's modernization model will be explicitly different from the Western model. Nevertheless, the longer-term perspective we use, the more grounds we find to include China (as well as Russia) in a broadly defined Global North. To reach a strategic compromise between Washington and Beijing would require political will, commitment, patience, stamina, and flexibility from both sides, but the contours of such a compromise are more or less clear. At the same time, even some general understanding of a possible North–South compromise is lacking. There are no grounds to hope for the Global North to come up with a comprehensive large-scale development assistance program for the Global South along the lines of the Marshall Plan offered by the United States to Europe in the aftermath of the Second World War. Quite on the contrary, we cannot rule out yet another rise of racism and xenophobia that would distance the Global North from the Global South even further. Amid such conditions, the world in throes of "globalization 2.0" might witness deeper integration of the Northern economies parallel to curtailing economic, political, and even humanitarian connections to most developing nations, tighter border controls in the North, and new restrictions on trans-border migrations.

The critical challenge of "globalization 2.0" is not about pulling the laggards in the South up to the level of the leaders in the North. It is impossible for one simple reason—to extend the living standards of the Western middle class to all inhabitants of Earth would require imposing exorbitant pressures on the planet's resources and dooming our planet's ecosystem to irreversible degradation. It is also impossible because the liberal model of today's North is not as efficient as it used to be in its heyday. The North is gradually losing its monopoly on modernity and is, therefore, less and less regarded by the Global South as a model to follow. In addition, over time, the geographical division between the North and the South becomes more porous. The North is expanding to the South—through huge ultramodern metropolitan areas in South Asia, the Middle East, Africa, and Latin America, through new sectors of economy and through new consumption patterns. The South, in turn, is infiltrating the North with its migration flows, lifestyles, culture, and religion. A "civilizational divorce" between the North and the South is next to impossible; if humankind fails to agree on some civilizational synthesis within the next couple of decades, "globalization 2.0" will definitely fall short of accomplishing the most fundamental mission of the twenty-first century.

Global Governance: History, Logic, and Trend

Zhang Yuyan

In recent years, the term *global governance* has been frequently used by the circle of international studies. The grand background of the emergence of global governance is that, first of all, global problems have become increasingly prominent with deepened economic globalization. Drawing so many concerns around the world, global governance, as both the solution and process of addressing global problems, lies against another general backdrop that various kinds of worldwide challenges can only be solved, or at least alleviated, through the joint efforts of all countries. The *global* nature of both international challenges and corresponding solutions, together with major players in this game trying to maximize their own interests by handling global problems, brings the study of international affairs into a new historical period.

Similar to the development of many other scientific disciplines, before the emergence of a full-fledged or widely recognized new paradigm for research, the best approach to study global governance is, through the process of describing its historical origin and evolution, to use the existing analytical framework and conceptual system to examine major fields or key issues, such as global monetary and financial governance, international trade and investment governance, world environment and climate change governance as well as international coordination of macroeconomic policies. At the same time, we should also be aware that as the connotation in global governance, like *a basket*, becomes increasingly complicated, the call for the theoretical layout and normative establishment of global governance has so naturally become evident, together with people's rising aspiration to give a clear-cut boundary of definition for the scope of global governance.

One philosophy for the theoretical advancement of global governance research is to interpret *global governance* as various players providing international public goods or club products through collective actions and, on this basis, establishing a set of logical frameworks to deal with a wide variety of international agendas or

---

Z. Yuyan (✉)
Institute of World Economics and Politics, Chinese Academy of Social Sciences, Beijing, China

© China Social Sciences Press 2023
Institute of Russian, Eastern European and Central Asian Studies, CASS and Russian
International Affairs Council, *Global Governance in the New Era*,
https://doi.org/10.1007/978-981-19-4332-4_2

global challenges. In addition, a large number of cases for global governance, where players, particularly state actors, participated in the game, are also *gold mines* that are valuable subjects to study for the refinement of and analysis of concepts, the generation of meaningful propositions, and the examination of existing theories or hypotheses.

A Historical Review of Global Governance

Generally, people are living in an era of ongoing globalization, especially in an economic dimension. The *globalization* mentioned here mainly refers to the historical process during which interconnectivity or interdependence among world countries and regions are continuously on the rise, with a refined division of labor among countries or economies, reduced institutional and technological barriers across the globe that once restricted the cross-border free flow of factors, and a growing consensus that more and more imperative global challenges require collective responses by all. It is generally believed that globalization originated from *the Great Geographical Discovery* in the late fifteenth century grew rapidly with the colonial expansion of European powers and reached its first culmination in the second half of the nineteenth century. Approximately one century and a half ago, Karl Marx and Frederick Engels pointed out in *the Communist Manifesto* that *the need for a constantly expanding market for its products chases the bourgeoisie over the entire surface of the globe. It must nestle everywhere, settle everywhere, and establish connections everywhere.* At that time, the classic writers not only saw the various phenomena that people call *economic globalization* today but also revealed the essence behind, that is, the economic globalization of that era was nothing but bloody or blatant expansion and robbery done by the capitalist mode of production. Given that competition under *the law of the jungle* often results in a lose–lose situation, thereby failing to achieve the maximization of self-interest, rules for trade and capital flow that constrain vicious competition, such as some bilateral or multilateral agreements by imperialist states, have come to the fore. In a sense, these international agreements or treaties can be regarded as the nascent form of global governance.

The outbreak of World War I disrupted the process of globalization dominated by imperialist powers, which in turn severely damaged such a rudimentary form of global governance with no law-binding force, few participating countries and limited coverage. During the two world wars, most of the world's major industrial countries pursued a beggar-thy-neighbor philosophy for trading policies. Later, the outbreak of World War II and the subsequent havoc on humanity finally gave people the awareness of the vital importance of peace, as well as the urgency to rebuild their homes and bring life back on track. This is the historical background of the first international monetary and financial conference in human history held in Bretton Woods, New Hampshire, the United States in July 1944 by representatives of the world's major countries, except the Axis powers or the defeated countries. At this meeting, countries not only established an international monetary system centered on the US dollar, namely *the Bretton Woods System,* but also paved the way for the subsequent establishment of a worldwide mechanism for peace, with the United Nations as its cornerstone.

The Cold War, following the end of World War II, divided the world into the West and the East, led by the United States and the Soviet Union, respectively. Global governance that had just started on its historical journey was replaced by two parallel and confrontational governance systems. Although there was an antagonistic feature of *divided global governance* during the Cold War, the level, scale, and coverage of global governance have been unprecedentedly improved during this historical period. The status of the United Nations as the main platform for global governance has been confirmed, and the functions of the Bretton Woods System have been strengthened, both with more participants for broader representation and a growing number of agendas that they have handled. In 1988, the Basel Committee, composed of the central banks of ten major industrialized countries, announced *the Basel Accord* (i.e., *Basel I*) as an important step forward in the supervision of transnational banking or global governance on international banking and finance. In view of these facts, the international dynamics during the Cold War can be roughly regarded as a fledgling period for global governance: Its overall framework was already in place, albeit its functions were frequently hampered by a confrontation between the two opposing blocs.

The end of the Cold War marked the beginning of a new era for the world. With the fall of the Berlin Wall in 1989, the clear division and opposition between the East and the West became a thing of the past, with the West, headed by the Unites States, overnight becoming the dominant force for worldwide political and economic affairs. In a sense, for the first time ever, human beings had the opportunity to answer the call of history and build a world with deeper economic integration and more guarantee for security. After fears of the next world war have largely subsided, there have been talks of how to reap and exploit *the dividends of peace* brought about by the end of the Cold War, especially how to dismantle the barriers against trade and investment to expand the market size and enjoy the benefits of the ensuing *gains from trade.* The transformation and upgrading of the General Agreement on Tariffs and Trade (GATT) into the World Trade Organization (WTO) in 1995 and China's accession to this organization in 2001 can be regarded as typical examples for the acceleration of globalization and the consolidation of global governance. In addition to apparent economic interests, Western developed countries, led by the Unites States, also have a less perceived yet more ambitious goal, that is, after the end of the Cold War, leveraging favorable international institutions to include and integrate new members, such as China, Russia, and countries in Eastern Europe and Central Asia, into the international system dominated by themselves. In this process, global governance begins to show one of its features as an *instrument.*

Instead of arguing that the 2008 financial crisis ushered in a new era of global governance, it is rather fair to say that this crisis has inherited or strengthened both the process and function of global governance from the previous period. While the *Basel II* formed in 2004 and the *Basel III* introduced in 2010 have obvious differences in terms of the philosophies for banking supervision and policy inclinations, as the latter pays more attention to the flexibility of supervision and emphasizes the importance of market competition, the two are almost the same, however, in terms of the institutional construction to deal with global financial risks. Influenced by this crisis, therefore, the ministerial meeting by finance ministers and central bank governors from the 20 countries has been upgraded to the Group Twenty (G20) summit, a historic move that symbolizes the improvement and consolidation of global governance. Apart from the financial crisis, other factors, from various aspects and to different extents, have also drawn worldwide attention to global governance: continued change of power relations among major countries after the Cold War; increasingly severe global issues such as climate change and terrorism; negative consequences by the acceleration of globalization since the fall of the Berlin Wall (such as the widening gap of income among different countries or different groups of people within a country); and worldwide challenges brought by the advancement of science and technology in the past 30 years, especially the breakthrough and coverage of IT technologies (such as cyber-security threats and the general awakening of people's awareness of human rights). Furthermore, criticisms of and worries about the retreat of its global responsibility by the Trump administration also reflect deep worldwide concerns for global governance from another perspective.

In a stricter sense, participation by the People's Republic of China in global governance began with its return to the United Nations in 1971 with a regained legal seat, marking China's official debut on the global stage. From the early 1970s to the late 1980s, with the restoration of such legal status in the UN and the overall alleviation of rivalry between the two blocs, China began to participate in the operation of international mechanisms, yet to a limited extent. With the advancement of reform and opening up, as well as the acceleration of economic globalization, China has played a deeper and broader role in international affairs since the 1990s. During the Asian financial crisis from 1997 to 1999, China's deed not only contributed positively to helping Asian countries cope with such a quagmire and get out of the crisis but also demonstrated China's self-confidence and sense of responsibility as a regional power for both regional and global governance. Since the beginning of the twenty-first century, with steady improvement of economic development and growing overall national strength, China's willingness has become more active toward its participation in global governance. In 2001, China successfully joined the WTO, which was regarded as a historic milestone event in the integration of China's economy into that of the whole world.

The international financial crisis triggered by the US subprime mortgage crisis in 2008 pushed the G20 mechanism to the forefront of global governance. Given that the G20 has already become one of the most important platforms for global governance, China, as the world's third-largest economy, would naturally play an indispensable and proactive part in this regard. In 2013, Chinese President Xi Jinping proposed *the Belt and Road initiative*, which provides new momentum and novel avenues for promoting and optimizing global governance. In 2014, China proposed the establishment of the Asian Infrastructure Investment Bank (AIIB). As the first international multilateral financial institution initiated and successfully established by China, the AIIB can, to some extent, be regarded as another landmark for China's participation in economic globalization and worldwide economic governance after joining the WTO. In summary, the proposal of the Belt and Road initiative and the establishment of the AIIB, together with China's signing of *the Paris Agreement* on climate change in April 2016, have illustrated ever stronger relations between China and the world.

At the G20 Hangzhou Summit in 2016, China successfully conveyed to the world its philosophy of dealing with global issues as well as its pursuit of a stronger voice and more rule-making rights for developing countries and emerging economies. At the World Economic Forum in Davos in January 2017, Chinese President Xi Jinping elaborated on the defects of the current framework for global economic governance: For example, it fails to address such a new worldwide landscape, with insufficient representation and poor inclusiveness; trade and investment rules fail to keep up with new realities, featuring exclusiveness and fragmentation; and the global mechanism for financial governance has not answered the new needs, making it difficult to effectively address the frequent turbulence in the international financial market, the accumulation of asset bubbles, and other worldwide challenges. Later, in a speech at the UN headquarters in Geneva, President Xi Jinping first systematically elaborated on a plan for the construction of *a community with a shared future for mankind* in terms of partnership, security, economic development, inter-civilization, and ecological progress, therefore providing an outline for the long-term vision of global governance.

Issues and Logic of Global Governance

Sixty years ago, Harvard Professor Thomas Schelling pointed out in his book *the Strategy of Conflict* that the motivation of players to participate in the game and the choice of game strategies are highly related to both *common interests* and *conflicting interests*. To illustrate the coexistence of these two kinds of interests, Schelling discusses such an experiment in the book: Two strangers may share 100 USD on the condition that the sum of their respective written expectations must be less than or equal to 100. Otherwise, neither of them will get a penny. The two players must cooperate or take into account the welfare of the other to receive the number of dollars they expect, which shows that there is *common interest* between these two partici-pants. In terms of the specific distribution of income, however, when one person gets more, the other gets less, which shows that this is *a zero-sum game*. That experiment has proven the coexistence between common interests and conflicting interests, while this logic is also true with the actual situation for global affairs: Even if a person is in pursuit of maximized self-interest, it is often sensible to take into account the inter-ests of the gaming opponents. The results of the experiment of two people sharing 100 dollars mentioned above have also confirmed this argument, as the vast majority of participants wrote down 50 as their expected amount.

The coexistence of common interests and conflicting interests is true not only for individual actors but also for national players whose objective is also to maximize self-interest. Global pursuits, such as reaching peaceful coexistence, fighting climate change, protecting the ecological environment, building cyber-security, combating terrorism, money laundering and other forms of transnational crimes, establishing a fair and open trade and investment system, and consolidating the international monetary and financial system, are all related to both the present and future well-being of all mankind. The control and resolution of these global issues, however, go far beyond the capacity of one or some countries, thus making extensive international cooperation a necessity. Every country, therefore, becomes a stakeholder, which means that there are *common interests* among nations. At the same time, the realization of peace, the response to climate change, the acquisition of an open trade and investment system, and the maintenance of stability for the international monetary and financial system are *not free lunches* but *costly undertakings*. Once cost sharing is involved, conflicts between stakeholders begin to emerge, with game playing and even fierce bargaining being inevitable.

What makes the case even more complicated is that the solutions to these global issues are typically about the provision of public goods. Taking into account the non-exclusivity of global public goods, such as maintaining a peaceful environment and curbing climate change, that is to say, any country or individual can benefit for free, all players are invisibly motivated to try their best to let *others* bear the cost of providing public goods and make *themselves* free riders. One of the consequences is the insufficient supply of global public goods, which can be manifested, for example, in the outbreak of wars or the escalation of threats for warfare, in the unrestricted emission of carbon dioxide in large quantities, in the rampage of terrorism, and ultimately in the general damage to the welfare of all mankind. To illustrate this phenomenon, a series of concepts or theories have been formulated, such as the *challenge for collective action*, the *prisoner's dilemma*, the *market failure*, the *tragedy of the commons*, or the *fallacy of composition*.

The increasingly serious issues that must be solved are, in nature, *global*, calling for correspondingly *global* cooperation by countries around the world. In a given jurisdiction, one of the usual solutions to *common problems* is to establish a unified and authoritative central government that captures resources through mandatory taxation to provide public goods for people in this place. However, this principle would fail to function on a global scale with sovereign states, as it is not feasible to establish a world government under current circumstances. To solve global problems, people have to find another way. As an alternative to building a world government, *global governance* comes to the forefront on the international stage. Hereby, *global governance* refers to the aggregate of self-enforcing institutions established by state or non-state actors to solve a wide variety of global issues. These institutions are based on negotiated consensus among various stakeholders, which, in essence, is nothing more than an equilibrium solution framed by various actors in making a balance between common interests and conflicting interests.

There are many kinds of global issues, and a particular global issue means different degrees of interest to different national actors. A typical example is *the United Nations Convention on the Law of the Sea* (UNCLOS). For sea-bound countries such as Japan and landlocked countries such as Mongolia, the significance of UNCLOS is obviously quite different. The difficulty of eliminating or mitigating a given global problem can determine the cost of global governance, while the huge disparity in national size or negotiating capacity of various actors will also profoundly affect the depth and breadth of their participation in global governance. With different internal power structures and decision-making mechanisms as well as varied degrees of social cohesion and stability, each actor further has its own way of behaving on the international stage. Meanwhile, many giant multinational corporations with huge financial capacity or religious groups with a strong power of mobilizing their followers have different pursuits of interests or orientations on values, therefore playing an important role in the global arena. These points can roughly explain the following phenomenon: Global governance takes various forms, and its efficacy is uneven. The absence or insufficiency of global governance, namely *governance deficits*, is common, which makes it even more difficult to carry out collective actions based on consensus.

In regard to *collective action*, Schelling's student and later colleague Mancur Olson cannot be missed. Five years after the publication of his teacher's *Strategy of Conflict*, Olsen published his doctoral dissertation under Schelling's guidance, *the Logic of Collective Action*, in which he elaborated on and further developed some of Schelling's ideas. His insightful proposition can be summarized as follows: Common interest is only a *necessary condition* but *not a sufficient condition* for the formation of collective action. There are two sufficient conditions in this regard: One is a small number of players, and the other is the existence of so-called *selective incentives,* which contains two interrelated meanings. One is that players who participate in collective actions can obtain higher expected benefits than those who do not, and the other is that players who do not participate in collective actions may face extremely high opportunity costs or even punishment. When the number of players in the game is small, selective incentives will be strengthened because in this case, each player's relative share of the output of the collective action increases; at the same time, each player's contribution to the product of collective action will be easier to observe, thereby helping to reduce free rides. Meanwhile, the transaction costs of reaching consensus and, ultimately, collective action are also lower when the number of players is small.

The goal of global governance is to provide global public goods. In addition to the *undersupply* of global public goods due to market failures, we have also seen an adequate or *oversupply* of certain global governance goods, such as some biased or partial international trade and investment rules. The mechanism of their occurrence can be fully explained in Olson's *Logic of Collective Action*. In the absence of sufficient incentives and a world government, a small number of conscious, capable, and highly staked players will form small-scale collective actions based on cost–benefit calculations, actively providing specific public goods that can maximize gains or minimize losses. Once a small interest group driven by a certain selective incentive takes up dominance, the resulting global governance in the form of international rules will be *non-neutral* or *partial*, and dominants may even advance their own interests at the expense of most other stakeholders. Here, *global public goods*, taking the form of international institutions or orders, are actually the *instruments* used by a specific interest group to achieve their goals. The question is why do those national actors, whose interests are damaged, still accept such international institutional arrangements that are unfavorable to them. The immediate answer is that acting together to challenge international institutional arrangements of this kind will also encounter collective action problems.

Considering that it is extremely difficult to form global collective actions, especially because the world is essentially a monopolistic and competitive market, most of the collective actions on global governance are *small-scale* ones, for which the G20 is a representative example. The emergence of regional governance, advocated by regionally dominant powers, is another example of this kind. The issue arising from the phenomenon above is the tension between *incentives* and *fairness* or, more commonly referred to as, the *trade-off between effectiveness and representation* in global governance. Managing these tensions is a challenge for humanity, and the corresponding result largely relies on the wisdom, open-mindedness, responsibility, and courage of all players, especially major powers. Here, China's traditional way of thinking is rather insightful and constructive, with the ultimate pursuit of *a modest plan between extreme solutions,* whereas everyone takes into account the feelings of other stakeholders during rule-making negotiations instead of trying to silence the other side and win a zero-sum game.

Criteria are indispensable in the process of thinking about global governance. When each player's contribution to the provision of global public goods and its benefits from within are marginally equal, it can be said that global governance of such kind is in *equilibrium* or in an *ideal state* because at this point, each player maximizes the benefits they may obtain from providing public goods, thus truly achieving their own interests and ensuring happiness for all. In the mechanism design theory in economics, *governance equilibrium* is roughly equivalent to *incentive compatibility.* In such an international system, issues such as free-riding, moral hazard, and adverse selection that hinder collective action conducive to the promotion of common interests have all lost their basis for existence. Although it is very difficult to achieve governance equilibrium in reality, describing the ideal state in a theoretical way provides us with a useful yardstick for analyzing the pros and cons of different forms of global governance and exploring ways to improve them. In principle, at least, it should be the goal of all players to perfect current global governance that falls behind the ideal case.

In today's world, power relations among major players are undergoing profound changes. Some emerging economies become more indispensable to the solution of international issues, while their stake in the current international system is also significantly increasing, with stronger awareness to safeguard and expand their interests by upgrading the global governance system. Against this background, it is so understandable that demands to adjust the current international order and gradually neutralize global institutional arrangements continue to emerge. However, countries with large vested interests in the current system of global governance aim to maintain the status quo. If the dominants of the current international system or global governance mechanism can keep pace with the times and follow the trend, as well as negotiate and cooperate rationally in cost sharing, benefit allocation, and balancing rights and responsibilities with those now indispensable players who then used to be marginal participants, then *selective incentives* will be transformed into *compatible incentives*, with substantially greater legitimacy and effectiveness of current and future global governance.

Various international organizations co-founded by sovereign states, such as the UN, the WTO, and the IMF, are mainly responsible for the specific roles of global public goods providers. Once an institution becomes an international organization, its functioning and efficiency will draw global attention. Since the outbreak of the global financial crisis in 2008, some international institutions have been widely criticized for their inadequate early warning and follow-up response, reflecting that they do have some room for improvement in the provision of global public goods. For various international organizations as agents and state actors as principals, there are important ways to approach governance equilibrium, such as to continuously improve negotiating rules and decision-making procedures of international organizations, to increase the efficiency of implementation, to build better mechanisms for the appraisal and evaluation of performance, to prevent themselves from being excessively bureaucratic, and to eradicate the soil for rent-seeking due to improperly established rules.

In *the Strategy of Conflict*, Schelling has also discussed an important phenomenon overlooked by classical economics: The creation and destruction of wealth and order are highly asymmetric processes. The wealth accumulated by millions of people over many years can be destroyed by a child's mischief while playing with fire. According to his calculations at the time, a worker with only a high school diploma could earn just a few thousand dollars a year, but he could destroy thousands of times more if he wanted to. A person would so willingly become a blackmailer if he can obtain a fraction of the wealth that he threatens to destroy. Schelling's reminder is highly relevant: After all, there are individual players across the globe who can destroy the world or cause great harm to human beings in one way or another. It is undoubtedly a lofty cause for the benefit of mankind to let players such as terrorists behave in an expected manner within fair and effective global governance. It would also be a meaningful undertaking if we could in turn enrich economic theory with insights gained from the study of global governance.

Today, the interdependence among countries has reached an unprecedented height, with both problems and corresponding solutions being *global*. Although each country has its own national interests, they are not competing parties in the negotiation but cooperators for shared destiny, as Jean Monnet, who actively promoted European cooperation after the end of World War II, put in his autobiography *Europe's First Citizen*. Forming global collective action sometimes requires making deals, negotiations, and compromises among various stakeholders. However, we cannot be satisfied with this, but to keep a higher pursuit: The solution of a global issue shall never be achieved by the compromise of another one; rather, the challenge facing any single country shall be regarded as a challenge for the whole world. To achieve this goal, a few key state actors need to have a broader mind and play a more responsible role.

Current Defects and Future Development of Global Governance

In the past few decades, with joint efforts by the international community, global governance has been continuously developed and improved. At the same time, however, with increasingly serious existing challenges and newly emerged global problems, the pressure and challenges faced by global governance are increasing as well, with a stronger contradiction between the increasing demand for global governance and the insufficient supply of global public goods. The basic reason behind this is that the existing global governance system cannot keep up with the changing trend of the times and is therefore incapable of dealing with global issues.

First, global governance is still far from achieving *full coverage* of global issues in various fields. The *blank spots* in global governance involve the following: first, the lack of consensus among countries on issues such as the digital economy and broader cyberspace regulation and the absence of some key powers in international agreements such as climate change. As public goods in nature, global governance has its inherent logic for insufficient supply. To be more specific, being roughly defined as the global public good, global governance has typical non-exclusive features. The maintenance of world peace, the stabilization of global trade and the financial system, and the promotion of sustainable human development all require high costs but indiscriminately benefit all countries. Even if a country does not contribute to the provision of these products, it can still enjoy the benefits free of charge. This leads to the *collective action problem*, which is bound to constrain the supply of global public goods and eventually lead to a *governance deficit*.

Second, many existing global governance systems or mechanisms are outdated and no longer authoritative, becoming instruments for safeguarding and expanding the interests of a few countries or groups with vested interests, even with the emergence of *governance rigidity*. The current global governance system was mainly established after World War II and was dominated by developed countries. After the establishment of these mechanisms, they have, to some extent, played an active role in dealing with global issues and maintaining world peace, stability, and development. At the same time, however, it should also be noted that conflicts and even wars in some hotspot areas continue to occur one after another that various forms of trade, investment, and financial protectionism are still prevalent and that challenges in emerging fields such as climate, environment, cyber-information, polar areas, and the outer space are increasing day by day. The outbreak of the international financial crisis in 2008 and the poor international public health cooperation to address the COVID-19 pandemic in 2020 have profoundly exposed the outdated and inefficient part of the existing global governance mechanism that fails to adapt to the new needs of world dynamics.

Third, the United States, as a key power, not only refuses to assume its responsibility of a major power but also takes suppressing other countries as its diplomatic priority. Since Donald Trump took office in the United States, China–US relations have undergone profound changes, and the process of economic globalization has almost been interrupted by the game of great powers. As the international division of labor and professionalization in manufacturing reach the highest level in history, the interdependence among major powers is yet highly asymmetric, and the potential benefits of global governance with non-neutral characteristics are huge. Therefore, there will inevitably be countries or blocs that regard global governance as a *weapon* to strengthen themselves and suppress competitors. For the major part of its foreign policies toward China, the Unites States hopes to use a set of the *reformed* or *renewed* version of international economic rules to fix China at the middle or low end of the global value chain while ensuring that its own long-lasting enjoyment of huge profits and the so-called *security* brought by high technological advantages. Furthermore, this will probably continue to be the dominant ideology of the Biden administration.

Fourth, the reform of global governance has been initiated but takes extremely slow steps in some areas. In the face of difficulties and crises, all countries in the world are aware of the necessity and importance of reforming and improving global governance. President Xi Jinping has repeatedly pointed out that with the increase in global challenges, it is the general trend to strengthen global governance and promote corresponding reforms. However, due to the obstruction by countries or blocs with vested interests represented by the United States and Europe, the structure of some global governance mechanisms has not been substantially changed for a long time. Even if consensus has already been reached for those reforms, it is often so difficult to be implemented in a timely and effective manner. The twists and turns of the reform on IMF quota and voting rights are, without a doubt, good examples of this point.

Fifth, there are significant differences in the goals or demands of various state actors, making it difficult to reach an agreement. Throughout the world today, the demand for the reform on global governance is stronger than ever. In an abstract sense, almost all countries have the willingness or expectation to advance global governance and build a safe, free, just, and prosperous world. However, when it comes to specific goals, there are many differences or even conflicts among ideas by different countries. Regarding priority and interpretation, different countries, or even the same country yet in different historical periods, would have different understandings. This means that in the next five to ten years, the competition between different governance models and governance priorities will undergo fierce competition, with countries striving to fight for the right to speak in the reform on global governance mainly manifested in the creation, control, application, and interpretation of international rules.

Against the background of major changes unseen in a century, there are roughly four scenarios for the future trend of global governance. First, the COVID-19 pandemic crushes and shatters the existing regional, multilateral, and global systems so that countries around the world adopt beggar-thy-neighbor policies or even enter jungle-like wars. Hegemonic countries become unscrupulous, taking *power is truth* as their fundamental norm in handling international relations. Second, the multilateral or global system completely collapses or exists only in name, while world multi-polarization, characterized by games between major countries, presents a regional grouping trend. At the same time, regionalism itself will also be reorganized: some mechanisms will be strengthened, some created, some reorganized, and, possibly, some abandoned. The third is the emergence of two or more parallel systems that are marked by at least partial decoupling of industrial chains. The result is that the multilateral system is dismembered or diluted, while the criteria for such division are multifaceted, mainly including the understanding and implementation of system rules; economic, social, and political factors; and other aspects such as civilization and ideology. Parallel systems can be further divided into balanced parallel systems and imbalanced parallel systems with comparable strength or incomparable strength of each system. Fourth, the process of re-globalization has been started. As the common enemy of the whole world, the COVID-19 pandemic, especially its huge short-term impact, has awakened mankind as people deeply felt that they should have long ago formed a community with a shared future but they have yet failed to do so. What we should do and can do is joining hands to consolidate, improve, and innovate the existing global multilateral system. Comparatively speaking, the probability of the first scenario is much lower, while in the latter three scenarios, the consolidation and expansion of regional cooperation as well as the reform and improvement of the existing multilateral system might be better choices for China. The ultimate case, however, to become mainstream depends on competition among major economies, especially China and the United States.

"Black Swans" of Globalization

Alexey Fenenko

The global coronavirus lockdown has divided the expert community into those willing to see nation states regain their prerogatives and those who favor establishing a prototype of a global government. This divide has got the better of two other points of concern. The former is that societies in all developed countries have demonstrated high mobilization potential. The latter is that our civilization went through an incredible experiment within a mere month. For the first time after World War II, the most liberal democracies in the U.S. and the EU saw food rationing and severe movement restrictions.

In spring 2020, the cause was the need to combat the pandemic, but prospectively, a system of mobilization can easily serve as an alternative to globalization. At the same time, the image of a mobilizational future, while it seemed to have become a thing of the past, is becoming very realistic.

How Many Globalizations?

The contemporary expert community and, to a large degree, the public consciousness have been brought up with the linear image of progress, one that presents the world as moving from backward forms and relations toward more progressive ones. (Hence the surprise of both authors and readers, "How is that even possible that [...] can happen in the twenty-first century..."). The idea that globalization is possibly coming to its end appears improbable to most of our contemporaries. We have managed to forget that there had already been three or four globalizations in the past. Each appeared everlasting to its contemporaries, and their end seemed unthinkable; yet, each of them did end.

A. Fenenko (✉)
Russian International Affairs Council, Moscow, Russia

© China Social Sciences Press 2023
Institute of Russian, Eastern European and Central Asian Studies, CASS and Russian International Affairs Council, *Global Governance in the New Era*,
https://doi.org/10.1007/978-981-19-4332-4_3

Today's scholars frequently dub the Hellenistic era of the third–fourth centuries BC "proto-globalization." After Alexander the Great's campaigns in the fourth century BC, the Mediterranean and the Middle East evolved into a single economic and political space with common-type economies, political regimes, political cultures, and a single language. A merchant or an artisan could freely, without any restrictions, move their goods from Carthage to the Indo-Grecian kingdoms. This space was held together by Mediterranean routes running through Rhodes, Alexandria, Carthage, and Sicily. Ships traveled thanks to a system of lighthouses that formed a belt around the Mediterranean, serving as the technological underpinning of the Hellenistic globalization.

A distinctive feature of the Hellenistic period was the ubiquitous spread of the classical Greek language and culture, coupled with a cultural interpenetration between Greece and the Orient. The colossal libraries of Alexandria and Pergamon open to all free citizens were intellectual pillars of this proto-globalization. The two most powerful non-Greek states, the Roman Republic and Carthage, were also involved in the Hellenistic space. For an educated Roman or Carthaginian, not speaking the Hellenic language and failing to know Greek philosophy was like not having basic English reading skills for our contemporary. Over the course of his lifetime, a free citizen could change many states. Everywhere, he saw roughly similar cities and lifestyles, he spoke the same Hellenic language, he read the same papyri, and he encountered the same political systems, a mix of the ancient Greek poleis and the ancient Eastern monarchies.

In the first century BC, the Roman type of globalization supplanted the Hellenistic one. Western Europe, the Mediterranean and the Black Sea region became a single economic and cultural space. The Hellenic language and Greco-Roman culture dominated everywhere. A free citizen could travel unobstructed from the British Isles to *Panticapeum* (today's Kerch), from Myra in Asia Minor to *Colonia Claudia Ara Agrippinensium* (today's Cologne). The Roman edition of globalization peaked in 212 AD, when Emperor Caracalla introduced Roman citizenship for all the free people of the empire. It stood to reason that Christianity became established in the Roman Empire 150 years later as a religion that posits everyone's equality before God. An educated Roman of the late fourth century would probably see his world perishing and several barbaric kingdoms being installed in its place as a grim fantasy. Yet, the Second (378–382) and the Third (395–410) Gothic wars abolished the "Roman globalization" in a matter of a few short years, paving the way for the Great Migration.

Local "globalizations" happened within any imperial unions of the Middle Age: in the Caliphate (seventh–ninth centuries), China's Tang Empire (seventh–ninth centuries), the Mongol Empire and the *Pax Mongolica* it established (thirteenth–fifteenth centuries), with whom Catholic Western Europe would actively interact. Each of these empires formed its regional space with unified trade and economic ties, common language, and culture. In the High Middle Ages, Western Europe was effectively a single political space connected by a system of feudal relations and opposed to other civilizations. These phenomena were rather regionalization within empires than a true globalization. Nevertheless, contemporaries had a hard time

"Black Swans" of Globalization

imagining any of these systems coming to an end: For the people of those times, they were a reality and a norm to linger on for centuries.

The nineteenth century, an era between the end of the Napoleonic wars and the start of World War I, when the world gained economic unity, truly became the "first globalization." The "first globalization" had its material and technological framework: the global financial system resting on the gold standard. The British Bank took the first step toward creating it, when it introduced gold backing for the pound sterling in 1816. Since then, the British pound became a global means of payment. Exchange rates of other currencies correlated with the pound as well as with gold prices. Paris Accords of 1867 shaped the global monetary system. Each currency had to have gold value, which allowed for establishing its gold parity. If a state's currency had no gold value, its financial transactions on the global market were executed through a currency to which its financial system was "tied."

Like today, the economic system of that globalization was rooted in free movement of capital, goods, and services. Back then, this system was referred to with the English word "free trade." The countries unwilling to open their gateways to the "free market" quickly ended up waging the Opium Wars and getting shelled, like Nagasaki in 1864—developments that forced them to remove customs barriers. A loan from a German or Swiss bank could easily be taken out in St. Petersburg or in Paris. An English-made suit or Zeiss optical instruments could be purchased in Rome, in Bucharest, or even in Nagasaki. The degree of interconnectedness of the nineteenth century world is perfectly reflected in a passage by the French sociologist Gustave Le Bon, who wrote in 1896: "Having waited for three months, and being in urgent need of the metal, I wrote to a firm in Berlin. Although this time the order was only of a few francs, I received a reply by return of post, and the [metal], worked up into the required dimensions, was delivered at the end of a week. ... The consequence is that German firms are springing up in Paris every day, and the public is obliged to have recourse to them, despite its patriotic reluctance. You go to one for an insignificant purchase, and soon you go nowhere else."

These ties were not just local trade between neighboring countries—they were transnational. Let us give the floor to Le Bon again. "A year ago," we read in the *Journal*, "a merchant of South America wished to export some American lambskins to France and Germany. He was put in communication, for this purpose, thanks to the officious care of our consul and our minister of commerce, with one of our commission agents. The American merchant then dispatched a consignment of twenty thousand skins to the French house and, simultaneously, an equal consignment to a German house in Hamburg, with whom he had an understanding. A year went by; the two houses sent in the accounts of the sales." Since the early nineteenth century and until 1914, global trade grew nearly 100-fold. As regards the transnationalization of ties, the idea of "monopolistic capitalism" with monopolies being almost equal to states was put forward in the early twentieth century. The idea of replacing states with transnational corporations was developed over a hundred years ago.

The idea of today's globalization based on the Internet and a free transfer of information has become a cliché in political science. The nineteenth-century globalization was based on a free transfer of information as well, via the telegraph. It developed at a pace equal to the pace of the Internet's proliferation. Since the early 1830s, German states, Russia, and Great Britain adopted the electric telegraph. In 1843, the Scottish physicist Alexander Bain patented the electric telegraph, which made it possible to transfer images. In 1858, a transatlantic telegraph connection was established. Then, telegraph came to Africa, and relay stations in Egypt and in Malta made it possible to establish a direct telegraph connection between London and Bombay. It was the invention of the telegraph that made it possible to disseminate information rapidly and to set up regular steamer and train traffic—two key modes of transportation in the nineteenth century. As for the freedom of information, it matched today's standards, sometimes exceeding them. For instance, during the Crimean War, British and French newspapers were sold in St. Petersburg, something unthinkable for the wars of the twentieth century.

American political scientist James Rosenau suggested that a tourist and a terrorist are the symbols of international relations in the new globalized world. To put his comparison to test, we only need to read Fyodor Dostoevsky's novels about Europe in the 1860s, where Baden-Baden and Nice were chock-full of tourists and of outright "network terrorists" like Stavrogin and Verkhovensky. "Millennials live on credit in rented apartments, use car sharing, work in co-working environments, while everything they earn goes into traveling. They have no ties to anything, they own nothing, they have no property. They do not create property either, the only thing they are engaged in is self-expression," says Evgeny Krutikov, a military expert from Russia. But is it not the spitting image of the nineteenth century world where all kinds of Erast Fandorins and Prince Florizels spent half their lives traveling around the world in search of adrenaline rush? No one thought about expired visas or imported weapons, since everyone in the nineteenth century could own arms. There were no specific restrictions on movements: A Russian officer strolling around Paris or Nagasaki was just as common as an Austrian officer at a ball in Paris or St. Petersburg, and a Prussian archeologist needed no visas to go up the Egyptian pyramids or to drink coffee with Omar Pasha.

The nineteenth-century globalization left us an amazing artifact, Jules Verne's novel *In Search of the Castaways*, where the English Lord Glenarvan and his companions freely traveled in 1864 along the 37th parallel. They did not need to take vacation or an unpaid leave at work; they did not need to apply for visas and worry about their expiration dates. While traveling, they never had trouble sending a telegram from Patagonia or Australia, and they could always get a fresh newspaper. No one prevented them from taking their personal weapons into other countries; no one demanded that they fill out customs declarations. The characters never had any problems with the locals: Everyone spoke English or French. Similarly, in another book by Jules Verne, *The Carpathian Castle*, no one ever wondered how a Hungarian count freely imported weapons into Italy. Today's global world does not have half the freedoms of the free world of the nineteenth century.

Critics object that the nineteenth-century globalization was elitist, while today's globalization is popular. In fact, the situation was almost exactly the opposite: The U.S., Australia, New Zealand, and South Africa were established by European migrants precisely in the nineteenth century. Italian, Polish, Irish, Jewish, and

Hungarian poor could move across the Atlantic or Indian Oceans to settle abroad without any visas or green cards. German immigration into Russia was so large that it virtually spanned all population groups: from officials and aristocracy, to peasants along the Volga. There was no such concept as "illegal migration": Any migrant was an eagerly awaited settler, and a country's prosperity was measured in its population figures. Intoxicated with propaganda clichés, we do not notice that our globalization never fully returned us the freedoms of the nineteenth century.

Andrey Kortunov, Russian political scientist, offers interesting data that proves the superficial nature of our globalization, "Currently, roughly 20% of economic output across the globe is exported, while only 17–19% of tourists cross their countries' borders. On average, transnational corporations produce only 9% of their products outside their country of origin, while roughly 7% of phone call minutes are international and only 3% of people live outside the countries they were born." I will add that if we take these indicators, the nineteenth-century globalization will prove to have had a far larger scale. Still, it ended in 1914: The world entered a 30-year period of isolated and protectionist national economies.

These examples demonstrate that globalization is as mortal as humans, peoples, and cultures are. The past had seen several globalization systems that ultimately crashed and burned. So, why do we think that the current globalization that in some ways does not even match the previous one is irreversible and permanent?

Whence Are Black Swans Coming?

Today's political science abounds with the "black swans" theory, coming from the economic risk theory. In 2007, the American sociologist Nassim Nicholas Taleb published a work titled *The Black Swan: The Impact of the Highly Improbable,* where he introduced the abbreviation TBS, The Black Swan. This abbreviation stems from a historical anecdote. Until 1697, people believed that swans could only be white—yet, the Dutch expedition of Willem de Vlamingh found a population of black swans in Western Australia. So, the phrase "black swan" came to mean an unexpected event, a "point of bifurcation" that changes the course of history in a radical and unexpected manner.

There is another way of looking at this theory, based on several ethical axioms that determine the very way of thinking about the TBS.

First, proponents of "black swans" believe sharp historic disruptions to be an anomaly and not the norm. TBS theorists cannot bring themselves to believe that only 70–80 years ago we lived in a world where the political map kept changing because of revolutions, wars, and upheavals. For instance, what we call "populism" and "inadmissible rhetoric" was the norm in the world between the two World Wars. It remains unclear why our world should be seen as permanent stability and not as a time between two instability periods.

Second, the "black swan" theory is explicitly ahistorical. It proceeds from the premise of the world history being a thing of the past, and of a radically new world having come into being after 1960 or 1970; this world does not and cannot have revolutions, wars, upheavals, ambitious, and aggressive politicians. There should be "permanent peace" with any crisis being an anomalous "black swan." Though, why exactly we should have entered a world without crises, wars, and revolutions after 1970 remains a question.

The "black swans" theory ignores the "back projection" method: A recognition of the fact that the world before us also did have societies that believed themselves to have achieved "permanent stability." During the "Age of Enlightenment," the Thirty Years' War (1618–1648) was seen as a "barbarity that would never happen again." The nineteenth century thought the Napoleonic wars would be "the last wars," and revolutions were an inadmissible sedition. (This is starkly reminiscent of the fashionable concepts of the need to preserve stability at any cost and "to be responsible"). The nineteenth century was also convinced that the humanity of the future would travel down the path of science, happiness, and progress, and when Fyodor Dostoevsky claimed the opposite, he almost appeared to be something of a weirdo. Do I need to remind the readers that when the era of World Wars arrived, it viewed the liberal and relatively peaceful nineteenth century as naïveté incarnate?

Third, the "black swan" concept means that the global world order established pursuant to the outcome of World War II is the norm for all time. Any shifts within its framework, be it the textbook collapse of the Soviet Union or 9/11, seems to be improbable, coming out of the blue. Nassim Taleb, the author of the theory, distinguished several types of fallacies that result in excessive confidence in one's own ability to analyze the future: (1) inclination to believe information coming from one's own environment and/or information field; (2) applying the game theory to real life; and (3) retrospective faith in predicting future events based on the analysis of the past ones. I would add the fourth fallacy, which is more important: belief that all historical upheavals were over after World War II.

This is where the paradoxical confusion of scientific categories on the one hand and moral and ethical categories on the other comes from. Columnists, scholars, and politicians often repeat the word "unacceptable." We see as unacceptable wars, climate change, economic crises, disasters… that is, essentially everything that has been happening for 5000 years. In the period of the relative stability of the 1970s, the public and the elites convinced themselves that all that was over for good, and we were living beyond world history. Having once believed in stable security, they considered its loss "unacceptable," which sounds highly naïve. The elites and the public in the "great powers" of the 1860s probably thought it "unacceptable" for the Vienna world order that had been forged in the Napoleonic wars to be undergoing transformations. The collapse of the Roman, Frankish, or British Empires was also unacceptable for some, which, by the way, did not prevent these empires from collapsing.

Popular discussions of combating "global challenges" is another example. We somehow forget that the very concept of "global challenges" can exist only within our Yalta-Potsdam world order that postulates equality of peoples and races and restricts states' sovereign rights to wage wars. The world order that postulates inequality of states and views expansion as natural does not have any global challenges. Transitioning to such a "non-Yalta" world order will mean eliminating the very notion of "global challenges." This scenario is unthinkable only if we believe that the world shaped pursuant to the outcomes of World War II is the norm for all times, until the end of the world. This thesis has already been put under question by the major crisis sparked by the Russian special operation in Ukraine which started on February 24, 2022.

It is far better to view "black swans" not as accidents, but as the result of processes in society or in inter-country interactions taking a definite shape. The collapse of the USSR gave shape to the processes that had been transpiring in the late Soviet society; 9/11 was the conclusion of America's policies in the Middle East; the financial crisis of 2008–2009 resulted from free transnational capital flows within the Jamaica financial system. It is quite possible that the current pandemic and the unprecedented lockdown regime it prompted is not a black swan that has come out of the blue, but the conclusion of the processes that had been brewing under the cover of globalization.

The Four Alarm Bells for Globalization

A couple decades ago, political scientists heatedly discussed the basis of globalization: Is it the speed of information transfer or increasing transnational connections? In fact, these are all consequences of the free trade regime that is globalization's true foundation. Its foundations were laid down in the mid-1940s with the adoption of the General Agreement on Tariffs and Trade (GATT) that was transformed into the World Trade Organization (WTO) in 1995. Simultaneously, the 1944 Bretton Woods Conference established institutions that monitored global capital flows and states' financial policies. The foundations of globalization were finally cemented at the Jamaica Financial Conference that established a system of floating exchange rates and free trading (FOREX). Information technologies (IT) or artificial intelligence technologies (AI) simply provided the system with the requisite technologies.

When the World War II victorious powers created this system, they strove to fill in two gaps in the previous globalization. First, they introduced a target loan system controlled by the IMF and the World Bank with a view to preventing other countries' MIC from creating an alternative to the MIC established by victorious powers. Second, they created a system for issuing stabilization loans intended to prevent another Great Depression of 1929–1933. Simultaneously, the IMF's expanding lending system made most developing countries "eternal debtors" that had no chance for an economic breakthrough.

These are the rules that were legitimized by the famous Washington Consensus of 1989 that postulated the increased role of market relations, maintaining the free trade regime, and reducing the importance of the public sector. The Washington Consensus meant changes in the structure of national economies. These changes entailed reducing public property and state investment projects. It made it harder to build industrial complexes and, consequently, to create military potentials alternative to G7's potential. At the same time, liberalizing foreign trade system and attracting investment reduced states' capability to control national economic systems. Developing countries were evolving prerequisites for the appearance of new social group geared toward transnational connections and certain consumption standards.

American economist Manuel Castells predicted the collapse of this system back in 2000. He was the first to point out that the global economic system contains an insurmountable contradiction. The global services economy requires an increasingly greater money supply so that consumers could unfailingly pay for the services. However, it is only national governments that can increase money supply and that requires increasing national control over monetary policies. This phenomenon was objectively taking the global economic system toward collapsing into national and regional sectors. Amid the triumphant expansion of the dollar zone and the institution of the euro in the 1990s, the "Castells' paradox" remained virtually unnoticed. In the meantime, it began to come true.

The first alarm bell for globalization rang after 9/11 that affected American public's attitude to globalization. In the 1990s, the U.S. perceived globalization as a historically progressive phenomenon based on liberal principles. On January 24, 2000, President Bill Clinton in his annual State of the Union address even said that globalization was in line with the U.S. national interests. In the fall of 2001, American experts started saying that under certain conditions, globalization might prove dangerous for the US. On September 20, 2001, in his State of the Union address, George W. Bush said it that the time when states ceded their sovereignty to supra-national bodies was over, and now was the time to take sovereignty back. His statement had practical consequences: On October 24, 2001, U.S. Congress passed the Patriot Act that envisaged:

- tightening the U.S. visa regime via expanding the powers of the border and customs control services;
- expanding secret services' control over the media in matters of preventing propaganda of terrorism;
- special services were granted control over IP databases of their employees;
- U.S. President was granted the power to sack and appoint attorneys general (was in effect until 2007).

In 2002, the Patriot Act served as basis for creating the Department of Homeland Security. Its task was to prevent terrorist attacks in the U.S. and minimize the damage they cause. In 2004, the office of Director of National Intelligence was established as a cabinet-level position with the power to coordinate the activities of all special services. Simultaneously, the National Counterterrorism Center was being established. Formally, the director was granted extensive powers ranging from monitoring the funding of intelligence services to coordinating their relevant operation plans. These steps taken by the Republican administration shaped new agenda in discussions on globalization: The possibility of partially restricting civil rights to protect the state from terrorist attacks.

The U.S. example proved relevant for other states that imposed control over the freedom of movement. Economists continued talking about globalization and the "free world," although the state was step-by-step winning back its positions. When traveling to the U.S. or Canada, we had to name our future address at the departure airport, to show a copy of the invitation, to provide contact information for the party that sent the invitation, and then take off our coat and shoes to go through metal detectors. To receive a U.S. visa, we were fingerprinted, and our irises were scanned, to be checked at the border. Naturally, "millennium" liberals claimed that those were all temporary steps, explained the tightened controls away by the "U.S. specifics" or else they said things would change once George W. Bush and the neocons were no longer in power. For a while, it was possible to somehow explain away the paradox of border and customs controls being tightened instead of relaxed amid globalization. Yet, de-globalization was picking up steam.

The second alarm bell that showed the limits of the current globalization was the inability to develop a full-fledged WTO charter. To remove this obstacle, a round of talks was launched in 2001 in Doha, Qatar's capital, but the negotiations did not produce any tangible results. Its participants faced three problems: food security, copyright laws (blocking the possibility of creating large national manufacturing sectors without relying on investment policies), and introducing a single energy tariff system which would put some countries at disadvantage due to their different climate conditions. The participants failed to handle these problems, which showed that most countries within the Jamaica system were not going to fully abandon protectionism.

The global financial crisis of 2008–2010 sounded the third alarm bell. It was not only the matter of the relatively mild global debt market meltdown. What was far more important was that the crisis rehabilitated state intervention into economy. In the fall of 2008, Henry Paulson, the Secretary of the Treasury, presented a plan that envisaged governmental subsidies to large businesses and the Federal Reserve System buying back the debt obligations of problematic banks. As part of its implementation, Congress adopted the Emergency Economic Stabilization Act; it served as basis for establishing the Office of Financial Stability. Other countries traveled the same route: 15 EU states agreed to introduce the system of state guarantees for bank loans; Russia's government provided liquidity for the banking system and "mildly" devalued the ruble; Beijing adopted the program of re-orienting China's economy toward domestic demand and switching some dollar reserves into gold. 2010 Basel III international accords mandated that lending organizations create an additional buffer capital and introduce caps on financial leverage allowed to financial intermediaries in order to prevent new unsecured derivatives from appearing. Nation states were gradually assuming the functions of economic regulation, which in itself ran contrary to the ideology of "globalization without borders" based on transnational corporations and "new actors."

Another result was that the 1989 Washington Consensus, justly dubbed "globalization rules," was eroding. It should have been replaced with the Seoul Consensus, a series of statements on the principles for reforming the international financial system adopted at the G20 Seoul Summit on November 11–12, 2010. Yet the Seoul declarations certainly failed to fully supplant the Washington Consensus. At the same time, they were a no-confidence statement to it. The Seoul declarations put a question mark over every decision in the Washington Consensus. If what is needed is ensuring "stable, sustainable, and balanced growth," then clearly the preceding economic growth did not meet those standards. If developing countries needed to be involved as equal partners, the Washington Consensus system was by definition unequal. So, the Washington Consensus was clearly delegitimized. Yet nothing appeared in its place.

The fourth alarm bell for globalization rang in 2014 when Russia and the West imposed economic sanctions and embargoes on each other. It was not only the long-term nature of these restrictions that constituted a problem for the globalization model. Of far greater importance was Russia's decision to create its national payment system. The world was gradually losing a single financial system based on two global currencies: the dollar and the pound sterling. Even more importantly, these systems emerged while the WTO system was in place: Essentially, great powers were going back to protectionism, bypassing the free trade regime. President Donald Trump's subsequent trade wars with the EU and China only continued and further developed the returning protectionism.

The wars of sanctions had another significant consequence. None of them resulted in transnational corporations rebelling against their governments, although the globalization theory claimed that they should have done so. Transnational corporations agreed to lose markets (and major profits with them) and complied with the decisions of the leaderships of the U.S., Germany, Italy, Russia, and China. Transnational business turned out to have been subjugated to nation states' policies and essentially did not create any alternatives to these leaderships. The statements that the world of states were being replaced with the world of corporations ("the new Middle Age") turned to be a major exaggeration. Corporations are still playing by the rules of and within the boundaries set by national governments.

For the last 20 years, the large-scale globalization project was gradually shrinking, and nation states were growing stronger inside it. So far, these developments did not extend into the private sphere, which created the illusion of globalization standing firm, but this extension had to happen sooner or later. The question was only of the exact moment when the strengthening nation states would overpower the globalization project. We may have approached this threshold in 2020.

A Non-global Alternative

These trends have deeper foundations identified by the German sociologist Karl Mannheim: Since the late nineteenth century, the world has been going through an unprecedented ascendance of statism as the strengthening of the state's functions. Three trends underlie this phenomenon. First: urbanization-generated transition to mass society that requires governing large masses of people. Second: the emergence of a more technologically prolific civilization that requires tighter centralized planning of the entire production cycle and transportation. Third: transition from aristocratic society to bureaucratic society where a strong state acts as the distributor of social spending. Today's "global freedom" that scholars from the liberal school of thinking like to talk about are just a pale shadow of the truly global freedoms of the nineteenth century.

Restrictions in the global economy have also grown instead of decreasing. Let us browse the novels of Charles Dickens and Émile Zola, or Karl Marx's Capital, and we will notice with no small surprise that the Vienna world order had virtually no barriers for the movement of capital. Nothing prevented a British entrepreneur from opening a branch of his firm in Hong Kong or Nagasaki; nothing stood in the way of a French banker buying shares in a German company or playing the stock market at the Vienna or Madrid exchange. A Russian merchant did not need any visas to travel to the World's Fair in Paris or London and close any deals he pleased there. No government had the power to cancel such a deal if, for instance, this particular member of the bourgeoisie said something politically incorrect in the media or had problems with his sources of income. Marx considered the 1863 global "cotton crisis" in detail, but he never envisioned nation states levying duties on cotton imports or even prohibiting its exports into individual "undesirable" countries. In the today's world of the alleged globalization, this level of economic freedoms is unthinkable. Today's liberal globalization failed even to restore the nineteenth century level of global freedoms, and it is already highly unlikely to restore it in the near future.

This context affords us a different perspective on whether globalization is reversible. Let us imagine our world where we cannot purchase foreign goods in our own country. We will be surprised to realize that there is no longer any trace of globalization. Abolishing free movement of goods removes the need for a global reserve currency and free currency conversion: Why do we need so many global trade deals amid universal protectionism? Abolition of free movement of capital will result in the transnational sector crashing and many related professions becoming a thing of the past. Restoring the real sector and restoring manufacturing will be the alternative to social collapses, which will require some form of mobilization.

"Mobilization" narrowly construed means a sum total of steps intended to switch a state's military and institutions into the military emergency mode. Broadly understood, a "mobilization project" is a wide-ranging use of military (force) governance methods intended to achieve certain goals. Until recently, the notion of mobilization has appeared somewhat outdated: The momentum still kept afloat the cult of globalization, openness, and all kinds of rights. However, the experience of combating the pandemic proved that mobilization projects are back.

This mobilization has had two consequences. Short term, it demanded that citizens of all developed countries radically overhaul their way of life. We are not talking only restricting their rights to move and to leave their homes; citizens also had to switch to remote work and change their lifestyle doing their shopping online and visiting only the stores in their own neighborhood. Long term, however, we could be talking the disappearance of a whole group of professions in the services sector. Abolition of mass tourism will result in the death of tourism and hotel sector business, and reduced contacts with other states will result in a decreased demand for translators/interpreters, lawyers, shop assistants, tour guides, etc.

Such a transition may generate a social shock. However, the experience of socioeconomic hardships at the time of the perestroika, the collapse of the USSR and

Yugoslavia, and the Balkan wars of the 1990s has shown that today's societies are quite capable of surviving these shocks. In the latest iteration, these shocks were to be undergone for the sake of the relevant countries joining globalization (it is another matter on what terms they joined the globalization and in what capacity), and now shocks may be undergone in order to abandon globalization. Naturally, it will involve social shocks, a drop in the quality of life for some social groups, changed political regimes and maybe disintegration of individual states. But who says that these phenomena have become a thing of the past after 2000?

There are nuances, though. One country, even a large one, exiting the globalization process will not signify the collapse of that process. It is more likely that the country itself will become an international outcast with all attendant consequences. Or else, such a country should have a tremendous potential for it to destroy globalization. We are talking the destruction of the very fabric of international interactions, i.e., the principles of the freedom of trade. Only in that case, a new, non-liberal economic system may be formed.

* * *

It is not some "black swans" coming out of the nowhere that are bringing about the decline of globalization. This decline is underlain by an objective process: The destruction of the global economic space amid simultaneous bolstering of the technological space for state control. By the early twenty-first century, the development of information technologies allowed for rapid manipulations of public sentiments and electoral votes, which in and of itself boosted the state's regulation potential. Today's mobilization experience can easily become a weapon of sorts for transitioning from the world of globalization to the world of nationally oriented economies that is essentially already happening.

The state governance theory proposes three efficiency criteria: (1) Purposes of governance accord with the political culture of a given country; (2) once this correlation has been found by the political elites, it remains stable; and (3) state institutions have resources for such governance. Compared to the most recent "anti-globalization" wave of the mid-twentieth century, today's level of AI development allows for a sharp increase in the potential of such governance at the national level. The early 2020s approach the period of this potential being implemented. It is only the question of the event that will legitimize the transition that has long been brewing.

A World on the Verge of Total Chaos

Nikolay Plotnikov

International security is being seriously tested. Thousands of people in various regions are struggling to survive, fearing for their safety and for the safety of their loved ones.

Apparently, new shocks seem to be coming. Corruption has proliferated across the planet, with no one—not even the United States or the European Union—able to curb it. Many people around the globe live in poverty, which creates fertile ground for radicalism. International organizations and states as institutions are becoming increasingly impotent, while non-state actors, including terrorist groups (such as Islamic State, Al-Qaeda, Boko Haram, and Al-Shabaab[1]), structures such as Open Society Foundations run by George Soros, the Rothschild Foundation, the Rockefeller Foundation, Bill Gates' business empire, and social networks (Twitter, Facebook, YouTube, etc.), are growing in strength and influence over global processes.

U.S. Policy

Despite the exacerbating domestic crisis, the United States continues to insist on its superiority, refusing to take stock of the policies of other countries, primarily those of Russia and China. Washington believes that the U.S. should demonstrate its exceptional leadership to the world and promote a liberal world order.

---

[1] Terrorist organizations banned in Russia.

The article was originally published in Russian in Mezhdunarodnaya zhizn, https://interaffairs.ru/news/show/29449.

N. Plotnikov (✉)
Russian International Affairs Council, Moscow, Russia

© China Social Sciences Press 2023
Institute of Russian, Eastern European and Central Asian Studies, CASS and Russian International Affairs Council, *Global Governance in the New Era*,
https://doi.org/10.1007/978-981-19-4332-4_4

The U.S. attempts to hold onto its positions by introducing disruptive technologies in the sphere of artificial intelligence, walking out of international arms control and non-proliferation agreements. The U.S.–Russia relations are at their lowest ebb since the Cold War. Washington's reluctance to launch dialog with Moscow, build relations on the basis of mutual compromise and take Russia's interests into account makes improving relations nigh on impossible.

The U.S. politicians see Russia as Washington's primal enemy. In an attempt to curtail Russia's foreign policy and prevent its economy from flourishing, Washington is increasing its sanction pressure, inciting conflicts near Russia's borders (for example, supporting the war in Ukraine) and provoking political instability in Russia (financially supporting non-systemic opposition).

The Increasing Activity of Non-state Actors

Non-state actors are stepping up their activities in global affairs. We are primarily referring here to terrorist organizations, such as the Islamic State, Al-Qaeda, Boko Haram, and Al-Shabaab, whose emergence is a direct result of the general collapse of statehood.

In the Middle East, Syria, Iraq, and Yemen have suffered most as a result of terrorist activities. In Northern Africa, it is Libya. The authorities of these countries have lost their monopoly on legitimate measures in domestic and foreign policy. Non-state actors are unable to even partly fulfill the functions of the state. Their activities are mostly limited to collecting taxes and doling out punishment against dissenting jihadists, which leads to deepening chaos and further fragmentation of states.

Modern terrorist organizations are no longer small groups of poorly armed but wealthy people. They are well-organized structures with extensive networks, multimillion-dollar incomes, and specialized divisions. They are constantly looking for new forms, methods and techniques to make a greater impact on a large scale. They learn from each other, adopt the most efficient practices and try not to repeat the mistakes of their predecessors.

The Islamic State and al-Qaeda are adapting to the new conditions following their defeats in the Middle East. Once the idea of creating an Islamic State in Iraq and Syria fell apart, their leadership switched focus to other countries, covering a huge area from Africa (Libya, Morocco, Tunisia, Somalia, the Democratic Republic of the Congo and Mozambique) to Asia (Afghanistan, Pakistan, Sri Lanka, the Philippines and Malaysia). The main goal of jihadists is to carry out strikes on economic centers to spark instability. Burning forests and agricultural fields and poisoning domestic animals have become common.

Other non-state actors contribute to the destruction of statehood and the erosion of state borders: tribal and ethnic groups and organized criminal organizations involved in the trafficking of drugs, weapons, people and human organs and the smuggling

A World on the Verge of Total Chaos 41

of consumer goods. Depending on the situation, they act by themselves or alongside stronger organizations.

Trade Wars, Economic Sanctions, and the Shadow Economy

In economics, trade wars, and economic sanctions have become the norm. As for sanctions, the United States is the undisputed leader here, with Washington's NATO allies often finding themselves on the receiving end of these restrictive measures. The United States uses sanctions to force others to take political and economic actions that would benefit Washington. A vivid example here is the sanctions against Nord Stream 2, which affect the interests of EU companies.

Now, the United States has started a trade war with China. Trade wars, however, are a double-edged sword. An escalating trade war with China could result in Beijing's restricting U.S. imports of rare earth metals, which are crucial to consumer electronics, military systems and medical research. However, it is the consumers who will suffer most of all.

The energy sector is experiencing a shortage of resources, and hydrocarbon supply routes between producing and consumer countries are becoming increasingly vulnerable.

Most major fields with proven oil reserves are located in the Middle East, Venezuela, Canada and Russia. The reserves are rapidly decreasing given the rate of economic development and explosive population growth. New supplies are increasingly difficult to find. According to estimates based on proven reserves and current consumption levels, we will only have enough oil for another 45–50 years (coal and natural gas are predicted to last slightly longer, approximately 60–70 years).

The issue of ensuring the safety of oil tanker transportation is particularly relevant, accounting for over 60% of global oil trade. Approximately 90% of Middle East oil passes through a few "bottlenecks" of global maritime shipping: the Hormuz, Bab al-Mandab Strait, Malacca and Gibraltar straits, the Suez Canal, the Bosporus, and the Dardanelles. Pressure on any of these waterways could hit global oil and liquefied natural gas trade and the commodities markets.[2] The episode with the Ever Given container ship blocking the Suez Canal is worth mentioning, as it was holding back goods worth approximately $9.6 billion per day, costing the Suez Canal some $14–15 million per day.[3]

Pipelines are also a viable target for terrorists, as their length makes it difficult to ensure their safety.

The shadow economy is flourishing as well. Its size is inherently difficult to measure, but it is deeply ingrained in every country without exception. Most of the shadow economy remains focused in Sub-Saharan Africa, Latin America, and the

---

[2] The cost of the Suez Canal blockage//BBC news. March 29, 2021. URL: https://www.bbc.com/news/business-56559073.

[3] Ibid.

Caribbean. It draws people into criminal relations, creates conditions for organized crime to prosper, undermines the administrative functions of the state, and deprives it of a significant part of its revenues to exacerbate socio-economic issues. The shadow economy permeates banking, investment and commodities trade, undermining the confidence of people in their governments.

Transnational Organized Crime

Transnational organized crime (TOC) is inextricably linked with the shadow economy. Criminal groups create extensive networks for their nefarious activities: drug trafficking, migrant smuggling, money laundering, and trafficking in drugs, humans, human organs, firearms, counterfeit goods, natural resources, wild animals, and valuable cultural artifacts.

TOC is a huge business, accounting for up to 7% of the global GDP. From 2015–2016, it was estimated at $3.6–4.8 trillion.[4] TOC is able to adapt quickly to markets, giving rise to new types of crime. It is also particularly prevalent in conflict regions, notably in Syria and Iraq.

There has been an increase in intellectual property crimes, cyber theft from bank accounts of organizations and individuals, money forgery, and the production of fake alcoholic beverages and food.

Depletion of Natural Resources

The excessive exploitation of natural resources has led to a huge shortage. Large and profitable deposits in all countries with a developed extractive industry are becoming depleted, leading to climate change and the degradation of flora and fauna. As a result, more than 31,000 of the planet's 30 million known species of animals and plants are now endangered, 8% of all known animal species have disappeared and 22% are in danger of extinction.[5]

Approximately half of the forests that originally covered the Earth's land surface are gone.[6] One of the main reasons for this was the clearing of forests for agricultural land due to population growth.

---

[4] Transnational Organized Crime and the Impact on the Private Sector//Global Initiative. December 7, 2017. URL: https://globalinitiative.net/analysis/transnational-organized-crime-and-the-impact-on-the-private-sector-the-hidden-battalions/.

[5] UN Report: Nature's Dangerous Decline "Unprecedented"; Species Extinction Rates "Accelerating"//UN. URL: https://www.un.org/sustainabledevelopment/blog/2019/05/nature-decline-unprecedented-report/.

[6] Toolkit and Guidance for Preventing and Managing Land and Natural Resources Conflict. Extractive Industries and Conflict//UN. URL: https://www.un.org/en/land-natural-resources-conflict/pdfs/GN_Extractive.pdf.

Increased deforestation leads to an annual increase in greenhouse gas emissions of 12–17%. According to the World Health Organization, nine out of every ten people on the planet breathe air with high levels of pollution, and 7 million people die from air pollution every year.[7]

In the next 100 years, the Earth may run out of phosphorus reserves, which are needed for plants to grow. A missing solution to the problem may lead to conflicts similar to wars over oil and fresh water. The disappearance of phosphorus could result in the extinction of humankind.

The struggle for natural resources leads to the redistribution of spheres of influence and wars. Forty percent of all civil wars fought over the past 60 years have been connected with this.[8] At the same time, natural resources themselves have been used as a source of financing wars.

Food Shortage

There has been a steady increase in the number of starving people since 2014. In 2019, just before the coronavirus pandemic, 690 million people worldwide were undernourished. The number is expected to surpass 840 million by 2030, especially in regions where civil wars are unfolding and where catastrophic climatic events tend to happen more frequently.

The COVID-19 pandemic has increased the risk of a global spike in food prices. In the poorest countries, food makes up to 40–60% of the consumer basket. Approximately 60% of people living in Africa and South Asia cannot afford a healthy diet. The world is on the verge of a global food crisis.[9]

Water Scarcity

In addition, the world is running out of drinking water. One in four of the world's 500 largest cities are in water stress. Drinking water reserves have almost dried up in Cape Town, and the situation has reached the point of crisis in Bangalore, Beijing,

---

[7] UN Report: Nature's Dangerous Decline "Unprecedented"; Species Extinction Rates "Accelerating"//UN. URL: https://www.un.org/sustainabledevelopment/blog/2019/05/nature-decline-unprecedented-report/.

[8] UN Report: Nature's Dangerous Decline "Unprecedented"; Species Extinction Rates "Accelerating"//UN. URL: https://www.un.org/sustainabledevelopment/blog/2019/05/nature-decline-unprecedented-report/.

[9] Hunger is Rising, COVID-19 Will Make it Worse//UN. URL: https://gho.unocha.org/global-trends/hunger-rising-covid-19-will-make-it-worse.

Sao Paulo, Cairo, Jakarta, Istanbul, and Mexico City. London may face a serious water shortage before 2040.[10]

Groundwater has become the only source of water for 2 billion people across the planet. However, more than 30% of the world's largest groundwater systems are in a disastrous state. The largest pools of groundwater are rapidly becoming depleted. At the same time, the global demand for water is increasing by approximately 1% per year.[11]

The increase in water demand follows overall population growth, economic development, changes in eating habits and climate change. By 2030, the global water demand will be 40% higher than it is today. Climatologists predict that by 2050, when the global population reaches 9.4–10.2 billion, slightly more than half of it will live in regions with a shortage of water.

The Middle East is home to 11 out of the 18 most water-stressed countries. Lack of water is one of the causes behind the numerous conflicts in the region. Prolonged droughts in Syria, Iraq and Iran are forcing rural dwellers to move to cities, increasing the number of people living in poverty and sparking their radicalization.

Non-renewable aquifers—the main source of water for some countries in the Middle East—are shrinking. While for rich countries such as Saudi Arabia, Qatar, Kuwait, and the United Arab Emirates it is easier to solve the water issue by investing in desalination and improving infrastructure to reduce water losses, nations mired in conflict (Yemen, Syria and Iraq), as well as Jordan, which has taken in a huge number of refugees from Syria and Libya, and the Gaza Strip, find themselves unable to do the same.

The population in most countries of the Middle East is growing, while the amount of water is dwindling. The situation is aggravated by the ineffective use of water resources due to outdated technologies. Water losses in some countries are as high as 60%.[12]

The Environment

For the environment, problems associated with climate change, deforestation, desertification, use of household waste, environmental pollution (including pollution of the world ocean), and proliferation of diseases that threaten the health of people, domestic animals and crops are only getting worse. Global warming is causing more intense and destructive droughts, hurricanes and heatwaves than ever before, and this is happening with alarming regularity.

---

[10] Water Scarcity Looms in London's Future//Circle of Blue. March 28, 2018. URL: https://www.circleofblue.org/2018/world/water-scarcity-looms-in-londons-future/.

[11] Overview//WWF. URL: https://www.worldwildlife.org/threats/water-scarcity#:~:text=Agriculture%20consumes%20more%20water%20than,areas%20and%20floods%20in%20others.&text=By%202025%2C%20two-thirds%20of,population%20may%20face%20water%20shortages.

[12] Water Scarcity Looms in London's Future//Circle of Blue. March 28, 2018. URL: https://www.circleofblue.org/2018/world/water-scarcity-looms-in-londons-future/.

Urbanization has been leading to the destruction of natural landscapes, which are now blemished with buildings made out of concrete and brick. This interrupts the natural water cycle, leading to floods. Increasing population density means more gas emissions, greater air pollution and an increase in the volume of household waste.

Deforestation and forest fires are responsible for more than 10% of greenhouse gas emissions, a number that will only rise as forest area decreases.[13] The depletion of forest cover destroys the habitats for wildlife, whose population has shrunk by more than 50% since 1970. Around one million species are on the verge of extinction.[14]

Global warming is causing sea levels to rise, which may lead to catastrophic consequences for humankind. Today, approximately one in ten people lives less than 10 m above sea level. By 2050, a number of coastal cities and small island states will experience annual flooding.[15]

The melting of the permafrost in the Arctic means that increasing levels of methane and carbon dioxide are emitted into the atmosphere, accelerating global warming. Glaciers in the Himalayas and the Hindu Kush supply water to nearly 2 billion people. The rate at which they are melting bears the risk of a shortage of drinking water.

Demographic and Migration Issues

The world faces increasing demographic imbalances and large-scale migration processes. While the number of people living on the planet is growing, this growth is uneven. In developed countries, it is slowing down, with retirees making up an increasing proportion of the population. Meanwhile, in poorer countries, where a significant part of the population lives on less than $2 per day, the opposite seems to be the case: a growing population with an increased number of young people. This, as well as limited employment opportunities, makes the youth susceptible to radicalization, and terrorist organizations recruiters take full advantage of this.[16]

Demographic trends suggest that the global population may reach 10–11 billion people by 2100, with more than 3 billion living in Sub-Saharan Africa and 1 billion

---

[13] 15 sources of greenhouse gases//Allianz. September 12, 2014. URL: https://www.allianz.com/en/press/extra/knowledge/environment/140912-fifteen-sources-of-greenhouse-gases.html.

[14] 68% Average Decline in Species Population Sizes Since 1970, Says New WWF Report//WWF. September 9, 2020. URL: https://www.worldwildlife.org/press-releases/68-average-decline-in-species-population-sizes-since-1970-says-new-wwf-report.

[15] Ranking of the World's Cities Most Exposed to Coastal Flooding Today and in the Future//OECD. December 4, 2007. URL: https://www.oecd.org/environment/cc/39729575.pdf.

[16] World Bank Forecasts Global Poverty to Fall Below 10% for First Time; Major Hurdles Remain in Goal to End Poverty by 2030//The World Bank. October 4, 2015. URL: https://www.worldbank.org/en/news/press-release/2015/10/04/world-bank-forecasts-global-poverty-to-fall-below-10-for-first-time-major-hurdles-remain-in-goal-to-end-poverty-by-2030#:~:text=PRESS%20RELEASE-,World%20Bank%20Forecasts%20Global%20Poverty%20to%20Fall%20Below%2010%25%20for,to%20End%20Poverty%20by%202030.

in the Middle East.[17] This kind of population growth raises a number of questions: Are we capable of sustaining decent living conditions for this many people? How will rapid population growth impact the environment? How will it affect the struggle for access to agricultural land, natural resources, and water?

Mass migration is primarily caused by low standards of living, conflicts, violence, climate-induced disasters and environmental changes. In 2020 alone, some 37 million people migrated from low-income countries and countries ravaged by civil war and conflict.[18]

Cyberthreats

Information technologies continue to develop at an exponential pace. They are introduced into all spheres of life: economy, industry, education, healthcare, culture, the services sector, etc. A disruption in the functioning of any of these could have catastrophic consequences. This is why many countries are developing cyberweapons, whose use for political and military ends has become a part of everyday life. They do not require declaring war or violating state borders. Cyberweapons can be used "as a matter of course," inflicting serious material and reputational damage on the enemy. A prime example of this is the alleged cyberwar between Israel and Iran.[19] In late April 2020, a cyberattack was carried out against Israel's water distribution networks and sanitation systems. Hackers attempted to shut down the pumps and penetrate the system that monitors chlorine concentration in tap water. Cyber defense systems identified and blocked the attack before it could cause any significant damage.

Israeli operatives concluded that the attack was too sophisticatedly executed for amateur hackers and must have been the work of the Iranian state. It is unclear whether the attack was a response to Israel's repeated strikes against Iranian targets in Syria or whether it was a new tactic aimed at opening a cyber-front against Israel. In any case, it posed a threat to civilian infrastructure and was taken very seriously in Israel, as tampering with the chlorine content of drinking water threatens the lives of civilians. This was therefore a biological attack as much as it was a cyberattack. The attempt to hack into the water distribution networks made Israel see Iran as a threat of a different kind.

Israel did not wait long to retaliate. On May 19, 2020, The Washington Post reported a hacker attack on Iran's Shahid Rajaee port terminal in Bandar Abbas.

---

[17] The World Population in 2100, by Country//Visual Capitalist. September 2, 2020. URL: https://www.visualcapitalist.com/world-population-2100-country/.

[18] International Migration 2020 Highlights//UN. January 15, 2021. URL: https://reliefweb.int/report/world/international-migration-2020-highlights-enruzh#:~:text=In%202020%2C%20nearly%20177%20million,upper-middle-income%20country.

[19] Officials: Israel linked to a disruptive cyberattack on Iranian port facility//The Washington Post. May 18, 2020. URL: https://www.washingtonpost.com/national-security/officials-israel-linked-to-a-disruptive-cyberattack-on-iranian-port-facility/2020/05/18/9d1da866-9942-11ea-89fd-28fb313d1886_story.html.

The port, located in the Strait of Hormuz, serves up to 60% of Iran's trade turnover and houses a strategic naval base. The attack caused a great deal of damage to the terminal. The port's computer systems were down for two days, creating massive backups on the waterways and traffic jams on roads leading up to the facility, leading to significant delays in the transportation of goods and passengers. The Iranian side worked feverishly to contain the attack, minimize the damage and restore port operations as quickly as possible. However, their countermeasures mostly proved to be futile, suggesting that extremely sophisticated and effective cyber weapons had been used in the attack.

The exchange of cyber strikes pushes the situation into a more dangerous and uncontrollable area.

* * *

We are living in a world that faces an unprecedented number of threats. The current situation, aggravated by the coronavirus pandemic, leaves many deprived and exasperated by the uneven distribution of wealth, unable to meaningfully participate in social life. This leads to anger, distrust to the authorities, anarchistic sentiments and a disregard for laws.

To prevent the world from spiraling into an uncontrollable tailspin, we need to come together to end civil wars and violence, repeal sanctions, solve food and water problems, fight poverty and protect the environment. Restoring people's faith in international law and the state allows us to curtail radicalization in poor countries and stabilize the migration situation around the world, which reduces the mobilization of terrorist structures.

Open Multilateralism: Evolutionary Results of the International Institutions

Idea and Act: Multilateralism in the Governance of Eurasia

Zhuangzhi Sun

As the Cold War came to an end, a complex array of changes began to emerge in the political landscape of international relations in Eurasia. After the breakdown of the Soviet Union, the Commonwealth of Independent States (CIS), a regional organization led by the Russian Federation, came into existence. The CIS has established a huge body of permanent institutions and, further, even a joint armed force. As time goes by, the traditional approach for regional cooperation turns out to be insufficient for the developmental pursuit of these newly established countries and the multilevel needs of regional governance. Meanwhile, the Shanghai Cooperation Organization (SOC), together with other multilateral mechanisms, has come to the front as a brand new example for regional cooperation. With two major powers in this place, such as China and Russia shouldering more responsibilities, a new model of regional governance has taken shape and begun to play a constructive role in this regard.

A Distinctive Regionalization Process of Eurasia

In 1991, 15 newly established countries, each being independent sovereign states, appeared in the geographical space after the dissolution of the Soviet Union. Inheriting its legal status in the international law system, the Russian Federation summoned the Commonwealth of Independent States (CIS) with Ukraine, Belarus and other countries in hope of a peaceful separation among the republics. However, regional cooperation actually lagged behind. In the mid-to-late 1990s, Russia proactively led the establishment of several subregional multilateral mechanisms, such as the Customs Union, the Eurasian Economic Community, and the Collective Security

---

Z. Sun (✉)
Institute of Russian, Eastern European and Central Asian Studies, Chinese Academy of Social Sciences, Beijing, China

© China Social Sciences Press 2023
Institute of Russian, Eastern European and Central Asian Studies, CASS and Russian International Affairs Council, *Global Governance in the New Era*, https://doi.org/10.1007/978-981-19-4332-4_5

Treaty Organization. However, these mechanisms encountered multiple practical difficulties and have not addressed the fundamental concerns for regional governance.

Development of the CIS and its Dilemma of Regional Governance

On December 8, 1991, leaders of Russia, Ukraine and Belarus met in Belovezh and signed an agreement declaring that t*he Soviet Union, as a subject of international law and a geopolitical reality, would cease its existence.* The agreement also announced the establishment of the Commonwealth of Independent States (CIS), with a coordination body located in Minsk, the capital of Belarus. On December 12 of the same year, leaders from five Central Asian republics, including Kazakhstan, issued a statement in Ashgabat, expressing their willingness to participate in the CIS as *equal founding countries*, a de facto move showing their malcontent against the unilateral decision by the three Slavic countries. On December 21, leaders of 11 republics, including Azerbaijan, Armenia, Belarus, Kyrgyzstan, Moldova, Kazakhstan, Russia, Uzbekistan, Ukraine, Tajikistan, and Turkmenistan, met in Almaty and passed the *Almaty Declaration* which, together with other related documents, declared the formal establishment of the CIS and the cessation of the Soviet Union. Georgia, as an observer state, sent representatives to attend the meeting and it was not until December 1993 that this country, which was in the midst of both internal chaos and external threats, became a full member of the CIS. The CIS, in essence, was a transitional international organization to replace the Soviet Union, without a clear direction for its future development.

The establishment of the CIS did not mark the beginning of a new form of regional cooperation but rather served as a *caretaker agency* for the newly established countries to carve up the heritage from the Soviet Union, with continuous conflicts surpassing cooperative consensus among its members. The three Baltic countries, which also sit within the geographic space of the former Soviet Union, did not join the CIS but instead entered into the European Union and NATO. In August 2005, Turkmenistan announced its withdrawal from the CIS for the preparation of becoming a state with permanent neutrality. In August 2008, Georgia, which went to a *Five-Day War* with Russia over the South Ossetia issue, decided to withdraw from the CIS and completed all procedures required by August 18, 2009. In March 2014, Ukraine also announced its withdrawal from the CIS due to the annexation of Crimea by Russia. At this moment, there are actually only 9 founding members of the CIS, accounting for just three-fifths of the total.

In 1993, the disintegration of the *ruble* area cut off the ties that the CIS relied on to maintain the close economic relationship. Russia was unwilling to offer financial support to the newly established countries as the former Soviet Union did, and was also reluctant to yield absolute control over this region, particularly its superiority in terms of military and security. Admittedly, the CIS served as a unique platform and balanced the special relations among members of the former Soviet Union: based on a number of documents, some overarching principles of political and economic interaction among its members have been pinned down, guaranteeing the most fundamental rights and interests of the newly established countries. However, regional governance requires the formation of behavioral norms that all parties abide by at all levels, yet the CIS countries, obviously, gradually distanced themselves from each other in terms of politics, economy, society, and culture, even with emerging armed territorial conflicts, which means that regional governance did not actually come onto the agenda during this period of time.

A Regional Economic and Security System Led by Russia

In 1992, the CIS countries signed a collective security treaty in Tashkent, Uzbekistan. Since each CIS country started building its own defense system, unified armed forces did not exist for long. Russia has basically inherited the military strength of the Soviet Union and is now still responsible for regional air defense and even the security of some countries' external borders.[1] In the early 1990s, a large-scale bloodshed broke out between Azerbaijan and Armenia regarding sovereignty over Nagorno-Karabakh. In Georgia, Abkhazia and South Ossetia, seeking greater autonomy, confronted their central government. Tajikistan also experienced a civil war. Russia intervened in all those conflicts, yet not through any multilateral mechanism. Therefore, although the ceasefire was achieved, anti-Russian sentiment has been growing in many CIS countries.

Facing the eastern expansion by NATO and the European Union, Russia has felt increasing geopolitical pressure and thus sped up regional cooperation with its absolute dominance, with handling the economic crisis through integration as the first step. In March 1996, Russia, Belarus, Kazakhstan, and Kyrgyzstan signed an agreement to establish a customs union, which aims to coordinate the economic policies of these four countries and scale up the process of regional cooperation. In February 1999, Tajikistan joined this union. In October 2000, the five countries mentioned above signed another treaty to reshape this customs union into the Eurasian Economic Community. Later, Uzbekistan applied to join the Eurasian Economic Community in October 2005 and became an official member in 2006 but shortly after that, Uzbekistan proposed to cancel its membership in October 2008.

The Collective Security Treaty, signed in May 1992, came into effect in 1994 and was valid for the next five years. Armenia, Belarus, Kazakhstan, Kyrgyzstan, Russia, and Tajikistan renewed the treaty in April 1999, but Azerbaijan, Georgia, and Ukraine did not. On May 14, 2002, the Moscow Conference on the Collective Security Treaty adopted the resolution on the establishment of the Collective Security Treaty Organization (CSTO). On October 7 of the same year, the contracting parties signed an agreement on the legal status of the CSTO and articles of this organization

---

[1] Refers to borders with non-CIS countries.

in Kishinev. Uzbekistan returned to the organization on August 16 2006. The CSTO is, in essence, a military-political group that has established a rapid responding force and often holds joint military maneuvers, playing an increasingly important role in regional security affairs. However, in June 2012, considering its cooperation with Western countries, Uzbekistan decided to withdraw from the CSTO.

The establishment of the Eurasian Economic Community and the Collective Security Treaty Organization led to great fragmentation within the CIS, with countries siding with Russia joining the Russian-led regional mechanism. Russia's initial purpose was to restart the integration of the post-Soviet space, strengthen its regional influence, and provide strong strategic support for restoring its status as a great power. However, some CIS members have firmly embarked on a path to get rid of Russia's influence or even become anti-Russian after the color revolution under the instigation of the West. The remaining countries also have no intention of completely siding with Russia. As a result, such a regional mechanism of governance dominated by Russia appears to be in the form of multiple concentric circles: the CIS is at the outermost periphery which still has some values but cannot play a constructive role in promoting multilateral cooperation in the region; the Eurasian Economic Community plays a leading role in economic affairs; and the CSTO serves as the pillar of regional security governance. Russia has even considered replacing these two organizations for regional cooperation with a more unified Eurasian Union, but such a proposal was strongly opposed by its allies such as Kazakhstan and Belarus. Therefore, Russia started the Eurasian Economic Union in January 2015 to replace the Eurasian Economic Community in the first place.

Development of Regional Governance at Different Levels

Out of the need for self-improvement through collective unity, a series of moves have also been made in subregional cooperation in the CIS region. For example, in 1994, Kazakhstan, Uzbekistan, and Kyrgyzstan signed an agreement on the establishment of a unified economic zone. After Tajikistan joined this agreement in 1998, the organization became the Central Asian Economic Community. With the expansion of cooperation, it was renamed the Central Asian Cooperation Organization in 2002. With the encouragement of the European Union and the United States, Georgia, Ukraine, Moldova, Azerbaijan, and other countries have tried to walk out of the sphere of influence by Russia and forge closer ties with Europe. In October 1997, leaders of Georgia, Ukraine, Azerbaijan, and Moldova participated in the European Commission summit in Strasbourg, France, and decided to build a regional organization codenamed GUAM, taking the initial letter of each country's name. When Uzbekistan joined in 1998, GUAM became GUUAM. In June 2001, the five presidents of GUUAM member countries signed *the Yalta Charter*. In June 2002, Uzbekistan announced the suspension of its participation in the activities by this organization and, in July 2002, the presidents of Georgia, Ukraine, Azerbaijan, and Moldova held a meeting in Yalta and signed multilateral cooperation documents such as the agreement on the establishment of a free trade area. In 2005, Uzbekistan finally withdrew from the GUUAM, which reverted to GUAM again.

There are two utterly different trends regarding the multilateral system in the Eurasian region. One is a Russian-led multilateral organization and the corresponding process for regional integration, which has yet to encounter great difficulties in practice. The other, on the contrary, is a subregional collaboration that aims to be de-Russified and come closer to the West, hoping to strengthen independence as nation-states but also facing immense hardship. After Vladimir Putin came to power, Russia has pursued stronger and more assertive foreign policies and attached greater importance to the leverage of Russia-led regional organizations to take control over the political, economic and security affairs in this region. With the establishment of the CSTO, Russia also persuaded the Central Asian Cooperation Organization to join the Eurasian Economic Community. In regard to the economy, Russia promoted the launch of the CIS Free Trade Area. Unfortunately, Russia's attempt to build a regional governance system on its own has, in reality, been hampered in many ways.

In the 1990s, the cooperation between China and Russia at the regional level was rather small and limited, mainly in the form of diplomatic dialogs and consultations. For example, in 1996, when the two countries formally established their Strategic Partnership of Coordination, China and Russia also launched the "Shanghai Five" mechanism, inviting Kazakhstan, Kyrgyzstan, and Tajikistan in Central Asia into the group, so that countries could better eliminate problems left over from the Cold War, build military mutual trust in bordering areas and start disarmament in a coordinated way. This mechanism is actually a further continuation of the original China-Soviet negotiation, realized in a unique manner of bilateral mechanisms among five countries. Ultimately, the Shanghai Cooperation Organization was formally established, as these five countries increasingly focus on regional issues and prepare to make concerted efforts to maintain stability in Central Asia.

Establishment and Development of the Shanghai Cooperation Organization

In the millennial turn, Eurasia faced many uncertainties regarding economic development and regional security. Hotspot issues, such as the chaos in Afghanistan, have brought unprecedented challenges to regional stability. The process for regional governance in Eurasia encountered new challenges but saw new opportunities as well. The Shanghai Cooperation Organization (SCO) was then born against such a special international background and has soon covered the largest area, involved the largest population, and showed the greatest potential in Eurasia. Due to huge gaps in the political, economic, and social development of its member states, newly emerged problems brought about by its expansion as well as internal political crises in some of its member states, the SCO now faces growing obstacles to achieving effective regional governance. However, the SCO upholds a new cooperative perspective for the changing realities in this region. It has already achieved great and tangible achievements and received even more expectations for further accomplishment.

Exploring New Models of Regional Cooperation

As a new type of regional organization born after the Cold War, the SCO has gone through an extraordinary path of development. The SCO is one of the first regional organizations to explicitly propose combating international terrorism and assisting young Central Asian countries in dealing with nonconventional security challenges. It plays a unique role in bringing common development and shared growth to all members, with deep participation in the betterment of regional governance and, further, even global governance. In the hinterland of Eurasia with complex and fast-changing vicissitudes, the SCO stands firm in opposing power politics and interventionism, representing the interests of emerging markets and developing countries in international affairs. In addition, China's philosophy of multilateral diplomacy is fully demonstrated through cooperation among SCO members, advocating the idea of a community with a shared future as the key for regional integration.

In retrospect of two decades of development, the success of the SCO can be categorized into the following aspects: first, it has formalized the principles for maintaining regional peace and security and realizing common prosperity with the "Shanghai Spirit", i.e., mutual trust, mutual benefit, equality, and consultation, reflecting distinctive characteristics of this historical period and promotes new philosophies for security and cooperation; second, a series of important political declarations and legal documents have been adopted by the SCO, covering various fields of cooperation such as politics, security, economy, and humanities, which exemplifies member states' views on the international climate; third, the SCO strives to maintain the unity among its member states to safeguard the authority of this multilateral system and the international law, taking targeted measures to eliminate various kinds of hidden dangers; fourth, the SCO helps to improve multilateral cooperation by holding a meeting to pool together heads of state and leaders of government to make decisions on major issues, complete the expansion of membership, and welcome new observers and dialog partners so as to continuously broaden the scope and space for multilateral cooperation; fifth, the SCO has initiated and developed a set of multilevel and multisector cooperation paradigms, with dozens of ministerial-level conferences and cooperative frameworks for different purposes, with additional efforts to establish effective working platforms and safeguarding mechanisms; sixth, the SCO has established permanent institutions such as the Secretariat and the Regional Anti-Terrorism Agency, obtained legitimate status based on international law, and built extensive contacts with other multilateral organizations or worldwide agencies, like becoming an observer of the United Nations General Assembly.

The cooperation among SCO member states features pragmatism with tangible results. In the economic field, after signing the outline for multilateral economic and trade cooperation, SCO member states have also formulated implementation plans and safeguarding mechanisms. Seven working groups have been built to carry out specific cooperation in energy, trade, transportation, agriculture, telecommunications, etc. In regard to security, after signing *the Shanghai Convention on Combating Terrorism, Separatism and Extremism*, SCO member states continued to introduce conventions on anti-drug, anti-terrorism, and anti-extremism as well as the design of security cooperation. Substantial cooperation in joint law enforcement, anti-terrorism exercises, information exchange, and personnel training has been carried out as well. As for people-to-people exchange, the SCO launched meetings for culture, education, science and technology, health, tourism, and environmental protection, established a network-based SCO university, and held large-scale exchange events such as youth dialogs and media forums. The industrialists' committee and the banking consortium have also come into being to continuously expand local cooperation. After the outbreak of the international financial crisis, multilateral cooperation by the SCO became more focused and deeper. The statement issued by heads of government in November 2020 placed special emphasis on safeguarding the economic sovereignty of SCO member states and promoting settlement in local currencies.

Proposing New Concepts for Improving Regional Governance

The SCO is not a conventional alliance of states but a novel type of regional organization with new methods for cooperation, new concepts for development and new norms for policy-making. It is impossible for the SCO to repeat other international organizations in terms of character or function; rather, the SCO aims to establish a distinct regional mechanism. Additionally, as an inter-governmental organization for cooperation, the SCO will not establish supranational institutions and will not violate the national sovereignty of its members. The SCO has created a new model for countries in the region to conduct civilized dialog and achieve shared growth, which is conducive to promoting the democratization and multipolarization of international relations as well as establishing a new reputation by member states as defenders of regional stability.

To improve regional governance, it is essential to build a good structure, establish well-designed institutions and set reasonable goals to reach consensus and seek extensive cooperation among countries in this region. Facing new problems and emerging challenges in global and regional governance, Chinese leaders, through the SCO as a platform, put forward a concept for global governance featuring extensive consultation, joint contribution and shared benefits at the 2018 Qingdao Summit, as well as an initiative to build an SCO community with a shared future, providing a China's Plan and SCO's Proposal for improving global governance. At the SCO summit in November 2020, the Chinese President Xi Jinping gave further details on building a community of health, safety, development, and people-to-people exchange. In fact, this covers the most urgent agendas for regional governance at this moment.

The new concept of regional and global governance advocated by the SCO believes that international cooperation should build fairness, maintain genuine multilateralism, oppose the Cold War mentality, say no to trade protectionism, and reduce the widening wealth gap between developed and developing countries, particularly by giving developing countries and emerging economies equal opportunities for growth. This is also how SCO differentiates itself from other international organizations dominated by Western countries. The SCO member states do not belong to any bloc of developed Western countries, so they can indeed represent the interests of most countries in the world and their policy propositions on international affairs reflect the voice of justice. As President Xi Jinping noted at the 2019 Bishkek Summit, facing increasing global challenges, the SCO must demonstrate its due international responsibility, adhere to the global governance concept of extensive consultation, joint contribution and shared benefits, step up coordination and collaboration, safeguard the international system with the United Nations at its core, advocate multilateralism and free trade, and promote the development of the international order in a more just and reasonable direction.[2]

SCO as an Example for Improving Regional Governance

The SCO adheres to the principles of equality and openness without targeting any third parties. This organization explores new ideas for regional cooperation, not by alliance but through partnership, seeking to enrich and deepen multilateral cooperation in various fields and at all levels. China-Russia comprehensive strategic partnership of coordination is the cornerstone and prerequisite for the smooth development of the SCO, and the two leading countries have strengthened their coordination on major issues, resolved potential conflicts through the Belt and Road initiative and the Eurasian Economic Union, and carried out policy communication in key areas such as economy, trade, investment, finance, and people-to-people exchange. In addition, China and the Eurasian Economic Union have signed economic and trade cooperation agreements. The SCO has therefore become an important platform for strategic planning integration by its member and observer states. Since its establishment 20 years ago, the multilateral cooperation within the framework of the SCO has fully reflected the common interests and shared concerns by countries and peoples in the region, with its international influence and reputation continuously on the rise.

From the perspective of regional governance, the SCO's contribution lies not only in eliminating conflicts and managing differences but also in laying a solid political and legal basis by signing important documents with binding forces, such as *the SCO Charter* and *the Treaty on Long-Term Good-Neighborliness, Friendship and Cooperation.* In addition, the SCO leaders' summit always expresses views on

---

[2] "Staying Focused and Taking Solid Actions for a Brighter Future of the Shanghai Cooperation Organization—Remarks by Chinese President Xi Jinping at 19th meeting of SCO Council of Heads of State", *People's Daily*, June 15, 2019.

important regional or even international issues in the form of political declarations and makes decisions or plans for multilateral cooperation in important areas. In 2021, the hasty withdrawal of US troops brought huge and growing chaos to Afghanistan. After the Dushanbe Summit, a special summit on this challenge between the SCO and the Collective Security Treaty Organization was held. The former summit adopted 30 documents, including *the Dushanbe Declaration on the 20th Anniversary of the SCO, the 2022–2024 SCO Program on Cooperation in Combating Terrorism, Separatism and Extremism,* and *the 2022–2023 Cooperation Plan for Safeguarding International Information Security,* and so on. During the latter summit, countries fully discussed the situation in Afghanistan and prepared to take measures to push for a smooth transition in Afghanistan as soon as possible.

The SCO wants a regional governance system that remains open, stays non-confrontational and does not target any third parties, focusing on improving a network of partnership; strengthening regular exchanges with subordinate agencies of the UN, playing a more proactive role in regional and international affairs, and working together to promote long-lasting peace and common prosperity in the world. The SCO has established cooperative relations with other regional organizations such as the CIS, the CSTO, ASEAN, the Eurasian Economic Union, and international financial institutions such as the World Bank, the International Monetary Fund, and the Asian Infrastructure Investment Bank. Internally, the SCO encourages non-governmental exchanges among member states and creates a good social basis for fostering friendship from generation to generation.

Regional Governance Under New Circumstances in Eurasia

The overlapping influences of the COVID-19 pandemic and the changes unseen in a century have had a great impact on the international landscape as well as the process of regionalization and globalization. Many international organizations have been badly affected, while some major countries have also proposed new initiatives for regional cooperation. Challenges for regional governance in Eurasia come not only from the uneven development among countries in the region, or differences in policies and interests but also from the manipulation and penetration by external forces. Since it is almost impossible to comprehensively address security concerns or solve economic governance issues under a single, unified framework, it is only feasible to form a multilevel and multifield cooperation approach in the first place.

New Challenges for Regional Governance in Eurasia

First, globalization and regionalization have encountered adverse currents: in disre-gard of the universally recognized norms of international law, the US continues to bully other countries; populism begins to emerge across Europe; and Cold War mentalities and protectionism have created obstacles for multilateral cooperation. After Joe Biden took office, the US continued to carry out a dual containment against both China and Russia by calling together anti-China and anti-Russia alliances, which led to the escalation of geopolitical confrontation in Eurasia.

Second, the authority of the United Nations and other international organizations has been damaged. To seek their own interests, some major powers have trampled on the principles of cooperation established by the UN Charter. The United Nations and other multilateral mechanisms have also lost their dominance in resolving international hotspots. The Nagorno-Karabakh conflict in 2020, for example, reflects the declining capability of international organizations to address regional conflicts.

Third, due to major crises coming one after another, a country in this region would find it difficult to take care of itself, not to mention forming cooperative synergy with other neighboring countries. They act separately and thus cannot establish close and effective cooperation: examples include the financial crisis, the COVID-19 pandemic, increasingly rampant international terrorism, global threats by climate change, severe drug crimes and thorny environmental issues, etc.

Sovereign states are important actors for regional governance, so relations among states and development within states will inevitably exert an impact on regional cooperation. The common ground among major powers in Eurasia is huge, together with rich resource reserves and developmental space in this region. At the same time, however, both internal and external environments are very complex. The influences of various external forces are intertwined and often collide with each other, while contradictions and differences left over from the old times are clustered and concentrated, creating conflicts and disputes among countries within the same region, many of which even go beyond the border of Eurasia. Due to the inability of various countries to build a functioning social security system in the process of national transformation, injustice and inequity are prominent in these societies. Moreover, the COVID-19 epidemic has further magnified various social contradictions, so a *deficit of governance*, i.e., inability to internal govern, has brought new challenges for inter-governmental cooperation.

Integration and Coordination of Major Diplomatic Initiatives by China and Russia

In Eurasia, China, Russia, the United States and the European Union have all put forward targeted initiatives for regional cooperation out of different strategic considerations. China's Belt and Road initiative and a community with a shared future for mankind have far-reaching influence. Russia has put forward a strategic concept called the Greater Eurasian Partnership with the Eurasian Economic Union as its cornerstone. Meanwhile, the United States has launched the Blue Dot Network and Indo-Pacific Strategy. The European Union has put forward a number of Central Asian strategies. Other countries in Eurasia would often pursue balanced diplomatic policies: on the one hand, they attach importance to the cooperation with China and Russia; while on the other hand, they also seek support from the West. For example, Kazakhstan once proposed a Road to Europe action plan, while Uzbekistan places great emphasis on the military exchanges with the United States. In addition, the United States, the European Union, Japan, and India have established the 5 + 1 format mechanism with Central Asian countries. The United States issued a new Central Asia strategy in February 2020, posing a direct challenge to the strategic interests of China and Russia in Central Asia.

In response to these circumstances brought by the competition and cooperation of major powers, the leaders of China and Russia signed a political statement in 2015 on the integration and coordination between China's Silk Road Economic Belt and Russia's Eurasian Economic Union. This would mainly include: expanding cooperation on investment and trade, optimizing trade structure; facilitating mutual investment, boosting cooperation on capacity, implementing large-scale investment projects, jointly building industrial parks and cross-border economic cooperation zones; strengthening interconnectivity in terms of logistics, infrastructure for transportation and multimodal transport; carrying out joint infrastructure development projects to expand and optimize a regional production network; establishing trade facilitation mechanisms in areas with fully-developed conditions; creating a favorable environment for the development of small and medium-sized enterprises that can play an important role in regional economic development; promoting the expansion of settlement in local currencies for trade, direct investment and loans; strengthening financial cooperation through financial institutions such as the Silk Road Fund, the Asian Infrastructure Investment Bank and the SCO Interbank Consortium; and promoting regional and global multilateral cooperation to achieve harmonious development.

Strategic integration is not only about the connection of multilateral cooperation platforms and projects at the regional level, but also about the cooperation of long-term national development plans, making itself a brand new concept for international relations and inter-governmental cooperation. In regard to the Belt and Road initiative, this relates to economic and trade cooperation, including bilateral cooperation, multilateral cooperation and even global cooperation at different levels, as the fundamental purpose is to achieve common economic development. Later, the integration gradually covered people-to-people exchange and political dialogs. Furthermore, Chinese leaders have pointed out that the Belt and Road initiative could be brought in line with even broader developmental and cooperative plans such as agendas by the United Nations, particularly by bringing part of the United Nations 2030 Agenda for Sustainable Development into the Belt and Road initiative.

Multilateral Cooperation for Better Regional Governance

Some existing multilateral mechanisms and frameworks in Eurasia mainly include the Shanghai Cooperation Organization led by China and Russia, whose cooperation scope could further extend to South Asia and West Asia after its expansion; the Eurasian Economic Union and the Collective Security Treaty Organization led by Russia with constant turmoil; the GUAM Group, which serves as a geopolitical instrument, having a distinct pro-European and anti-Russian feature; several dialog mechanisms in Central Asia, established by multiple external major powers with five countries in this place, remaining as a manifestation of diplomatic conversations and political consultation; and other informal mechanisms, including the Central Asia Regional Cooperation Summit initiated by Uzbekistan.

The geopolitical and geo-economic landscape in Eurasia has taken on a new form and shows new features. China and Russia cooperate with each other with an indeed close partnership, but each of them has its own strategic considerations. Russia tried to leverage its Greater Eurasian Partnership to form a multilateral cooperation system that best serves its interests, but it also faces great challenges in finding a reliable foothold. Meanwhile, although the United States has withdrawn its troops from Afghanistan, it has no intention to give up its presence in this region: the US tries to re-deploy its strategic layout in Eurasia by relying more on the EU and NATO to contain China and Russia. India, Japan, Turkey, Iran, and even Poland are all eager to infiltrate some different parts of Eurasia, hoping to strengthen their own regional influence. The ongoing confrontation between Russia and the West in Eurasia is a huge headache, with Ukraine and the Black Sea being the focuses of contention at this very moment.

Regional governance is an integral part of global governance. As Eurasia itself is closely linked with surrounding regions and faces growing challenges and threats from multiple directions, acting as a whole is definitely conducive to ensuring the interests of countries on this land. The SCO is highly likely to become the most important supporter for a new model of regional governance, because it can continuously propose new philosophies for cooperation, adjust its cooperation goals according to the changing realities in this region, and establish close ties with many important international organizations and multilateral mechanisms to promote cooperation in various fields. In addition, member states of the SCO can thoroughly discuss regional issues among themselves and support each other on the broader international stage. They have deeper, broader, and richer cooperation, so they stand ready to participate in improving the regional governance system. However, this region also faces some difficulties, such as insufficient capacity for action, difficulty regarding coordination in various fields and differences in the strategic interests of major powers.

Conclusion

Regional governance differs from ordinary multilateral cooperation because it is not only about the cooperation at the political and security levels but also about long-term stability and common development across this region. This requires the joint participation of governmental institutions, non-governmental organizations and civil societies, especially by strengthening the interaction in the social sphere and at the local level, to form a multidimensional structure of an enriched cooperation model. Eurasian countries have close social ties, diverse cultures and many cross-border ethnic groups. Thus, regional cooperation in Eurasia has geographical and institutional advantages that are readily in place. Improving regional governance requires that various multilateral mechanisms coordinate with each other, coexist in harmony and carry out cooperation.

Regional governance works in a similar logic as regionalism and multilateralism do. It requires considering and handling political, economic, and social affairs from a regional perspective, reflecting the overall interests and shared progress of the region. Generally, regional governance refers to such a form of multilateralism under which geographically adjacent or close countries (usually three or more countries) come together. The act is made due to the increasing degree of interdependence, out of the need to maintain their own interests, and through formal or informal mechanisms, so that they can manage complex interrelations, deal with challenges inside and outside the region together, seek cooperative spontaneity and conduct policy-making to share consensus, make common arrangements and deal with mutual relations under this framework.[3] In this sense, the basis and premise of regional governance is multilateralism, and regional governance, in turn, is an in-depth practice of multilateralism at the regional level.

Geographical proximity is the spatial advantage for the emergence and development of regionalism. Geographically adjacent countries are more inclined to develop a sense of intimacy and belonging, as they share something in common in history and culture. Political, economic, and security interdependence is another realistic factor for the emergence of regionalism.[4] Regionalism is often manifested in the form of regional integration, and each level of cooperation has some specific content and format. Regional governance in the Eurasian hinterland has unique characteristics, and the goal is also to achieve political, economic, and cultural closeness and even mutual integration at various levels, even though this kind of integration among countries faces very complex problems.

To improve the regional governance in Eurasia, countries should first enhance mutual trust and respect each other, particularly in terms of social systems and cultural background; second, form stable relations featuring interdependence and common development by using strategic bilateral and multilateral mechanisms to enhance cooperation among regional countries; third, develop widely accepted principles and institutions for effective multilateral cooperation. Chinese leaders proposed building a community of a shared future for the SCO; cultivating the soil of non-governmental friendship among member states; forming multilateral cooperation mechanisms and partnership networks in various key directions; enriching the scope of our cooperation; and, finally, playing a leading and exemplary role in building a new model of international relations that features mutual respect, equality, mutual benefit, openness, and inclusiveness. The success of regional governance lies in truly benefiting all peoples within this region and realizing shared prosperity for all countries on this land.

---

[3] Smith [1], C.77.

[4] Yang and Li [2].

References

1. Smith, M. 1997. Regions and regionalism. In *World politics*, eds. B. White, R. Little, and M. Smith. Macmillan Press LTD.
2. Yang, Yi, and Xiangyang Li. 2004. Regional Governance: From the perspective of regionalism. *Journal of Yunnan Administration College* 2: 50.

International Institutions in Contemporary Global Politics

Irina L. Prokhorenko

A distinguishing feature of the modern international system amidst economic and political globalization is the growing number and variety of nonstate actors. A special place among these is held by international (multilateral) institutions, which, in addition to informational and communicative institutions, also carry out regulatory functions. This concerns not only international intergovernmental organizations (such as the United Nations) and nongovernmental entities (such as the International Committee of the Red Cross), but also organizational structures that are considered international organizations *sui generis*. These are informal global governance forums (G7, G20) and other quasi-organizations (interparliamentary institutions, intercountry formats such as BRICS), intergovernmental and nongovernmental international conferences, regional integration groups (the European Union, ASEAN, subregional integration initiatives) and such novel integration formats, for instance as mega-regional agreements (the Regional Comprehensive Economic Partnership, the Comprehensive and Progressive Agreement for Trans-Pacific Partnership).

State-centric methodological approaches to international relations, such as political realism and neorealism, view international institutions as secondary to states as the main actors of international affairs. Consequently, they do not pay proper attention to the issues of functioning, autonomy, legitimacy and effectiveness of these institutions. However, the indisputable academic achievements of organizational theory and

---

I. L. Prokhorenko (✉)
Russian International Affairs Council, Moscow, Russia

© China Social Sciences Press 2023

Institute of Russian, Eastern European and Central Asian Studies, CASS and Russian International Affairs Council, *Global Governance in the New Era*, https://doi.org/10.1007/978-981-19-4332-4_6

constructivism—sociological institutionalism[1] and the spatial approach in particular[2]—have provided researchers with a new perspective on various international institutions, viewing them as social organisms, organizational fields and transnational political spaces of communication and interaction. Scholars study issues of organizational management and their interaction both among themselves and with the international environment, institutional structure, image, culture, identity, and transformation factors.

In the last 15 years, the so-called managerial concepts of international organizations have also gained traction. They define international organizations as institutions of cooperation between states contributing to the resolution of common tasks to improve the global system. Another popular idea is the "agora concept"—the notion of public space where problems of international importance are discussed and may be resolved.[3]

The constructivist and spatial aspects of the analysis of international institutions are becoming even more appropriate due to the emerging global governance system,[4] understood as resolving global problems (described as "major challenges" in the strategic documents of the Russian Federation); managing global risks related to threats to nature, human health and nutrition, sustainable development, balanced global financial system; and achieving common goals through the concerted efforts of states and organizational structures, including international institutions.

Traditionally, international institutions cannot be viewed as legitimate without member states consenting to their actions. New approaches imply that international nongovernmental institutions are by nature relatively independent both administratively and functionally, and those established by states gain greater autonomy as they evolve and enhance the supranational component of their economic and political governance model (as, for instance, the European Union does) and thereby their growing agency in global politics. This confirms the conclusions of many researchers concerning the current trend toward the crisis of a state as a social institution and an international relations actor.

The most apt and succinct definition, proposed by Russian economist and European integration specialist Olga Butorina, describes regional integration as "a model of a conscious and active participation by a group of states in the processes of global stratification produced by globalization." Its main goal is to create a successful stratum that is, to strengthen the standing of an alliance in those areas that are particularly important at a given stage of globalization. The objective of each individual state is to ensure the most favorable strategic prospects for itself. Essentially, integration allows participants to maximize the benefits of globalization while limiting its negative impact. Integration is intended to resolve regional development problems.

---

[1] Prokhorenko [1].

[2] Strezhneva [2] and Prokhorenko [3].

[3] Klabbers [4] and Kuteinikov [5].

[4] For more on the phenomenon and practices of global governance see: Baranovsky and Ivanova [6].

In addition to resolving international crisis situations, international organizations, international conferences and exclusive clubs set themselves the goal of formulating global challenges and searching for collective answers and solutions to world problems and global development issues. Such problems directly affect most countries and people and are augmented by globalization processes per se, such as growing economic and political interdependence and the systemic nature of their effect on regional and national processes. These problems, including pandemics, epidemics and dangerous diseases, natural and man-made disasters, environmental degradation and climate change, uncontrollable migration and population growth, food insecurity, WMD proliferation and the risk of their unsanctioned use, international terrorism and religious and ideological extremism, transnational crime and corruption, water scarcity, energy and other natural resources, require maximum possible international cooperation. It is also obvious that it is impossible to clearly differentiate global and regional problems.

As international institutions evolve and develop, they become complex collective agents, gaining awareness of their status as integral structures, and simultaneously presenting themselves to the world as such—as bodies capable of developing and implementing long-term behavioral strategies. States play an ambiguous role in relation to such nonstate actors: on the one hand, they have the will and resources needed to control their activities; on the other hand, for some states, involvement in such organizational structures can increase their international authority, influence, and even survivability, while for other states with a claim to regional and global leadership participation means being able to use various forms of leverage (whether soft or hard).

The first case can be exemplified by the supranational component in the European integration project. The French initiative to create the Economic and Monetary Union can be viewed in the context of the complicated domestic situation in the 1980s, combined with the French standing in global economy and world politics. In turn, Spain's commitment to developing the European community (in that regard, Spain is often dubbed not merely a Euro-optimist but a Euro-enthusiast) is largely explained by the complicated relationship between the center and regions in the highly decentralized Spanish "state of autonomies" with its strong traditions of particularism and separatism.

The second case is vividly exemplified by the policy of the United States in the context of the changing world order after the end of the Cold War. The gradual, yet relative weakening of the superpower, which is frequently measured by the dynamics of the country's share in the global GDP, does not cancel out the leading role that the United States plays in global finance, trade, science and technology. The fact that it will continue to play this role for the foreseeable future makes the United States a source of major shocks on the international arena (given that the U.S. foreign policy is geared toward unipolarity) and a potential agent of collaborative interaction with other participants in international affairs.[5] This can be observed, on the one hand, in the decision of the Democratic Joe Biden Administration to rejoin the Paris

---

[5] Baranovsky [7].

Agreement and the World Health Organization following the departure of the United States from both under Republican President Donald Trump. On the other hand, the same trends appear when we consider the causes that slow down the long-needed reform of the World Trade Organization as the global trade regulator.

Following Max Weber's ideas of a new type of legitimate authority—the rational-legal one typical for today's state and bureaucracy (as opposed to traditional authority and the charismatic authority)—and bureaucracy as an organizational phenomenon,[6] bureaucracy can be described as playing a key role in international institutions, largely determining the form and content of their activities and their organizational behavior, as well as creating and disseminating symbols, meanings, norms and rules and even formulating new interests for states.

At the same time, bureaucracy is not the only agent for creating new ideas and new social knowledge of multilateral organizations. Depending on their type and area of activity, they actively interact with national governments, industry-specific ministries and agencies, transnational corporations and other businesses, political parties and movements, various interest groups, civil society organizations, and the expert community, thereby assisting in the formation of transnational elites and a global community.

It is important to mention that some well-known concepts, solidly entrenched in today's political vocabulary, such as "development" ("sustainable" and "responsible"), "refugee," and "environmental migrant", emerged and became established precisely among international institutions. In turn, the universal values protected by international institutions are conducive to bringing national governments to understand the tasks of protecting human rights, countering climate change, ensuring national interests, and establishing state policy priorities. The role of international institutions in shaping the global agenda is great and as a result, they can influence the contents of the governmental, sociopolitical and academic discourse in various countries and regions of the world.

International rankings regularly published by some multilateral institutions deserve a separate mention. The most influential among them are the Human Development Index published annually by the United Nations Development Program and the Global Competitiveness Report developed by the World Economic Forum. Although such rankings are criticized for being politicized, insufficiently objective, and West-centric, they are an important leverage tool for international institutions to influence public opinion, the expert community that frequently uses them, and political decision-makers at various levels of governance.

A new trend in the organizational structure of multilateral institutions is the emergence of new dimensions or components in their activities due to the attention they pay to target audiences such as the expert community, women, young people, small-and medium-sized enterprises, and civil society. The lack of democratic legitimacy is a problem that must be grappled with—not only for the European Union as an elitist

---

[6] Weber [8, 9].

International Institutions in Contemporary Global Politics 69

project but also for other multilateral organizations that perform regulatory functions. This can be achieved through involving individual members or delegations of national parliaments of their member states in their activities.[7]

Such international global regulation institutions as the World Trade Organization, the International Monetary Fund (IMF), the World Bank (WB), and the G7 and G20 have created parliamentary networks,[8] national parliament speaker summits,[9] and other forms of interparliamentary cooperation. In particular, in 2002 the Inter-Parliamentary Union and the European Parliament spearheaded the Parliamentary Conference on the WTO, which now convenes annually but functions outside the WTO formal structure and has not yet gained the status and powers of a parliamentary assembly.

Such interaction includes various informal discussions that accompany the adoption of binding international decisions outside the state framework. They serve to set up venues for more formal communication that prepares global, nonbinding decisions on issues of common global importance.[10]

The transformational trends in the modern world order include, on the one hand, a long-term polycentric trend and, on the other hand, a clear outline of a new U.S.–China bipolarity. These are leading toward a restructuring of the international system, affecting global governance dynamics and the activities of international institutions—some of which (the United Nations and the World Trade Organization) have set themselves the tasks of reform, while others are expanding their institutional format and their areas of activity.[11]

Moreover, global problems that international institutions have effectively been established to handle create new incentives for multilateral cooperation, as well as new contradictions between states, thus exacerbating competition and promoting differences in world development and global governance issues. We cannot deny the existence of the deglobalization trend that emerged during the global financial crisis and received a boost during the COVID-19 pandemic, nor can we ignore the bias toward national concerns and foreign policy imperatives. At the same time, the international community has also received a number of positive signals. For instance, at the Glasgow Climate Summit in November 2021, the United States and China, the world's two principal greenhouse gas emissions "culprits," signed a declaration to take action to counter climate change.

---

[7] Nye [10] and Prokhorenko [11].

[8] The Parliamentary Network on the World Bank and IMF, established in 2000, is open for individual participation by members of national parliaments.

[9] G7 has held them since 2002, and G20—since 2010.

[10] Strezhneva [12].

[11] For instance, G20, which has ceased to be solely an exclusive club of heads of government or state, financial ministers and heads of central banks discussing financial policy issues.

References

1. Prokhorenko, I.L. 2014. Organizatsionnaya teoriya v analize global'nogo upravleniya [Organizational Theory in Global Governance Analysis]. *Vestnik Moskovskogo universiteta. Series 25. Mezhdunarodnye otnosheniya i mirovaya politika* 3: 150–173. (In Russian)
2. Strezhneva, M.S. (ed.). 2011. Transnatsional'nye politicheskie prostranstva: yavlenie i praktika [Transnational Political Spaces: Phenomenon and Practice]. Moscow: Ves' mir. (In Russian)
3. Prokhorenko, I.L. 2015. Prostranstvennyi podkhod v issledovanii mezhdunarodnykh otnoshenii [Spatial Approach in Studying International Relations]. Moscow. IMEMO RAN. (In Russian)
4. Klabbers, J. 2005. Two concepts of international organization. *International Organizations Law Review.* 2 (2): 277–293.
5. Kuteinikov, A.E. 2008. Novoe v issledovanii mezhdunarodnykh organizatsii [New Trends in Studying International Organizations]. *Mezhdunarodnye Protessy* 6: 60–69. (In Russian)
6. Baranovsky, V.G., and N.I. Ivanova. (eds.). 2015. *Global'noe upravlenie: Vozmozhnosti i riski [Global Governance: Opportunities and Risks]*. Moscow: IMEMO RAN. (In Russian)
7. Baranovsky, V.A. 2019. New international order: Overcoming or transforming the existing one. Social Sciences. *A Quarterly Journal of the Russian Academy of Sciences* 50 (2): 38–53.
8. Weber, M. 1946. *Essays in Sociology.* New York: Oxford University Press.
9. Weber, M. 1947. *The Theory of Social and Economic Organization.* Glencoe, IL: Free Press.
10. Nye, J. 2001. Globalization's democratic deficit: How to make international institutions more accountable. *Foreign Affairs* 80 (4): 2–6.
11. Prokhorenko, I.L., V.G. Varnavsky, M.V. Strezhneva, and E.M. Kharitonova. (eds.). 2020. *Mezhparlamentskie instituty v mirovoi politike [Inter-Parliamentary Institutions in Global Politics]*. Moscow: Ves' mir. (In Russian)
12. Strezhneva, M.V. 2018. Parlamentskie seti v transnatsional'nom ehkonomicheskom upravlenii [Parliamentary Networks in Transnational Economic Management]. *Vestnik Permskogo Universiteta. Seriya: Politologiya* 2: 5–20 (In Russian).

Reshaping Global Governance with Genuine Multilateralism

Zhongping Feng and Zhigao He

At this moment, globalization and global governance are progressing on a nonlinear, diversified and multidimensional trajectory, with the focus shifting from *who governs global issues* to *how to handle transnational affairs*. Multilateralism is one of the essential characteristics for the discourse of global governance, with its underpinning focuses on *which* kind of multilateralism the world should adopt and *how* to consolidate multilateralism of this kind. The current multilateral framework was established under the leadership of the United States after World War II. However, with the increasing prominence of global challenges, the rise of emerging economies and the surfacing of a large number of nonstate actors, the existing principles and mechanisms of multilateralism cannot address the requirements of new realities on global governance. Considering a shrinking window of opportunity for solving global challenges and maintaining the effectiveness of global governance, we need to take the initiative to explore more possibilities about multilateralism so as to further boost global governance.

Global Governance in the Dilemma

Global governance in the post-pandemic era needs to be built on genuine multilateralism, to face common interests for the whole world, to resolve power fragmentation and populist shocks brought about by globalization, to improve the legitimacy and effectiveness of governance, and to prevent the decline of the global governance order.

Z. Feng (✉) · Z. He
Institute of European Studies of Chinese Academy of Social Sciences, Beijing, China

© China Social Sciences Press 2023
Institute of Russian, Eastern European and Central Asian Studies, CASS and Russian International Affairs Council, *Global Governance in the New Era*,
https://doi.org/10.1007/978-981-19-4332-4_7

Shocks by unilateralism and protectionism on global governance. Global governance has already been shaken by a series of *zero-sum thinking* such as unilateralism, protectionism, xenophobia and nationalism, with an increasing number of governments failing to promise or support the establishment of stronger multilateral relations. At the same time, countries argue that globalization and global governance have violated their national sovereignty and limited democratic decision-making. It is clear that any single country or international organization cannot cope with this challenge alone, not to mention expecting unilateralism or hegemonic approaches for the guarantee of good global governance. Moreover, if there is a country that always maximizes its national interests on a global scale when facing worldwide challenges, it will be more difficult to achieve win–win ends through multilateral means. The most obvious example is that the strategic adjustment by the United States has greatly undermined the existing global governance system. In particular, the sudden and rapid strategic turnabouts by the Trump administration have become a major factor that put multilateral global governance in a dire dilemma. In addition to the brunt of unilateralism and protectionism, global governance also faces other challenges such as regionalized governance or, say, segmented governance like tectonic pieces. However, countries are now more interconnected than ever before, requiring global governance based on genuine multilateralism.

Dilemma by defects from the global governance system itself. The insufficiency of governance stems from, in part, the fact that transnational issues go beyond the capacity of governance by national or international institutions. In recent years, traditional multilateral cooperation has reached its ceiling, for example, it may take many years to reach an international climate agreement under the framework of the United Nations Framework Convention on Climate Change (UNFCCC), not to mention additional difficulties for the implementation of treaties of this kind; the Doha rounds of negotiations under the framework of the World Trade Organization (WTO) have been slow and even stalled.

There are two primary forms of endogenous competition within the existing global governance system: one is the *politicization of international authority*, and the other is *anti-institutionalization*.[1] It is precisely the increasing inability of the rules-based order (i.e., the liberal international order, or the open liberal order) dominated by the West to maintain the normal functioning of the system as well as the contest for influence and dominance by Western countries that leads to rising tensions, growing conflicts, closure of borders, end of globalization, interruption of multilateralism for win–win outcomes and, further, the disturbance in and decline of global governance. However, tensions within the global governance system have in turn necessitated the need for reform and adjustment to fix deficiencies in the current framework of global governance. Therefore, global governance in the forthcoming years will present a parallel of evolution and deterioration, as well as the coexistence of confrontation and cooperation.

---

[1] Zürn [1].

Challenges to global governance by unprecedented worldwide events such as the COVID-19 pandemic. The COVID-19 pandemic has accelerated the turbulent and fragmented trends in global governance that have already existed before the outbreak, such as the erosion of both multilateral rules and institutions as well as accelerated deglobalization. The pandemic has exposed the fragility of global trade, worldwide supply chains and international industrial chains, proving that territorial borders do not provide protection or immunity. The virus has brought heavy economic losses across the globe, putting the whole world economy into recession. According to *the World Economic Outlook Report* released by the International Monetary Fund (IMF) in October 2021, the global economy does recover in 2021 yet with a decreasing momentum, achieving a 5.9% annual growth rate (a 0.1% decrease compared with the expected figure calculated in July 2021). According to research by the German Development Institute (Deutsches Institut fur Entwicklungspolitik), the impact of the COVID-19 pandemic would put an additional 70 million people into *extreme poverty* around the world, living on less than two dollars a day.[2] This means that people labeled *extremely poor* (currently 600 million) will further increase by more than 10%, not to mention an even larger number of people categorized as *very poor*. Moreover, the pandemic has disproportionately affected people at different income levels, thereby exacerbating inequality. With the gender pay gap (women earned 84% of what men earned), females bear the brunt of economic and social aftermaths of the pandemic, as more women than men work in informal sectors and are more likely to lose their jobs. Meanwhile, the pandemic has further fueled unilateralism and protectionist tendencies. For example, some countries have leveraged this crisis of public health to instigate nationalist sentiments, with populism bringing new blows to the already fragile global governance and reinforcing its inherent dilemma.

Today's international community is more complex than ever, with intertwined global challenges such as sluggish economic growth, climate change, worldwide epidemics and pandemics, as well as refugee crises. Global governance is highly competitive, with a fundamental contradiction between the growing need for deeper cooperation and the declining willingness of the international community to take collective action. These challenges will also spill over to social and political dimensions of global governance, affecting the development of its structures and principles. Multilateralism, as an approach to bring better welfare for people from all nations, is now being replaced by another narrative that includes games among great powers, the return to geopolitics, the rise of unilateralism and the spread of populist movements. Therefore, global governance needs our urgent move to provide convincing narratives of norms and reasonable paths for cooperation.

---

[2] Negre et al. [2].

Global Governance Calling for Genuine Multilateralism

Different approaches have been proposed for addressing global challenges, such as multilateralism, regionalism, bilateralism, unilateralism and other complicated yet interrelated philosophies. Given the nature of international relations, bilateralism and unilateralism are foreign policy instruments commonly employed by nation-states: unilateralism is the preferred course of action for hegemonies yet with a poor degree of legitimacy that impairs the soft power of these states, while bilateralism, mainly through policy-making, means changing targets and priorities on a case-by-case basis. Given the challenges for world politics due to its specific structural features (distribution of power and diffused principles of sovereignty), multilateralism, i.e., the engagement of three or more players in international politics is an essential diplomatic strategy option for actors on the global stage. The United Nations, the World Bank, the International Monetary Fund and the World Trade Organization constitute the overarching framework of multilateralism. Moreover, the values, norms and principles of multilateralism have been enshrined in *the UN Charter*, the only universal statement of principles with constitutional value recognized worldwide.

Theoretical Interpretation of Multilateralism

The worldwide and interconnected nature of global challenges calls for solutions that transcend national borders. Multilateralism itself is an integrated approach that fosters partnerships among nations, regional institutions and international organizations to address shared global issues. John Ruggie believes that multilateralism has three underpinning characteristics: *indivisibility*, emphasizing that multilateralism is based on socially constructed public goods; *universal organizing principles*, putting multilateralism against discrimination; and *expansion of mutual benefit*, pointing out that multilateralism brings mutual benefit and shared growth.[3] Moreover, multilateralism means not only a specific diplomatic instrument, but also the commitment to certain principles, substantive goals and methods of foreign policy, together with a series of basic values. Multilateralism thus refers to the *combination* of coordinated diplomatic interactions by more than two actors with collective actions within the framework of international organizations. With certain principles and norms as guidance, multilateralism initiates actions that are in line with basic rules and regulations of these organizations.

Multilateralism is both a purpose and an instrument, therefore being both a philosophy and a strategy. Multilateralism not only means the regulation, institution and way of governance in world politics but also points out that countries seek to establish, maintain and develop a specific international normative order through concrete diplomatic means. In other words, multilateralism represents the approach through

---

[3] Ruggie [3].

which a country achieves its goals, as well as the system of rules and normative frameworks where such an approach is conducted.

On the one hand, multilateralism determines the way to implement a policy or a strategy, pointing to specific actions in diplomacy rather than the substance and aspirations of international politics. In short, multilateralism is a diplomatic instrument for global governance and international cooperation. The multilateralism pursued by the US is more of a strategic apparatus, focusing on instrumental attributes and strategic dimensions. For example, the American philosophy of international cooperation is inevitably influenced by its national conditions, state interests and political climate. When Europe and the US have conflicting interests, each of them will swiftly adopt a multilateral approach of its own. That is, multilateralism is not an end in itself, but a means for pursuing interests, ending up in institutionalized forms of cooperation through various types of state behaviors.

On the other hand, multilateralism, as a process, is always in pursuit of specific goals. Multilateralism involves certain procedures and principles, conveys norms and values, and is therefore closely related to the philosophy of international order. Therefore, multilateralism is not only a policy-making choice or a specific diplomatic approach, such as bridging differences, reducing tensions, giving specific status to a stakeholder and providing solutions, but also the correct and appropriate answer to today's political challenges worldwide, with an additional significance for normative values. Currently, the debate in this regard is not just about multilateralism itself and the corresponding foreign policies but also about *which* principle, value and international organization to choose for building the global order and shaping the international landscape.

There are various kinds of interpretations and classifications of multilateralism, and these criteria are relatively vague. The simplest classifications of multilateralism are based on number and scale, such as global multilateralism, regional multilateralism and mini-multilateralism. There are also classifications of multilateralism based on quality and nature. For example, Mario Telo points out the difference between two kinds of multilateralism, distinguishing traditional international multilateral cooperation that originated in the Westphalian paradigm from governance beyond the state, with the EU being a major practitioner and advocate.[4] In addition, there is also a distinction between true multilateralism (i.e., genuine and inclusive) and selective multilateralism.

As the world comes into a new era, multilateralism is characterized by new features such as the diversification of multilateral organizations, the growing importance of nonstate actors, the increased connectivity of policy agendas as well as the increasing depth and breadth of civic engagement. Vicissitudes in global governance and changes in the grouping of actors have created new demands for genuine multilateralism that would be an indispensable prerequisite for new agendas of global governance and a correspondingly institutionalized structure with authority (i.e., the coexistence of multilayered and multityped subjects) (Table 1).

---

[4] Tello [4].

Table 1 Typological analysis of multilateralism

Types of multilateralism	
Based on number	Based on quality
Westphalian paradigm	Governance beyond the state
As ends	As means
Based on strategies	Based on norms
Small scale	Big and complex
Exclusive	Inclusive
Global	Regional
Selective (hypocritical)	Genuine

Note This is a table made by authors themselves

Perceptions of Multilateralism by Major Actors

The perception of multilateralism by the US is inevitably influenced by its national conditions, state interests and political climate. When multilateral cooperation is not in the interests of its own, the US will never hesitate to adopt a multilateral approach with its own dominance or even to unilateralism. Stewart M. Patrick of the Council on Foreign Relations distinguishes four different categories of multilateralism during the Biden era[5]: *legitimacy*, with the world order represented by the UN Charter; *solidarity*, with a new form of reorganizing the international club; *dynamism*, for optimizing and updating the 19thcentury framework of the alliance among major powers; and *flexibility*, for adopting a point-to-point way of cooperation among its allies.

There are different views on multilateralism among Western countries. One is that multilateralism itself is not outdated at all and that the crisis for multilateralism comes not from the absence of multilateral rules but from the decreasing number of countries bound by multilateral rules. The reason for the danger and decline of multilateralism is that some countries have turned their backs on it or that it has become a tool for some countries to pursue their own specific interests. The reboot of multilateralism requires more commitment from individual countries. Another argument is that multilateralism is not only inefficient but also unable as well to maintain a rules-based international order. The restructuring of it requires a fundamental overhaul of the multilateral order. In reality, the US focuses on the second narrative, while the EU seems more inclined to follow the first, although there are signs that the EU is moving toward the second as well.

Multilateralism is part of the mainstream political discourse in Europe and the cornerstone of its diplomatic policies. The EU put forward the concept of *effective multilateralism* in its security strategy report in 2003. In June 2019, the Council of the European Union arrived at the conclusion for more actions to strengthen a rule-based multilateralism. The EU needs to promote multilateral solutions all the more, because

---

[5] Patrick [5].

effective multilateral cooperation is the best way to advance both national and collective interests. Strengthening the multilateral system by the EU will be based on three points: upholding international norms and agreements, extending multilateralism to new global realities, and reforming multilateral organizations in line with their aspirations.[6] In February 2021, the European Commission published *Strengthening EU's Contribution to Rules-Based Multilateralism*, a joint communication with the European Parliament and the EU Council. The document has redefined the EU's stance on multilateralism and corresponding strategic focuses, and set out both the direction and blueprint for actions to strengthen the multilateral system of the EU.

The EU adheres to two strategic priorities of multilateralism: the first is to promote global peace and security, and jointly tackle global terrorism and transnational crimes, while the second is to rebuild the global system for public health supply chains after the COVID-19 pandemic for a green, digital, inclusive and sustainable global recovery.[7] Apart from the EU as a whole, its member states have also proposed their own philosophies and methodologies about multilateralism. Germany and France proposed *the Alliance for Multilateralism* initiative,[8] as they observe that competition among great powers and the development of nationalism have led to the increasing fragmentation of the world order in terms of politics, economy and society. Some like-minded countries along with Germany and France are committed to promoting multilateralism, stabilizing a rules-based world order and adapting to new challenges. In May 2021, Germany published its first white paper on multilateralism named *International Cooperation in the 21st Century: A Multilateralism for the People* which will become *the guide to the conduct of Germany's foreign relations* and define the scope of Germany's participation in multilateralism.[9]

Russia's engagement with multilateral institutions is guided by the long-term vision of its foreign policy, particularly the shift in the international landscape from a US-led unipolar order to a multipolar one. Russia prefers the United Nations as the platform for multilateralism, and believes that multilateral cooperation through the UN can give full play to Russia's advantages, with the emphasis on *equality* among member states, the promises not to violate state sovereignty, and the commitment to agreement and consensus. It is rather understandable that Russia does not invest so much in multilateral cooperation in areas where it has no immediate interests or expertise, which is best exemplified by Russia's accession to the World Trade Organization.[10]

---

[6] Council Conclusions: EU Action to Strengthen Rules-based Multilateralism, June 17, 2019, https://data.consilium.europa.eu/doc/document/ST-10341-2019-INIT/en/pdf.

[7] European Commission, Strategy on Strengthening the EU's Contribution to Rules-based Multilateralism, February 17, 2021, https://eeas.europa.eu/sites/default/files/en_strategy_on_strengthening_the_eus_contribution_to_rules-based_multilateralism.pdf.

[8] Alliance for Multilateralism, https://multilateralism.org/.

[9] Federal Foreign Office, International cooperation in the twenty-first century: A Multilateralism for the People, May 19, 2021, https://www.auswaertiges-amt.de/en/aussenpolitik/multilateralism-white-paper/2460318.

[10] Gabuev and Chernenko [6].

Meanwhile, Russia does not fully recognize the current *rules-based* multilateral order, because *rules-making* is dominated by Europe and the US. In an international order that lacks governance based on international law and the principles of the UN Charter, Russia prefers a *combination* of coordination between great powers and multilateral cooperation to better guard against its own sovereignty and consolidate its status as a great power. Based on this perception, Russia believes that China and Russia should continue their coordination in international organizations, adhere to principles, and explain their positions to other countries in order to jointly safeguard multilateralism.[11]

With regard to multilateralism, China has gone through a long process: to learn, to conform and finally to firmly advocate for concrete actions. China has learned what multilateralism is and how to conform to this principle and is now a faithful advocator for this idea. Behind this process is the shift of China's diplomatic strategy from a passive *stimulus–response* way into an active attitude for *taking the initiative.* China believes that some Western countries have assembled small circles (i.e., blocs) in the name of multilateralism to engage in ideological confrontation, and opposes any act that undermines the international order or creates confrontation and division in the pretext of *rules.* In addition, multilateralism means following the purposes and principles of the UN Charter and conducting dialog and cooperation on the basis of equality and mutual respect. The UN should act as the flagship of multilateralism.[12]

In regard to policy-making, China takes the lead in designing and building multilateral cooperation mechanisms, with active diplomatic participation on its own. The 10 + 1 *mechanism*, established by China and ASEAN, the Shanghai Cooperation Organization (SCO) and other multilateral frameworks have altogether ensured the security and development of China and most of its neighboring countries. Moreover, China's promotion of multilateral institutions such as the BRICS mechanism and the Asian Infrastructure Investment Bank (AIIB) has contributed to the improvement of the global governance system.

As for theoretical exploration, China adheres to multilateralism with strong opposition against exclusion and discrimination to promote common aspirations such as peace, development, fairness, justice, democracy and freedom across the globe. China advocates inclusive multilateralism based on the common interests of mankind and promotes multilateralism with the following principles: *putting morality first with great importance attached to trustworthiness and righteousness; conducting equal consultation and persuading others with reasoning; maintaining harmony while allowing for difference; seeking openness and inclusiveness; promoting gradual progress and building broad consensus.*[13] China believes that *to practice genuine*

---

[11] Russian Ambassador to China: China and Russia insist on safeguarding multilateralism, People.cn, December 31, 2020, http://world.people.com.cn/n1/2020/1231/c1002-31985648.html.

[12] Ministry of Foreign Affairs of PRC: "Position Paper on China's Cooperation with the United Nations," October 22, 2021, https://www.fmprc.gov.cn/web/ziliao_674904/tytj_674911/zcwj_6 74915/t1916136.shtml.

[13] Department of Policy Planning of the Ministry of Foreign Affairs: "Deeply Advance Multilateralism with Chinese Characteristics under the Guidance of Xi Jinping Thought on Diplomacy," Study Times, October 25, 2019, http://www.qstheory.cn/llwx/2019-10/25/c_1125151043.htm.

multilateralism, we must pursue win–win cooperation but not zero-sum games, be fair and just without bullying others, focus on actions without empty talk, respect diversity and say no to the hegemony.[14] At present, unprecedented changes unseen in a century and the COVID-19 pandemic are intertwined, and challenges that bring the whole world into a period of turbulence with instability and uncertainty are on the rise. However, China's observation is that the trend of world multi-polarization will not be fundamentally changed at present nor for a long time in the future. As economic globalization has shown new resilience, the call for safeguarding multilateralism, strengthening communication and consolidating coordination has become stronger than ever.

Although it has become a consensus that multilateralism is *in trouble*, this does not necessarily mean that multilateralism is *outdated*. As there are multiple perspectives for multilateral theories and diversified forms of multilateral practices, countries need to reach a consensus on the normative basis and specific content of multilateralism, including what is the *core* of multilateralism, what *purpose* shall be achieved and what *interests and values* should be taken into account. Even if the global community has already arrived at some consensus on the principles, values and goals of multilateralism, agreements should equally be reached as much as possible regarding its specific implementation.

Approaches to Promote Multilateral Cooperation

The future international order needs to provide a set of norms and arrangements for a highly interconnected and interdependent world, which urgently requires the advancement of multilateral cooperation. It is easy to *call for* and *articulate* one's support for multilateralism, but how to *promote* multilateral cooperation is the greatest challenge lying ahead of the international community. Reshaping global governance and promoting a new round of globalization require immense dynamism unleashed from genuine multilateralism, in which major powers take the lead, regional organizations serve as links, developing countries constitute a cornerstone, and nonstate actors offer supplemental momentum so as to better realize the reform and improvement of global governance.

First, multilateralism calls for cooperation among major powers to take the lead in global governance. As an effective diplomatic discourse and policy instrument, multilateralism needs to rely on bilateralism to advance bilateral relations under the framework of multilateral cooperation. That is, without frequent and substantial bilateral interactions, multilateral cooperation and consultation will be unsustainable. Therefore, if bilateralism cannot be regarded as an integral part of multilateralism, the commitment made in multilateral negotiations cannot be guaranteed, not

---

[14] Xi Jinping: "Bolstering Confidence and Jointly Overcoming Difficulties To Build a Better World", *People's Daily*, September 21, 2020.

to mention the results of multilateralism being obtained. All-around bilateral cooperation is the foundation and, in turn, multilateral cooperation plays a role in boosting and innovating bilateral cooperation. Furthermore, better bilateral relations will help countries share information, build mutual understanding, eliminate misunderstandings and strengthen mutual trust to foster the atmosphere for cooperation and the convention for doing so, therefore boosting positive interaction between multilateral platforms and bilateral relations.

Genuine multilateralism relies on strong multilateral leadership, where great power cooperation can play an important role since multilateral agreements necessitate intensive bilateral diplomacy and major power cooperation. This requires major powers to jointly focus on the global agendas, set deadlines for negotiations, explore the possibility of reaching compromised solutions and effectively implement the agreements that have been reached, thereby enhancing the effectiveness of global governance. Therefore, major powers such as China, the United States, European countries and Russia need to enrich multilateral agendas, enhance strategic mutual trust, and enlarge political foundations for multilateral cooperation, particularly through stronger cooperation under the UN framework. After all, the United Nations is the broadest, largest and most authoritative intergovernmental international organization in the world, with unique influence that cannot be replaced by other international organizations.[15] At the same time, international organizations such as the International Monetary Fund, the World Bank and the World Trade Organization are all actors who maintain the existing international order. Different from traditional treaty-based international organizations, a large number of forum-based organizations without permanent institutions (such as the G7 and the G20) are playing an increasingly important role in global governance, so China, the US, European countries and Russia need to seek the largest common ground for multilateral cooperation on platforms of global governance.

Second, multilateralism requires regional organizations to serve as links in global governance. Regional integration moves ahead with the concurrence of globalization and fragmentation. A more regionalized global system is an ongoing norm in the post-Cold War world and regions are gradually recognized to be at intermediate or transitional levels between countries and the world, serving not only as geographical concepts but also as grounds for social interaction. *Multilateral regionalism* is becoming a bridge connecting regionalism and multilateralism, as well as a link between national governance and global governance. The relation between globalism and regionalism, is on the one hand, a trade-off where one's gain means the other one's lose: a shortage of public goods provided by globalism necessitates that by regionalism. On the other hand, however, the two are complementary to each other as well: globalization has given new connotations to regional integration, and at the same time, since global governance is too complex to understand and too difficult to manage for most countries, regional action becomes the second-best choice. Regional organizations ensure the free flow of people, capital, goods and services

---

[15] "China's Position Paper on UN Reforms", Xinhua Net, June 7, 2005, https://www.chinacourt.org/article/detail/2005/06/id/165465.shtml.

within a region to a certain extent. Regional organizations such as the European Union, ASEAN, African Union, League of Arab States, and the Community of Latin American and Caribbean States (CELAC) are becoming increasingly prominent and influential in regional and even global governance. As of June 2021, 349 regional trade agreements are in force, with larger coverage and greater scope.[16] Perhaps *regionalism* can better adapt to new changes in a tectonic-like pattern of the global society and the tendency of national populism.

Inclusive regional cooperation should be promoted with regional organizations for integration as anchors. By strengthening partnerships with regional integration organizations such as the European Union, ASEAN and the African Union, China has brought new impetus into regionalism and interregional cooperation based on the logic of functionalism and pragmatic progress, integrated informal institutionalism and flexible institutionalism, and balanced consensus-based pragmatism and flexible corporatism to realize effective interaction between regionalism and globalism in the process of multilateral cooperation. Recently, the EU issued *the EU Strategy for Cooperation in the Indo-Pacific Region*, emphasizing the promotion of regional governance with ASEAN as the midpoint. Given that *multilateral diplomacy* is the EU's preferred means of participation in the Indo-Pacific region and ASEAN is the cornerstone of the EU's partnership network, China and the EU, therefore, can jointly work and coordinate in the Asia–Pacific/Indo-Pacific region. In regard to Africa, China and the EU are exploring new forms of cooperation in a third-party market and consolidating China-EU-Africa multilateral cooperation in areas such as regional development assistance and infrastructure construction.

Third, developing countries constitute a cornerstone in multilateralism. Global development should adhere to the priority of growth, with particular emphasis on shared, balanced and inclusive development, to build a community with a shared future for all. *Inclusive development* requires all countries and all societies to share the benefits brought by economic globalization, with extra attention paid to the most vulnerable groups. From a social perspective, worldwide inequality is a byproduct of globalization, while the existence of marginalized individuals and societies is a threat to the stability of the entire world. Growing economic inequalities have been amplified and aggravated by this round of public health crisis, widening the political rift between winners and losers of globalization. The economic downturn brought by the COVID-19 pandemic is likely to intensify and last even longer, since, in a globalized world, the industrial chain, supply chain and value chain have been integrated into a worldwide loop where a defect at any link may result in a knock-on effect on the entire global economy. Facing the pandemic, countries tend to *isolate themselves*, which increases the possible risks of deglobalization, counter-globalization and even anti-globalization. Regionalization, nationalization and localization have altogether exposed the fragility of globalization. However, the new round of industrial revolution featuring intelligence, networking and digitization means that both the major direction and the mainstream philosophy of the future reform on global governance

---

[16] Regional trade agreements, World Trade Organization, June 15, 2021, https://www.wto.org/english/tratop_e/region_e/region_e.htm#committee.

must be *multilateralism.*[17] This calls for building inclusive global value chains, at the core of which low-income developing countries and their small and medium-sized enterprises (SMEs) can overcome barriers and get on board.

New growth is a means, not an end. There may be a trade-off between *fast recovery* and *smart recovery* in how to manage economic and social affairs after the pandemic. The economic and social consequences of the COVID-19 pandemic require national governments and the international community to share responsibility, not only through countercyclical action to stimulate growth, such as prioritizing investments to promote a green transition under *the Paris Agreement* but also by proactively supporting the well-being of people in lower-income areas. This requires deeper and broader social security as a priority, together with other policies to reduce inequality, such as progressive taxation and investment in rural infrastructure. After the outbreak of the pandemic, the international community took action. For example, the G20 pledged to put 5 trillion US dollars into the global economy to deal with the pandemic and its impacts. The International Monetary Fund and the World Bank helped their member countries respond to the virus through emergency financing and technical assistance. At the same time, large-scale recovery plans need substantial financial resources, but low-income countries face limited fiscal budgets, which will require external support through development cooperation or assistance in finance, technology and expertise. That is, the efficacy of global governance, to a certain extent, lies in how the world works on the weakest link: for example, the effectiveness of global public health governance depends on what the country with the least capacity did in this regard. China has actively participated in and implemented *the G20 Debt Service Suspension Initiative for Poorest Countries*, allowing 77 developing countries and regions to suspend debt repayment during the coronavirus pandemic.[18] In addition, China provided 2 billion US dollars in aid and helped fundraising for the WHO *Solidarity Response Fund* in China. Therefore, global governance needs a broader, deeper and more inclusive multilateral approach rooted in society and with more concern for each individual.

Fourth, multilateralism requires not only the participation of states in multilateral cooperation, but also that from nonstate actors. Changes in the global system (particularly the process of globalization) have led to an increase in the number and intensity of trans-sovereign issues and a growing demand for global public goods. Along with this trend is the institutionalized public–private cooperation within inclusive and multiagent institutions for global governance. Part of the goals of global governance can be achieved only by a new form of multilateralism with more participation by the private sector. One of the hallmarks of officially-led multilateralism today is nonpublic negotiation and bargaining among national government representatives or political elites, which is consciously isolated from public supervision or participation. Given the new changes in current world politics and some of its specific structural shifts, such as the *extension of power distribution*

---

[17] Fuzhan [7].

[18] China's State Council Information Office: White Paper on "Fighting COVID-19: China in Actions", June 7, 2020.

and the *proliferation of sovereignty principles*, the role of nonstate actors in multilateral cooperation is increasingly important. As the international community becomes more diverse with deepening interdependence among countries, the role and status of international organizations in global governance and international relations continue to rise. For example, international organizations cover a wider range of agendas and their governing functions have become more prominent. According to the 2020 statistics by the Union of International Associations (UIA), there are 73,000 international organizations from 300 countries or regions, 41,000 of which are active, covering both intergovernmental and nongovernmental sectors. At the same time, there will be 1,200 new ones every year.[19] These organizations give full play to the role of nonofficial or semiofficial institutions as well as rely on strong professional backgrounds and resources in this regard to build an all-round, multilevel and wide-ranging framework for multilateral cooperation.

Genuine multilateralism means not only shared efforts by both public and private actors, but also the equal participation of countries at different stages of development with different development models. First, genuine multilateralism can enrich representation by giving emerging countries a stronger sense of relevance and least developed countries a louder voice, therefore allowing all national and international actors to become participants in the rule-making process. Second, genuine multilateralism can bridge the gap of governance, especially by reducing the defects of *inadequate legitimacy for input, process and output* generated by global governance dominated by officially-led multilateralism. Third, genuine multilateralism can promote public–private partnerships in global governance, by rearranging rules of the game and institutional arrangements on the distribution of power, allocation of resources and state-society relations.

Moreover, genuine multilateralism allows all stakeholders to have equal voices and concerns, with representatives of nonstate actors engaged in the dialog. On the one hand, it can better reflect the needs and expectations of all participants on relevant issues and, on the other hand, it can prevent powerful countries or interest groups from controlling and manipulating the policy-making procedure. However, this does not necessarily mean that all participants will be part of decision-making, as too much input of ideas can result in confusion and fragmentation. Therefore, in the process of participating in multilateral cooperation, we must stipulate the rules and principles for nonstate actors to participate in diplomatic affairs. Otherwise, the competitive nature of relations will only hinder the implementation of multilateral cooperation.

---

[19] Union of International Associations, "The Yearbook of International Organizations", 2020, https://uia.org/yearbook.

Conclusion

Global governance in the post-pandemic era is the confrontation and coexistence between populism and corporatism, between nationalism and cosmopolitanism and between unilateralism and multilateralism. Increasing interdependence means stronger demands for global governance, and compared with the pursuit of short-term and immediate interests, countries can benefit more by jointly complying with a maintained international order and its rules. However, if global governance fails to address negative changes worldwide, the result would be a chain effect with complex and disruptive consequences, such as rising economic costs and political decay. Moreover, the current multilateral cooperation system faces the risk of the inability to contain the return of geopolitics and avoid great power competition, making it increasingly difficult to handle global challenges.

Genuine multilateralism, in this regard, is a possible way to reshape global governance, but it will also face challenges such as competition from other multilateral philosophies and the restriction from US unilateralism. The success of genuine multilateralism also depends on a number of prerequisites, such as full awareness and thorough analysis of the vulnerabilities and sensitivities of the parties involved, together with close attention to the stance and attitude toward inclusive multilateralism by other international actors. This includes, in particular, whether they have genuine interests, whether they have the willingness to compromise, whether they are ready to cooperate on a reciprocal basis, whether they have domestic support, etc.

At this moment, the greatest diplomatic concern for China is no longer how to integrate itself into the international order but how to find a balance between joining it and reshaping it. China is facing the *two great changes*, namely, the transformation of its own development and the change of the world structure, so we must strive to achieve a positive interaction between them. Furthermore, diplomatic philosophies featuring China's multilateralism, manifested by the idea of *cooperation and coordination for shared growth* from the Belt and Road initiative and the call for *a community with a shared future for mankind*, are becoming the core of its discourse for diplomatic affairs as well as its proposal for global governance.

References

1. Zürn, Michael. 2018. Contested global governance. *Global Policy* 9 (1): 138–145.
2. Negre, M., Gerszon Mahler, D., Lakner, C. 2020. *Covid-19, Poverty, and Inequality: Growing Inequality can Worsen the Pandemic's Effects*, Deutsches Institut für Entwicklungspolitik. https://www.die-gdi.de/en/the-current-column/article/growing-inequality-can-worsen-the-pandemics-effects
3. Ruggie, John, and Multilateralism Matters. 1993. *The Theory and Praxis on an International Form*. New York: Columbia University Press.
4. Tello, M. 2020. The development of European international relations theory and Sino-European dialog. *World Economics and Politics* 1.

5. Patrick, S.M. 2021. The four contending approaches to multilateralism under Biden. *World Politics Review.* https://www.worldpoliticsreview.com/articles/29675/on-foreign-policy-us-mulls-what-comes-after-the-liberal-international-order
6. Gabuev, A., Chernenko, E. (2019). *What Russia Thinks About Multilateralism, Project Syndicate.* https://www.project-syndicate.org/commentary/russia-multilateralism-international-law-by-alexander-gabuev-and-elena-chernenko-2019-08
7. Fuzhan, X. 2019. The new industrial revolution, global governance reshaping and multilateralism. *Economic Research Journal* 14 (6): 2–13.

UN Security Council Reform: Pro et Contra

Dmitriy Kiku

The decision to extend the mandate of the Organization for the Prohibition of Chemical Weapons (OPCW) on June 27, 2018, giving the Technical Secretariat the power to identify those responsible for using chemical weapons in Syria, served as a wake-up call in the context of the lengthy discussion on the need to reform the UN Security Council. Investing the OPCW with prosecutorial powers sets a precedent in the postwar period and is aimed at duplicating the Security Council's functions. Clearly, inspired by the decision, some countries have stepped up their efforts to reform the UN Security Council in terms of its membership and operating methods and have been pushing for a redistribution of powers among the Security Council and the General Assembly in favor of the latter.

Mission Impossible?

The repeated use of the right to veto by U.S. under Trump[1] in connection with Palestine during voting at the UN Security Council on draft resolutions that would go against their national interests is accompanied by the ongoing discussion on the need to reform the operating methods and membership of the Security Council.

Clearly, France could take advantage of the situation to promote the "Code of Conduct" initiative it put forward back in 2013 on the need for the five permanent members of the Security Council to voluntarily refuse to use their right to veto in cases

---

[1] Under the Obama Administration, the United States abstained from the vote on Security Council Resolution 2334 held on February 23, 2016, thus indirectly condemning Israel for establishing settlements on Palestinian territory.

D. Kiku (✉)
Russian International Affairs Council, Moscow, Russia

© China Social Sciences Press 2023
Institute of Russian, Eastern European and Central Asian Studies, CASS and Russian International Affairs Council, *Global Governance in the New Era*,
https://doi.org/10.1007/978-981-19-4332-4_8

where "mass crimes" were committed. According to some estimates,[2] 114 countries have already put their name to the initiative, although this is still shy of the two-thirds (128 votes) of the UN member states required to pass such an important decision. At the same time, France, along with all the countries that share its ideas, should bear in mind that three out of the five Security Council's permanent members—Russia, China and the United States—have rarely displayed unanimity on the issue, refusing to discuss the proposal put forward by the French side.

The election of Germany as a nonpermanent member of the UN Security Council for 2019–2020 gave Berlin yet another opportunity to make a point about the urgent need to expand the Council's membership and put forward its case for becoming a permanent member within it—both as a country in its own right and as a representative of the so-called "Group of Four" that also includes Brazil, India and Japan. However, due to German Ambassador to the UN Christoph Heusgen's confrontational rhetoric with regard to Russia and China, Germany's bid started losing support. "To my knowledge, the number of supporters of Germany's joining the UN Security Council seems to have sufficiently decreased. I think it is the best outcome of your work at the Council", said Chargé d'affaires of the Russian Federation to the United Nations, Dmitry Polyanskiy.[3] Deputy Chinese Ambassador Yao Shaojun remarked that "German membership at the Security Council has not stood up to the world' s and Council' s expectations. Thus, the German path to permanent membership will be difficult."[4]

In 2005, the Group of Four published a draft resolution of the UN General Assembly as part of the discussion on reforming the Security Council initiated by former Secretary-General of the United Nations Kofi Annan,[5] which proposed expanding Security Council membership to 25 that very same year.[6] The project envisaged the creation of six additional permanent seats on the Council (two for Asia, two for Africa and one each for Latin America and Western Europe) and four additional nonpermanent seats. The document included a provision stating that a review of the UN Security Council membership composition should be carried out 15 years after the adoption of the decision to expand it. The decision would have been considered adopted if two-thirds of the UN member countries had voted in favor of it. The next step would have been to elect the new permanent members by

---

[2] 114 countries have already supported the initiative of Veto powers limits, Liechtenstein said. RIA Novosti. September 23, 2017. URL: https://ria.ru/20170923/1505392044.html.

[3] Statement by the Chargé d'affaires of the Russian Federation to the United Nations, Dmitry Polyanskiy. United Nations Security Council. December 30, 2020. URL: https://undocs.org/S/2020/1257.

[4] Germany under fire from China and Russia at UN. EURACTIV.com. December 18, 2020. URL: https://www.euractiv.com/section/politics/short_news/germany-under-fire-from-China-and-russia-at-un/.

[5] In larger freedom: toward development, security and human rights for all. General Assembly, United Nations. March 21, 2005. URL: https://documents-dds-ny.un.org/doc/UNDOC/GEN/N05/270/78/PDF/N0527078.pdf?OpenElement.

[6] Security Council reform // General Assembly, United Nations. July 6, 2005. URL: https://www.un.org/en/ga/search/view_doc.asp?symbol=A/59/L.64.

direct secret ballot, and the necessary amendments would then have been written into the UN Charter upon ratification by the members of parliament of two-thirds of the member states, including all permanent members of the Security Council.

The so-called "Uniting for Consensus" group emerged as a counter to the Group of Four, counting such major regional competitors to the Group of Four countries as Spain, Italy, Argentina, Pakistan and South Korea among its ranks.

Uniting for Consensus included a so-called "intermediate model" of reform in their draft resolution for the General Assembly. According to this model, the UN Security Council should be expanded to 25 members, but the additional seats should be nonpermanent and for an extended term. Furthermore, these nonpermanent members should be given the opportunity for immediate re-election when this term ends. The Uniting for Consensus group also called for the permanent members of the Security Council to show "restraint" in regard to using their right to veto.[7]

African countries instead submitted their own draft resolution to the General Assembly calling for the Security Council to be increased to 26 members, with five nonpermanent and two permanent seats being given to representatives of this regional group.[8] In addition, the draft resolution called for the new permanent members to be accorded the same prerogatives as those of the current permanent members, including the right of veto.

However, none of these three draft resolutions was put to vote at the UN General Assembly, as their authors failed to secure the necessary support. There was a real threat that this most sensitive of issues might cause fracture within the United Nations. The decision was made during the 2005 World Summit to continue work on reforming the organization in the form of intergovernmental negotiations to find ways to bring the various positions into closer alignment.

Regarding the possibility of the current Secretary-General of the United Nations initiating a new round of reforms, it is important to remember his words in April 2018 about the Security Council being out of touch with modern realities and certain permanent members abusing the right of veto. The speech was made against the background of the worsening U.S.–Russia confrontation on the Syrian crisis. António Guterres also noted that a complete reform of the organization is impossible without first implementing changes to the work of the Security Council.[9] Many experts interpreted these statements as supporting the French idea of restricting the right of veto, which corresponds in principle with the position adopted by Uniting for Consensus and Portugal—Guterres' native country.

The extent to which the UN Secretary-General will be able to continue to the efforts of his predecessors, particularly Kofi Annan, to reform the United Nations

---

[7] Reform of the Security Council. General Assembly, United Nations. July 21, 2005. URL: http://csnu.itamaraty.gov.br/images/21._A_59_L_68_Uniting_for_Consensus.pdf.

[8] Reform of the Security Council. General Assembly, United Nations. July 18, 2005. URL: https://www.auswaertiges-amt.de/blob/231612/c0f60bf9389b16748e277453d04cd341/draft-resolution-african-union-data.pdf.

[9] UN Secretary General announced the beginning of a new cold war. Ria Novosti. April 23, 2018. URL: https://ria.ru/20180423/1519181166.html.

and the Security Council during his second five-year term (due in December 2026[10]) remains unclear, as it will take an enormous amount of time and effort.

Russian Interests

Russia has always advocated for making the UN Security Council more representative in nature while keeping it relatively compact in terms of membership to ensure an adequate and rapid response to contemporary challenges and threats. As far as Russia is concerned, the number of Security Council members should be in the "low twenties," which runs counter to the much-publicized proposals made by certain delegations and groups of countries to increase membership to 25 or 26.[11] To modify the working methods of the Security Council, Russia's interests are closely tied to preserving the status quo and the prerogatives of the permanent members, including the right to veto.

Clearly, the course taken by the Russian leadership at the beginning of the twenty-first century to support the members of the so-called "Group of Four"—Brazil, India, Germany and Japan—in their push to be included in an expanded Security Council setup has been adjusted somewhat in response to the development of the geopolitical situation and the nature of Russia's interaction with these states on the international stage. As Minister of Foreign Affairs of the Russian Federation Sergey Lavrov noted in May 2018, "countries such as India and Brazil are strong candidates for permanent membership in the Security Council."

Naturally, given that Berlin has slapped unilateral sanctions on Russia and considering Germany's dependence on the United States, we should not expect Moscow to pledge its support for the country's candidacy for permanent membership any time soon.

The lack of progress in the signing of a peace treaty between Russia and Japan, as well as Tokyo's territorial claims, were largely to blame for Shinzo Abe's ill-fated visit to Moscow in April 2013, when the Japanese Prime Minister failed to secure Russia's support for his country's candidacy for permanent membership in the UN Security Council.

It would be in Russia's interests to support the candidacy of Brazil, India (a nonpermanent member for 2021–2022) and South Africa—its partners in BRICS—as they all call for the comprehensive strengthening of international law. Ostensibly, BRICS could become an example for the formation of a new model of global relations that is built on top of the dividing lines of "east–west" and "north–south" and does not conform to the logic of military and political blocs.

---

[10] General Assembly Confirms Guterres as the UN Secretary General for the Second Term. UN News. June 18, 2021. URL: https://news.un.org/ru/story/2021/06/1404942 (In Russian).

[11] Statement by Permanent Representative V.A. Nebenzya at an informal meeting of the UN General Assembly on the issue of equitable representation in the UN Security Council, expansion of its membership and related issues. Permanent Mission of the Russian Federation to the United Nations. June 6, 2018. URL: https://russiaun.ru/ru/news/ga060618.

Non-neutral Global Governance and BRICS Cooperation

Xiujun Xu

Introduction

In June 2009, the leaders from Brazil, Russia, India, and China met for the first time in Yekaterinburg, Russia, and established a mechanism for holding regular annual meetings, thus transforming the BRICs (Brazil, Russia, India, China)[1] from a pure economic concept to a platform for international dialogue and cooperation. In less than two years, the BRIC club was expanded for the first time since its inception to include South Africa, the largest economy in Africa, as a full member, and the club of BRICs thus became the BRICS. South Africa's inclusion into the BRIC Group provides it with a more representative structure as a mechanism for cooperation among emerging economies. Geographically speaking, the five BRICS members come from Asia, Europe, Africa, and the Americas, among the five continents of the world; demographically speaking, the combined population of the BRICS countries is more than 50% of that of emerging markets and developing countries; in terms of land area, the total territory of the BRICS members accounts for approximately 40% of that of emerging markets and developing countries. The rise of the BRICS bloc indicates an increase in their comprehensive national strength, including economic, political, and cultural aspects, and marks the gradual shift of the BRICS countries' role in global affairs from the periphery to the center. More importantly, as the BRICS countries emerge as a powerful force in the world, it can bring some positive changes to the unreasonable structure of benefit distribution in the international community and unfair international rules.

The formation and development of the BRICS cooperation mechanism are instrumental in strengthening economic and trade cooperation and policy coordination

---

[1] O'Neill [1].

X. Xu (✉)
Institute of World Economics and Politics, Chinese Academy of Social Sciences, Beijing, China

© China Social Sciences Press 2023
Institute of Russian, Eastern European and Central Asian Studies, CASS and Russian International Affairs Council, *Global Governance in the New Era*,
https://doi.org/10.1007/978-981-19-4332-4_9

among the five countries. However, the international community has different perceptions and evaluations of the current situation and the future of the BRICS cooperation mechanism. Some optimistic analysts argue that, at the national level, the BRICS countries boast great potential for investment and promising economic development, which have paced the way for BRICS cooperation[2]; at the international level, the BRICS countries are expected to break the long-standing unfair monopoly of a few countries on global economic affairs. This represents the progress of the international community, and the BRICS will thus forge ahead with renewed vigor and vitality.[3] That being said, some pessimistic scholars emphasize the differences in political regimes, economic sizes, economic structures, and cultural traditions of the five countries, making it difficult for them to be united as one.[4] Among them, Joseph S. Nye, a leading American scholar, has written several times that the five countries would not form a close alliance because there is no "Mortar" for the BRICS Group to address their differences.[5] All these debates and disagreements actually center around one issue, which is how to evaluate the multilateral cooperation mechanism that these emerging regional powers have established and the far-reaching implications it exerts on the world today. This question not only entails an objective analysis of the present and the future of the BRICS countries but also provokes rational thinking about the changes of global governance mechanisms in the new era.

According to some power-based traditional theories, the international situation is portrayed as a comparison of power among states and the corresponding hierarchy of states in the international system.[6] As the US superseded the British Empire as a superpower after World War II and established its global hegemony, some scholars have been prompted to develop the "hegemonic stability theory" and the "hegemonic cooperation model", as a way of providing theoretical support for the so-called Pax Americana.[7] Charles P. Kindleberger, based on the public goods theory, first made his argument that a stable and well-functioning international economic system depends on a hegemonic state to bear the "public costs".[8] Logically, this means that for an open and free world economy, there needs to be a global hegemonic power to dominate and govern international affairs and that is how the international economic system can develop in a stable way. These theories did provide a concise explanation for the reality in the international community for some time. However, since the 1970s, the US as the global hegemon has been in decline.[9] Despite the ongoing debates about such a decline, it is an undisputed fact that the relative power of the US has waned. As a result, the hierarchical structure of global economic governance built on a hegemonic power has been increasingly challenged: on the one hand, the rise

---

[2] Sachs [2] and Elliott Armijo [3].

[3] Smith [4] and Ivashov [5].

[4] Tudoroiu [6] and Sharma [7].

[5] Nye [8, 9].

[6] Morgenthau [10] and Waltz [11].

[7] Keohane [12].

[8] Kindleberger [13].

[9] Wallerstein [14].

of a number of emerging economies has posed a threat economically to the absolute dominance of the hegemonic state; on the other hand, the waning of the hegemon's relative power has gradually weakened its ability to control the international system and driven up the cost of maintaining the established system. These challenges have increasingly laid bare the limitations of these power-based traditional theories. In this connection, it is imperative for us to rethink of the trends of the world structure in the future and develop new theories to explain and evaluate the emergence of trans-regional global governance mechanisms among emerging countries such as the BRICS.

In an increasingly institutionalized and interdependent world, international institutions are deeply embedded in the international community and state behavior is often subject to constraints established by these institutions. But in a more fundamental sense, international institutions reflect international actors' competition over their interests and demands. If we define the world structure as relatively stable or balanced relationships of powers and interests among states or groups of states in the world, then the status and role of states or groups of states in the world can be reflected by the relationships of powers and interests among them and can be changed as long as such relationships are changed. Taking this logic as a starting point, this paper attempts to examine the reality and future of the BRICS countries from the perspective of institutions and interests.

Multi-level BRICS Cooperation

In today's world, especially after the international financial crisis in 2008, the world has seen faster paces of political and economic adjustments. Amid the process, although developed countries still dominate the current international order, there are signs indicating that international political and economic center of gravity has begun to shift toward emerging countries. As a new force in global governance, the BRICS cooperation mechanism has turned out to be an important platform for consultation and dialogue among the five countries in addressing global issues, with great implications for global governance. Judging from the history of the BRICS cooperation mechanism, continuous progress has been made in its institutionalization in just a few years.

The Institutionalization Process of BRICS Cooperation

It has been a process for the BRICS group as a whole to grow from an investment concept to a multilateral cooperation mechanism for emerging economies that plays an important role in the international arena today. With 15 years of development, the BRICS countries have deepened their cooperation and bettered the mechanism. Once only meetings of foreign ministers were arranged under such a mechanism, but now it has grown into a multi-level cooperation mechanism with summits of Heads of States or Government at its core and many different areas covered.

First, multi-level dialogue mechanisms have been established. Since September 2006, when the foreign ministers from Brazil, Russia, India, and China met for the first time on the sidelines of the UN General Assembly, the BRICS dialogue mechanism has continued to develop, building a multi-level network of dialogue mechanisms covering various areas. In June 2009, the leaders from Brazil, Russia, India, and China met for the first time in Yekaterinburg, Russia, and the first meeting of the BRICS leaders after the entry of South Africa was held in Sanya, China, in April 2011. Since then, leaders among the BRICS nations have met annually in the above-mentioned five countries on a rotating basis. The BRICS countries have also established various high-level dialogue mechanisms, including meetings of BRICS high representatives for security issues, meetings of ministers in over ten specific areas, meetings of coordinators, occasional communication among envoys to multilateral institutions, and consultations of working groups. In addition, relevant departments and groups in the BRICS club have developed various forms of dialogues and exchanges, such as entrepreneur forums, cooperative forums, local government and city forums, think tank forums, financial forums, and business forums.

Second, the New Development Bank (NDB) was created in a bid to support infrastructure construction and sustainable development in emerging markets and developing countries, including the BRICS countries. Unlike international dialogue mechanisms such as the G20 and G7, the BRICS countries have founded a new type of physical institutions. In accordance with the Fortaleza Declaration issued at the 2014 BRICS summit, the NDB was founded with an authorized capital of US$100 billion, with contributions equally distributed among the five founding members, and it is headquartered in Shanghai, China. As a supplement to existing multilateral and regional financial institutions, the NDB, when established, promised to offer assistance for infrastructure construction and sustainable development projects to help emerging economies and developing countries through loans, guarantees, equity investments, and other financial instruments, as a way of promoting global growth. The NDB is also set to cooperate with international organizations and other financial entities and provide technical assistance for NDB-supported projects. Since the announcement of its operation in July 2015, the NDB has cumulatively approved a total of some 80 projects in member countries, with loans totaling US$30 billion. In September 2021, the NDB officially announced that it will add the United Arab Emirates (UAE), Uruguay, and Bangladesh as its newest members.

Third, deeper economic partnerships among the BRICS countries have been formed. Practical economic cooperation is a priority for the five countries, and it is also the most rewarding field witnessing the most fruits and closest ties among these nations. In July 2015, the BRICS leaders met in Ufa, Russia, centering around the theme of "BRICS Partnership—a Powerful Factor of Global Development", and reached a consensus on promoting the BRICS economic partnership. The Strategy for BRICS Economic Partnership was adopted by these leaders, setting out a comprehensive development pattern for the interconnectivity among the BRICS countries in terms of integrated markets, multi-tiered circulation networks, land, air and sea connectivity, and greater cultural exchanges. In November 2020, the 12th BRICS Summit was held virtually, and the Strategy for BRICS Economic Partnership 2025 was adopted. This document identified three key areas and their own objectives for cooperation, namely trade, investment and finance, digital economy as well as sustainable development. Also, it laid out a new road map for deepening the BRICS economic partnership in the next five years.

BRICS Cooperation Amid the COVID-19 Pandemic

The COVID-19 pandemic, coupled with changes unseen in a century, has dealt a heavy blow to the economy of the BRICS countries. At the same time, the pandemic has made it more necessary for these countries to deepen cooperation with each other, creating new opportunities for cooperation in certain areas. Specifically, this is mainly manifested in the following three areas.

First, international anti-pandemic cooperation has been actively advanced. In the face of such an unexpected outbreak of COVID-19, the BRICS countries have stood for science-based origin tracing, opposed politicization and stigmatization, and strengthened joint prevention and control. In this process, they have demonstrated their cohesiveness and supported each other's efforts in combating the pandemic by sharing information and experience. As for vaccine cooperation, the BRICS countries have continued to promote pragmatic cooperation in areas such as joint research and development, joint production, and mutual recognition of vaccine standards and have worked together to promote the design, production, and equitable distribution of vaccines as global public goods. The very aim of their efforts is to improve vaccine accessibility and affordability and provide momentum for developing countries' cooperation in fighting the pandemic. At the same time, the pandemic has also boosted cooperation among the BRICS countries in the field of traditional medicine, providing more approaches to address COVID-19.

Secondly, an impetus has been given to the BRICS countries to deepen digital cooperation. In the wake of the pandemic, the digital transformation of traditional industries in the BRICS countries has been significantly accelerated. They have poured more investment in digital infrastructure construction and joined hands to promote 5G network construction, application extension, technological development, and safety assurance. In terms of digital industrialization, the BRICS countries have continued to strengthen the role of information technology in serving pandemic prevention and control and economic recovery, offer more support for the big data industry and the Internet of Things (IoT) industry, as well as promote AI development. As for digital transformation of industries, they have been striving for deeper integration of the digital economy with the real economy, with priorities given to the development of digital agriculture, digital cultural industries, "Internet + health", and "Internet + tourism". With the BRICS countries taking a pragmatic approach to digital governance, their common efforts have produced great results in areas such as joint prevention and control for public digital security, standardized management of digital government services, smart upgrading of urban facilities, and digital market competition. At the same time, the BRICS countries have leveraged multilateral platforms such as the G20 to strengthen information exchanges and experience sharing in areas such as cloud computing, big data, e-commerce, and the platform economy, enhancing their discourse influence and rule-making power in the field of digital economy.

Thirdly, the pursuit of green development by the BRICS countries has sped up. The pandemic has made them more aware of the importance of green development, and they have thus enhanced cooperation in the field of sustainable development. In terms of green energy cooperation, they have helped each other achieve their respective renewable energy goals. In order to deliver on these targets, the BRICS countries are expected to increase their total installed renewable energy capacity to 1252 GW between 2020 and 2030, with 498 GW of newly installed capacity, accounting for about a quarter of the current global total of installed renewable energy capacity. The BRICS countries boast ample room for cooperation in areas of solar, wind, bio-, and nuclear energy. In terms of green manufacturing cooperation, they are working together to build a modern manufacturing model. In recent years, the BRICS countries have carried out more exchanges of information and technology on basic green manufacturing technologies such as green materials and green design, as well as the manufacture of environmentally friendly and green products with higher resource efficiency such as green cars and green refrigerators. In terms of green financial cooperation, the BRICS countries have been an active player in the building of a standardized green financial system. They have been working to conduct research on environmental, social, and governance (ESG) standards and sustainable finance, as well as contribute more to the development and principles of responsible financing and green finance at the country and cross-country level.

The Non-neutral Global Governance and the Demands of BRICS Countries

In the field of global governance, be it the United Nations Charter, the economic and financial rules under the Bretton Woods system or other prevailing norms in the current international community, they are all established under the domination of developed countries that firmly hold the whip hand over a number of major international institutions. Due to the non-neutral character, international rules and institutions have become important tools for developed countries to realize their own interests. As the BRICS countries' institutionalization process continues and their prominence in the international community rises, they are bound to bring changes to the current unfair and unreasonable world pattern of benefit distribution and reduce the negative impact of the non-neutral global governance. They are also making it clear that one hegemonic state or a hegemonic group of a few powers are unable to sustain the constantly changing international political and economic system, and in this process, the world pattern will be transformed from the traditional power-based type of domination and subordination to a more democratic type of equal participation and mutual benefits, which will be in line with the characteristics of the times.

From Non-neutral Institutions to Non-neutral Global Governance

Douglass C. North defines institutions as "rules of the game", which are "humanly devised constraints that structure people's interactions".[10] They include both formal rules, such as constitutions and laws, property rights institutions and contracts, as well as informal rules, such as norms, codes of conduct, and customs. In its most fundamental sense, an institution refers to a system of rules. By non-neutrality, it means that "diverse groups and individuals get different results from the given system. For those who have already benefited from the established system, or who may benefit from some future institutional arrangement, they are certain to do their utmost to defend or pursue it."[11] In other words, what is behind the system is the unbalanced distribution of powers and interests.

In this regard, we can understand it from the following two aspects: On the one hand, for the society as a whole, a certain system brings different potential gains or losses to different people or groups of people, with some benefiting and others suffering; on the other hand, for those benefiting or suffering groups or individuals, they differ in the relative gains or losses received. Moreover, institutional non-neutrality is not rare in human societies, not only within social groups and countries, but also in the international community. Despite the fact that most international institutions are established with the approval of participating countries and each country enjoys an equal status as written in such institutions, the rules under them and the decisions and actions taken thereunder usually lead to different extent of gains and losses for different participants.

In the era of economic globalization, the international structure differs from previous eras when nation states had a relatively low level of interdependence, so it is not determined by some pure summations of absolute powers, nor does it solely depend on the auto-distribution of relative powers among states. Rather, it takes the shape of an extremely complex network of the international community, embodied by various international institutions with various forms and functions. A rather comprehensive definition of international institutions has been given by Stephen D. Krasner, who considers them to be sets of implicit or explicit principles, norms, rules, and decision-making procedures around which actor expectations converge in a given issue-area of international relations,[12] where principles refer to

---

[10] North [15].

[11] Yuyan [16].

[12] Krasner [17].

beliefs of fact, causation, and rectitude, norms refer to standards of conduct established in the form of rights and obligations, rules refer to specific stipulations and prohibitions on certain actions, and decision-making procedures refer to the practice of making decisions and implementing collective policies. These systems of principles, norms, rules, and decision-making procedures may mean the cession of state sovereignty, infringement on state autonomy, and restrictions on state actions and, therefore, pose different challenges to nation states in their pursuit of interests.

As globalization deepens, human societies are gradually confronted with increasing global issues that respect no boundaries between countries. Such problems cannot be properly solved by any state alone and must be addressed with joint efforts. In this context, global governance comes into being, which refers to the practice that all governments, international organizations, and citizens carry out democratic consultation and cooperation so as to maximize the common interests. What stands at the core of global governance should be bettering a new international political and economic order that safeguards the security, peace, development, welfare, equality, and human rights of all mankind, including global rules and institutions governing international political and economic issues.[13] Hence, international institutions and global governance are quite inseparable. Despite all the flaws around their legitimacy, these international institutions have become an important vehicle for global governance amid globalization.[14] Indeed, global governance means coordination and cooperation based on a commonly agreed international institutional framework, which mainly relies on a network of institutions consisting of a number of formal and informal rules. In this connection, global governance can be seen as collective actions taken in international relations formed by a variety of preexisting international norms, standards, and mechanisms. However, global governance is labeled as "non-neutral" since the non-neutral nature of institutions, that is, actual benefits or losses to different countries or groups vary across the diverse global governance mechanisms.

The Interests of BRICS Countries in Global Governance

In the early 1990s, as the Cold War came to an end, the world gradually merged into one big unified market. In the decade that followed, the BRICS countries' intention to participate in global governance was not strong, so regarding their common interests in global governance, some scholars and analysts believe that as a cross-regional group of emerging economies, it is difficult for BRICS members to coordinate with each to identify common interests and they might find that their differences outweigh their consensus. Although such a statement exaggerates the divergence of interests among the BRICS countries, it is not unwarranted in a certain sense.

---

[13] Keping [18].
[14] Jiang [19].

For a long time, many have doubted whether the BRICS countries could build a community of interests due to the following factors. Firstly, trade links between them are still relatively loose, mutual investment still stands at a low level, financial cooperation is still in its infancy, and investment cooperation is yet to be enhanced. Secondly, there are major differences in politics and values between these BRICS countries. Among them, there are various social systems and political regimes, different religious beliefs and values, as well as diverse national identities and consciousness. Finally, constraints of the external environment also play a role. In many areas, the BRICS countries are subject to direct or indirect influence of developed countries. The developed western countries, which have long dominated the international economic order, are inevitably concerned about that their leadership in the global economy might be challenged by the rise of the BRICS countries. Hence, they do not want to see a united BRICS bloc as a community of interests.

Despite disruptions caused by the aforementioned factors, the BRICS countries are now in a position to participate in global economic governance due to dynamics of internal and external environment, being increasingly active in making their voices heard. What they have in common outnumbers their differences by a large margin, and they are gradually identifying their demands in a bid to change their long-standing unfavorable position in the global system. Such a weak position of the BRICS countries in global governance is increasingly highlighting the sensitive and fragile nature of their interests, which has put constraints on the further development of their economies. In many areas, such as leveling off commodity prices, preventing financial regulatory failures, establishing a rational exchange rate mechanism, breaking down barriers to investment and trade, and promoting trade balance, the BRICS countries are often in an adverse position, and in many cases, they are subject to others' "governance". More importantly, BRICS countries' status and role in the international community are largely mismatched with their strength as a result of the non-neutral nature of global governance and the dominance of the global governance discourse by countries with vested interests. However, in recent years, as their influence grows and global interests expand, the BRICS countries have used international platforms to put forward various proposals and propositions on global governance, expressing their own interests and safeguard their common interests as their prominence in the world continues to rise.

Firstly, practically speaking, the BRICS countries still need to drive their economic growth. In recent years, the BRICS countries have made major headway in economic development, and their overall share in the world economy has been on the rise. Besides, some BRICS countries have leaped ahead rapidly to occupy a pivotal position in the world economy. However, in terms of per capita income, they still lag behind their developed counterparts with a huge gap. In terms of the overall level of economic and social development, the disparity between the BRICS countries and developed countries remains relatively salient. The COVID-19 pandemic crippled the BRICS countries' economy to a great extent, highlighting their common interest in stabilizing the external environment, promoting global economic recovery, and maintaining rapid economic growth.

Secondly, the BRICS countries' interests would converge when it comes to addressing the challenges brought about by economic globalization. The deepening economic globalization has accelerated cross-border flows and allocation of goods, services, capital, technology, and information and has closely linked economic activities of various countries around the world. At the same time, however, economic globalization has also brought different types of risks and challenges internationally, giving rise to a series of global problems. For the growing BRICS countries, as their domestic economic systems are still fragile with somewhat flawed economic policies and institutions, they are more vulnerable to external economic shocks. As the whole is greater than the sum of the parts, the BRICS countries can band together to create synergy, so as to better safeguard their own interests and address global challenges.

Finally, the BRICS countries share the common aspiration to continuously expand their international influence and make global governance fairer and more rational. In the current international political and economic system, the US-led group of countries with vested interests remains the main beneficiaries, while the vast number of emerging markets and developing countries fails to enjoy fair treatment and exert influence commensurate with their own strength. This is mainly manifested in two ways: Firstly, the emerging and developing countries represented by the BRICS countries are in a subordinate position in the international monetary, financial, and trade system; secondly, the powers and obligations of them are not balanced in global governance mechanisms. The BRICS countries have undertaken too much responsibility in solving problems facing the whole international community, while their legitimate rights and say in these mechanisms are so limited. During the 2008 international financial crisis, while living with untold economic suffering, the BRICS countries made a great contribution to the global economic recovery. That said, they are still unable to monitor and restrain economic operations as well as financial and monetary policies of the developed countries, represented by the US, through corresponding international institutions. For this reason, the BRICS countries hold similar positions and have reached numerous consensuses on global governance reforms.

Inclusive Interests and the BRICS Countries' Cooperation

What the BRICS countries are building is a new type of partnership that reflects characteristics of our times, and they do not seek to form an anti-Western political coalition.[15] At the third BRICS Summit in April 2011, the five leaders made it clear that BRICS cooperation is "inclusive and non-confrontational" and that the BRICS countries stand ready to strengthen ties and cooperation with other countries, especially other emerging and developing countries, as well as relevant international and regional organizations.[16] It is clear that while conceiving and advancing BRICS

---

[15] Laïdi [20].

[16] Sanya Declaration—The Third BRICS Summit, *People's Daily*, April 15, 2011, Page 3.

cooperation, the five BRICS leaders have reached a consensus of pursuing inclusive interests.

Nonzero-Sum Game and Inclusive Interests in the Global Economy

A game can be understood as a "strategy" and "rule", and such games can be divided into zero-sum games and nonzero-sum games characterized by the benefits in different cases. In a zero-sum game, relationships between the parties are adversarial in a sense that one party's gains must come from another party's losses. However, in a nonzero-sum game, despite the fact that the total gains might be constant or vary as each party changes their mix of strategies, each party will benefit and a win–win scenario can be achieved for all parties. In the international community, countries around the world, as players in the global economy, are following no longer a zero-sum game but a nonzero-sum game that can be mutually beneficial and lead to a "all—or—nothing" scenario in more and more areas. This happens for the following reasons.

First, the global economy is becoming increasingly interdependent. Since the mid-twentieth century, economic globalization has swept through all developed capitalist countries and is gradually spreading to an even wider range of developing countries. The acceleration of globalization has led to closer economic ties among countries, making it difficult for a single country to control its economy by itself. Products cannot be produced without raw materials from other countries, foreign markets are stressed in products marketing, foreign capital needs to be absorbed while expanding investment, and coordination with other countries is necessary even when it comes to formulating national economic policies. Thus, globalization has become an irreversible trend in the world economy, under which process international economic exchanges are expanding, a number of international economic management organizations and economic entities are emerging, and regional economic integration is picking up momentum. It also leads to transnational exchanges, collisions, and integration of spiritual elements such as cultures, lifestyles, values, and ideologies. Nowadays, advanced technologies with information technology at its core are developing at lightning speed, narrowing the physical distance among countries. Countries and regions are becoming more closely integrated with each other, as they have increasingly intertwined relationships on the economic front and their economic activities tend to affect each other.

Secondly, industrial structures of various countries have become more complementary. Since the 1990s, a new round of global industrial transfer has sped up due to technological progress and the deepening international division of labor, resulting in an even stronger complementary effect of the global economy. Even gripped by various factors such as the financial crisis, the COVID-19 pandemic, protectionist measures and inward-looking policies, and regional and cross-regional industrial transfers based on the global division of labor have not been halted, while both intra- and cross-regional industrial structures have become much more complementary. On the one hand, the rapid pace of regional economic integration has accelerated the allocation of resources and the flow of production factors within regions, with the European Union, North America, and East Asia featuring the strongest momentum in terms of global industrial transfer, which has served to upgrade the global industrial structure. On the other hand, strengthened cross-regional economic ties have resulted in the global allocation of industrial chains and highly specialized international division of labor, mainly demonstrated by vertically structural complementarities in the division of labor between developed and emerging markets as well as the horizontally industrial ones among developed countries.

Thirdly, global issues have posed even greater challenges. Advancing science and technology and industrial development have increasingly enabled mankind to change nature, contributing to constantly developing material and spiritual civilization. But such progress has also brought along with it many negative effects on human society. In recent decades, we have seen more punishment from the nature, and a number of global problems have posed severe threats to societies. These are serious issues that are felt around the world, are pivotal to the survival and development of mankind, and cannot be solved unless all countries join hands with each other. Nowadays, global problems are more salient than ever before, and they mainly include population explosion, food shortage, insufficient energy supply, environmental damage, resource depletion, economic crisis as well as severe epidemics and pandemics. As these challenges threaten the common interests of mankind and relative solutions entail concerted efforts, their emergence has, in a sense, raised global awareness and encouraged countries to seek common ground so as to live together in peace. Such a trend has been conducive to changing, to a certain extent, the confrontational thinking of countries in politics and economics toward a new mindset of more cooperation, compromise, and concessions. In responding to global issues, countries' own development has gradually integrated into the whole world's progress, and countries in the world are gradually becoming indispensable to each other with their interests intertwined.

The fact that different economies are interdependent and complementary with intertwined interests dictates a foreign policy tone of cooperation, rather than competition, among the world's nations. Countries have not only common interests that they are expected to be defended together, but also inclusive interests that cannot be severed from each other. By inclusive interests, we mean a scenario where participants in the game are safeguarding their own interests in a way that does not hurt others' interests and may even work to their benefit, and their interests are therefore essentially in line with these of other parties. Inclusive interests, as non-exclusive and mutually beneficial interests, expand the connotation of common interest for national groups or other groups. On the one hand, the relationship between group members and non-members is not full of antagonism and competition, and while pursuing common interests, group members do not seek to benefit themselves at the expense of the interests of non-member states. On the other hand, group members and non-members can achieve win–win results, and the realization of common interests based on group members creates facilities for helping those non-members achieve theirs, ultimately leading to a mutually beneficial scenario. It is thus clear to see that inclusive interests mean to take a broader approach to relations of interests, which not only takes into consideration the common interests of group members, but also those of non-member states. Hence, it is even more important for emerging countries to pursue inclusive interests. Research has shown that while seeking their paths to leadership in global governance, emerging countries should take other countries' interests and perceptions into account, which is a necessary prerequisite for winning recognition, support, and allegiance of other countries.[17] Accordingly, in order to make cooperation mechanisms among emerging countries a success, inclusive interests must be regarded as both a necessary requirement and a realistic choice.

BRICS Cooperation in the Context of Inclusive Interests

Compared to traditional allies in the international community, BRICS cooperation does not target any other country, nor does it seek to obtain exclusive and one-sided benefits, which will not lead to a further division in the world benefit distribution. Indeed, cooperation among the BRICS countries serves the purpose of advancing broader cooperation and exchanges in the developing world, promoting a more rational global governance regime by addressing institutional deficiencies of the international community, and then fundamentally eliminating the roots of conflicts among various international actors and groups with distinctive inclusiveness. Specifically, such inclusiveness of the BRICS countries' cooperation is reflected in the following seven aspects.

First, the plurality of the BRICS members. Despite the fact that there are now only five BRICS member states, they come from different continents, including Asia, Europe, Africa, and the Americas, and all of them are major countries with great influence in their respective regions, representing the interests of other countries in each region to the greatest extent possible. When considering the differences of the five countries in terms of their domestic structures and national characteristics, such plurality is even more salient. The five countries have different political and judicial systems; economically, they feature different development models and economic structures and have varied levels of overall national strength and income per person; culturally speaking, they boast diverse cultural traditions, rituals, and religious beliefs. On this account, such diversity of membership of the BRICS Group fully demonstrates the openness and non-discrimination of the five governments' foreign policies. In this sense, the BRICS countries are not a narrow and exclusive interest group, but rather a cross-regional community of countries with diversified interests.

---

[17] Schirm [21].

Secondly, the openness of cooperation philosophy. As a coordination platform among emerging economies, the BRICS cooperation mechanism embraces the vision of openness and cooperation toward emerging and developing countries. Since its inception, the BRICS mechanism has received close attention from other emerging countries, with some of them expressing willingness to join the mechanism. BRICS further expands membership for the first time in three years that followed, with the admission of South Africa as a full member. This highlights the openness of the BRICS cooperation mechanism, making it possible for the group to admit other emerging countries with considerable GDP, population size, and regional and global influence as new members. They can establish new cooperation models such as the "BRICS+", which will make the BRICS mechanism more representative and influential in the world and serve to promote the cooperation among emerging countries and developing countries.

Thirdly, the win–win nature of cooperation goals. The BRICS leaders have reached a consensus that their cooperation is meant for a win–win result. BRICS cooperation is aimed at achieving "mutual benefits and common development". In the long-standing practice of conducting cooperation, a unique spirit has emerged in the BRICS countries' partnership, featuring "openness, inclusiveness, cooperation, and mutual benefits". On the premise of this consensus, the BRICS countries will remain committed to their common interests and strengthen coordination in the international economic, financial, and development spheres, so as to elevate the status and role of emerging countries and other developing countries in global governance, thereby helping establish a fair, equitable, inclusive, and well-managed new international political and economic order.

Fourth, the breadth of cooperation fields. It has been one of the fundamental principles of BRICS cooperation to carry out pragmatic cooperation in various areas. In the fields of trade and investment, all the five BRICS countries support global trade liberalization and investment facilitation and object to trade protectionism and unreasonable investment barriers; in the finance and currency domain, they are working together to promote effective regulation of global finance and diversify reserve currencies, and oppose financial altruism and monetary hegemony; and in the fields of science, technology, and climate change, the BRICS countries keep pushing forward the deepening of their cooperation.

Fifth, the multilayered structure of cooperation approaches. As the BRICS countries carry out various forms of cooperation, a multilayered cooperation framework has initially taken shape. Currently, a rather sophisticated four-pronged cooperation model has emerged, which is comprised of the BRICS Summits, Meetings of the BRICS Ministers, the BRICS Working Group Meeting, and The BRICS Civil Forum Meetings. Meetings of the BRICS Ministers mainly consist of the Meetings of Senior Representatives on Security Issues, Foreign Minister Meetings, Meetings of the BRICS Finance Ministers and Central Bank Governors, Meetings of the BRICS Trade Ministers, Meetings of the BRICS Health Ministers, Meetings of the BRICS Agriculture Ministers, etc. The BRICS Working Group Meetings are dedicated to such areas as agriculture, science, technology and innovation, and inter-bank financial cooperation; Civil Forums serve the purpose of enhancing cooperation and communication in business, city-to-city cooperation, sports, and culture. Various levels of cooperation between them have served as channels for governments, academic circles, business communities, and civil organizations to carry out effective communication, which have gone a long way toward better relations among them.

Sixth, the constructive nature of cooperation practices. As an important emerging force in the international community, the BRICS countries are placed to play a constructive role in the current international political and economic system, which can contribute to a fairer and more rational world order. When considering the historical trajectory of the west, it is clear that rising Western powers were inclined to resort to war and expansion as their way of transforming the global structure of benefit distribution, changing the world order, and then becoming hegemonic states. Different from these traditional Western states, the BRICS countries do not wish to scrap or uproot the current international system. While choosing to embrace and adapt to the current international system, the BRICS countries prefer to work with developed countries to reform the international financial and monetary system for the better, bring about comprehensive reforms of the United Nations, and enhance its central role in dealing with global threats and challenges. Cooperation practices of the BRICS countries have fully demonstrated that it is their wish to reform and contribute to the international system instead of overturning it.

Seventh, the non-confrontational character of cooperation strategies. What distinguishes BRICS cooperation from other mechanisms is that the five countries have managed to establish a new type of partnership dedicated to development and a non-confrontational strategy for cooperation. In this sense, the inception of such a mechanism is not at odds with the common interests of the broader international community, and they are rather compatible. Different from political and military alliances, the BRICS countries are banded together for development, which is a priority issue for both developed and developing countries. Since they want to remove barriers standing in the way of development, they have been working to establish inclusive partnerships within the BRICS Group, with other developing countries and between developing and developed countries.

The interests sought by the BRICS countries are not exclusive, but rather inclusive in many senses. Whether it is at the regional, trans-regional, or global levels, the BRICS countries have actively participated in and contributed to the global governance, and they do not seek to challenge the established international system. They are working on the one hand as a driving force for South–South cooperation and on the other hand as new sources of opportunities for enhancing North–South dialogue, coordination, and cooperation.

Conclusion

The non-neutral nature of the international system has contributed to an unreasonable structure of benefit distribution among members in the international community, which consequently leads to both favorable and unfavorable positions held by different blocs of countries. In the case of the BRICS countries, they are not holding a position that is commensurate with their overall strength in the current network of global governance mechanisms. There are usually two options at their disposal to get rid of their unfavorable position: They can either choose to make the non-neutral international system more responsive to their interests or create a new one that favors them. The BRICS countries, as a new force, have to compete with countries (blocs) with vested interests, and it is difficult for them to transform current global governance rules in the near future. In this sense, a more pragmatic and effective approach might be suitable for them, which means that they have to carry out in-depth cooperation, establish new non-neutral institutions to balance the current non-neutral global institutional framework, and push for institutional changes in their interests. These are indications that the BRICS cooperation mechanism only serves to better the current international system.

As the BRICS cooperation mechanism came into being and gradually gathers more momentum, it has not only helped step up dialogue and cooperation among the five countries but has also functioned as a platform for consultation and dialogue among developing countries and between developing and developed countries. As the five BRICS countries continue to deepen their cooperation, real benefits can be delivered to developed nations, other emerging markets, and developing countries. That said, since the BRICS mechanism is non-neutral in nature, other countries shall expect different absolute and relative gains from the five BRICS countries, which might result in conflicts of interest between them. In this connection, while the BRICS mechanism focuses on the five countries' demands, it must also be open and inclusive enough to reflect the interests of other countries as much as possible. By doing so, they can significantly soften the impact of dramatic changes in the world structure while pushing for incremental changes in the international system.

Currently, cooperation among the five BRICS countries is indeed confronted with tests and challenges, but they are expected to increase their economic strengths, further institutionalize their cooperation, implement what they plan on various issues, and actively explore new cooperation models such as "BRICS+" open for other countries' participation. With relentless efforts in these aspects, it is certain that the BRICS countries will play a more pivotal role in global governance, as they will help build a new world structure, establish a fairer and more rational international political and economic order, and create a new world featuring common prosperity and enduring peace.

References

1. O'Neill, J. 2001. building better global economic BRICs. *Global Economics Paper*, No. 66. New York: Goldman Sachs.
2. Sachs, G. 2007. *BRICs and Beyond*. London: Goldman Sachs.
3. Elliott Armijo, L. 2007. The BRICs countries (Brazil, Russia, India, and China) as analytical category: Mirage or insight? *Asian Perspective* 31 (4), 7–42.
4. Smith, J.A. 2011. BRIC becomes BRICS: Emerging regional powers? Changes on the geopolitical chessboard. *Global Research*
5. Ivashov, G.L. 2011. BRICS and the mission of reconfiguring the world: An alternative world order? *The 4th Media.*
6. Tudoroiu, T. 2012. Conceptualizing BRICS: OPEC as a mirror. *Asian Journal of Political Science* 20 (1): 23–45.
7. Sharma, R. 2012. Broken BRICs: Why the rest stopped rising. *Foreign Affairs* 91 (6): 2–7.
8. Nye, J.S. 2013. What's in a BRIC? *Project Syndicate.*
9. Nye, J.S. 2013. BRICS without Mortar. *Project Syndicate.*
10. Morgenthau, H.J. 1949. *Politics among Nations: The Struggle for Power and Peace*. New York: Knopf.
11. Waltz, K.N. 1979. *Theory of International Politics*. Reading: Addison Wesley.
12. Keohane, R.O. 1989. The theory of hegemonic stability and changes in international economic regimes, 1967–1977. In *International Institutions and State Power: Essays in International Relations Theory*, ed. R.O. Keohane, 74–100. Boulder: Westview Press.
13. Kindleberger, C.P. 1973. *The World in Depression, 1929–1939*. Berkeley: University of California Press.
14. Wallerstein, I. 2003. *The Decline of American Power: The U.S. in a Chaotic World*. New York, London: The New Press.
15. North, D.C. 1994. *Institutions, Institutional Change and Economic Performance*, translated by Liu Shouying, p. 3. Shanghai: Shanghai Sanlian Bookstore.
16. Yuyan, Z. 1994. Interest groups and institutional non-neutrality. *Reform* 2, 98.
17. Krasner, S.D. 1983. Structural causes and regime consequences: regimes as intervening variables. In *International Regimes*, ed. Stephen D. Krasner, 2. Ithaca: Cornell University Press.
18. Keping, Y. 2007. *"Introduction to Global Governance"*, *Chinese Scholars' insights into the World—Global Governance Volume* edited by Pang Zhongying, p. 24. Beijing: New World Press.
19. Jiang, Y. 2010. *Global Governance and China's Strategic Transformation as a Major Country*, 90. Beijing: Current Affairs Press.
20. Laïdi, Z. 2012. BRICS: Sovereignty power and weakness. *International Politics* 49 (5): 615.
21. Schirm, S.A. 2010. Leaders in need of followers: Emerging powers in global governance. *European Journal of International Relations* 16 (2): 197–221.

Balance of Power Versus Balance of Interest: Great Powers in Globalization

Illusions of a New Bipolarity

Alexey Gromyko

There is a certain foreign political dimension to the COVID-19 pandemic that is beginning to rear its head with increasing frequency and can thus explain the current behavior of states on the international stage. Coronavirus plays two largely contradictory roles—it accelerates some processes while at the same time putting the brakes on, or even halting, others. The former includes, among other things, the geopolitical plans of a number of states, while the latter includes finding solutions to global socioeconomic problems and domestic political processes. Many people start talking about a "new bipolarity." Are we truly seeing a revival of bipolarity, but in a modern form? That is, in the true definition of the word—is the world being split into two antagonistic systems?

It has become the norm in the western mainstream media, especially those media outlets that push the liberal political agenda, to separate the world into two camps. "China is on the way up and, thanks to Trump's trade war," CNN tells us, "the world is heading for an us-versus-them universe [...] There will be two camps, pro-America; pro-China [...]" Let us be clear, we are not talking about escalating tensions between two states here, but rather between two "camps."[1]

And now let us not forget that the only bipolarity that we have ever experienced was in the form of the U.S.–Soviet confrontation during the Cold War. It was marked by a gradual stabilization of international relations that culminated in the Helsinki Final Act of 1975. In other words, the logic of bipolarity entailed not only rivalry between the two global centers of power but also their joint activities to eliminate the threat of a major armed confrontation. However, relations between Washington and Beijing appear to be heading in a completely different direction. According

---

[1] Boris Johnson stakes future on Donald Trump after Brexit. The gamble may break Britain. CNN. August 24, 2019. URL: https://edition.cnn.com/2019/08/24/uk/johnson-trump-brexit-g7-gbr-intl/index.html.

A. Gromyko (✉)
Russian International Affairs Council, Moscow, Russia

© China Social Sciences Press 2023
Institute of Russian, Eastern European and Central Asian Studies, CASS and Russian International Affairs Council, *Global Governance in the New Era*, https://doi.org/10.1007/978-981-19-4332-4_10

to Graham Allison, "war between the U.S. and China in the decades ahead is not just possible, but much more likely than currently recognized."[2] It thus follows that interaction between China and the United States will lead to loosening, rather than a stabilization, of international relations.

There is also a more optimistic scenario, which would involve Washington agreeing to coexist with Beijing in a "competition without catastrophe."[3] The problem with this scenario is that any large-scale "rebalancing" will have to be carried out on conditions set by the United States.[4] However, given the current circumstances, such a rebalancing can only be achieved in a climate of equality or, more likely, under conditions that suit China. For this to happen, American foreign policy needs to return to some semblance of realism. However, this is beyond the scope of this article.

Are there any favorable "external conditions" for a bipolar world to take shape? Is there anything in the current international climate that would convince us to place our trust in China and the United States as the countries that are expected to lead these new poles? We should keep in mind that during the Cold War, the East and West continued to develop actively. Today, both China and the United States are shoulder deep in globalization. However, just look at what is happening to globalization. Economic, informational, technological, and other forms of competition are only growing. What used to be a self-regulating economic process is turning into a political instrument for suppressing business competitors, with unreasonable restrictions, the extraterritorial application of national laws, and actions in circumvention of the WTO rules in the name of "national security" becoming the norm. Many of the problems that led to the global financial crisis in 2008–2009 have not been properly addressed. The coronavirus pandemic promises even harder times. It turns out that, in its current manifestation, globalization is not a process that one country is able to steer; rather, it should be promoted by every country, and only by this way can they pursue their respective goals.

Some proponents of a new bipolarity might concede that deglobalization processes are indeed taking place right now, but in no way does this prove that the world is not being split in two and becoming bipolar in nature once again. The answer to this question would be that none of the world's most respected economists would challenge the idea that globalization is a representation of the interdependence of the modern world. We are talking about the specific ultraliberal form of globalization that has dominated for the last 30 or 40 years, exhausting its usefulness. There is no objective reason to expect a return to the old kind of bipolarity, which functioned as two parts of the world that existed almost in complete isolation from each other socially and economically under the leadership of the United States and the Soviet Union. Despite all the current trade, financial, and sanctions wars, the global nature of the market cannot be dismantled and returned to the Council for Mutual Economic Assistance and the European Economic Community, for example, which in any case had little to do with one another.

---

[2] Allison [1].

[3] Campbell and Sullivan [2].

[4] Campbell [3].

Illusions of a New Bipolarity

China and the United States are destined to have close economic ties, yet at the same time, they are sliding toward confrontation. Neither the first nor the second circumstance was characteristic of the confrontation between the United States and the Soviet Union. It turns out that the United States and China cannot exist in economic isolation from one another, nor can they build a kind of economic interdependence that would suit both sides, which has led to a kind of acute "ischemia" in the rivalry between the two countries. Even at the embryonic stage, this kind of bipolarity cannot offer stability to the world or anything that would even remotely resemble U.S.–Soviet relations.

One of the reasons why the rivalry between the Soviet Union and the United States grew into a standoff between the two poles was that external contours emerged in the form of socialist and capitalist camps, respectively. The events of the past 30 years show that the West, in the previous sense of the word, no longer exists. The dominance and economic might of the United States are very much on the decline, as its ability to use force effectively and maintain its leading technological status. Even the United Kingdom, traditionally Washington's closest ally, refused to support the White House in its war against the Chinese telecoms giant *Huawei*. According to the people of Japan, Canada, Germany, and France, the United States poses a greater threat to their respective countries than Russia and (with the exception of Japan) China.[5]

It is unclear exactly where the boundaries of the West begin and end. It is turning into a dual-core system with centers in Washington and the European Union that are undergoing strategic decoupling.[6] The United States has, since the presidency of George W. Bush, pursued a course of monetizing and pragmatizing relations with its allies, strategically leaving Europe. The European Union is trying to shed its image as a purely economic center of power through the idea of strategic autonomy and a common strategic culture. Europe will never again be the focus of the United States' attention, write *Foreign Affairs*, and so must ensure the survival of its own model to stake a claim to global leadership.[7]

For China's external contours, there is nothing here that resembles the socialist camp that existed under the auspices of the USSR. Political and ideological cohesion was key to the bipolarity that we witnessed during the Cold War. China has long surpassed the Soviet Union in terms of its economic influence, but politically, Beijing has very few allies, especially in regard to an out and out confrontation with the United States. This is perhaps the biggest difference between what we are witnessing today and the bipolarity of the past. When superpowers are not surrounding themselves with ideological blocs, bipolarity becomes nothing but two states getting into a bickering match, albeit with certain global attributes. China has perhaps one true strategic

---

[5] Munich Security Report 2019. The Great Puzzle: Who Will Pick Up the Pieces? MSC. URL: https://securityconference.org/assets/02_Dokumente/01_Publikationen/MunichSecuri tyReport2019.pdf.

[6] Gromyko, A. A. (2018). Splintered West: The Consequences for the Euro-Atlantic. Contemporary Europe, No. 4.

[7] Polyakova A., Haddad B. Europe Alone. What Cones After the Transatlantic Alliance. Foreign Affairs. July/August, 2019. URL: https://www.foreignaffairs.com/articles/europe/2019-06-11/eur ope-alone.

partner, and that is Russia. The United States, on the other hand, has many allies, although many of them, including France and Germany, are tired of being of their forced dependence on Washington.

Can the Russia–China tandem stake a claim to being one of the blocs in the new bipolar world? Most likely, not. As a rule, the poles can have only one indisputable leader. China–Russia relations are far from subordinate. They are good-neighborly relations. But the two countries pursue strategies that do not always coincide. The military and political standoff between China and the United States are largely focused in the South China and East China seas, thousands of miles away from Russia. Russia does not have any interests in that region. However, it is precisely here that China's most vulnerable geopolitical sore spots are located (Hong Kong, Taiwan, and the Paracel and the Spratly Islands). Russia has a zone of strategic tension of its own to the west, far away from China.

Another thing that we should keep in mind is that bipolarity was only possible in a world that was already split along ideological lines. However, the confrontation between socialism and capitalism is a thing of the past, and value differences have also receded into the background, making way for *realpolitik* and geopolitics.[8] Without an ideological confrontation, it is impossible to recreate the necessary conditions for the world to split into two camps. It is true that China and the United States have fundamentally different values and political systems, as was the case with the United States and the Soviet Union during the Cold War. However, these contradictions run nowhere near as deep. The United States remains convinced of its exclusivity and its God-given right to global leadership.[9] China, on the other hand, does not demonstrate any kind of messianism and, unlike the Soviet Union, does not promote socialist and communist ideas. Beijing does not rely on hackneyed ideological phrases; rather, it points to the effectiveness of its development model. The inescapable growth of competition between Beijing and Washington is not due to the irreconcilability of ideologies but rather to their geopolitical incompatibility, and this is simply not enough for the confrontation to transmute into a bloc-based rivalry.

However, many are still enticed by discussions of a new bipolarity, and there are many reasons why. Let us outline a few of them. First, the world order that existed during the Cold War was relatively simple. Second, people are motivated by anti-Chinese sentiments. That is, many associate the bipolarity of the Cold War with the eventual victory of one of the sides, and they hope that the United States will defeat China in much the same way that it defeated the Soviet Union. Third, it would seem that those who still believe in the return of a consolidated West under the leadership of the United States and the emergence of an anti-Western bloc led by China and

---

[8] The return of geopolitics had been a topic of discussion long before Donald Trump moved into the White House. See, for example, Larrabee S. Russia, Ukraine, and Central Europe: The Return of Geopolitics. Journal of International Affairs. April 15, 2010. URL: https://jia.sipa.columbia.edu/russia-ukraine-and-central-europe-return-geopolitics.

[9] The idea of American leadership appears 36 times in the country's 32-page National Security Strategy for 2015.

neighboring Russia see U.S.–China bipolarity as a viable option. Such conclusions are normally based on the immature and ideologically motivated idea of the world being split into "liberal democracies" on the one hand and "authoritarian regimes" on the other.

If the idea of a new bipolarity is untenable, then the possibility of a new Cold War, that is, the appearance of elements of the political, military, financial, and economic confrontation between Russia and the West, also has no substance behind. The phenomenon of the Cold War is inseparable from the post-war conditions that led to the emergence of U.S.–Soviet bipolarity. Its key parameters are well known, and almost none of them have been recreated. No one makes the claim today that there is a new geopolitical rift between Russia and the United States, and thus the West. The phrase "New Cold War" would still make sense with regard to the trajectory along which China and the United States are currently traveling. However, even then, it is used rarely and mostly by Washington.[10] Again, we need to keep in mind that the Cold War as an element of U.S.–Soviet bipolarity was a path to a certain balance of interests and not a slippery slope toward an open confrontation.

Regarding relations between Russia and the European Union, even given the depressing strategies pursued by both sides, the principle of a new bipolarity has not taken root. It is only under extreme duress and with extreme reluctance that the European Union has taken any steps against China. This was laid bare for all to see in the tragicomic story involving the EU report on disinformation about the COVID-19 pandemic. The handling of the coronavirus is leaving an increasing number of people in Europe with no illusions about the United States and the "shining city upon a hill," or indeed about the far-reaching ambitions harbored by Brussels. The point of view that the current state of relations with Moscow will only make the situation worse has been argued very articulately in a number of analytical works, not to mention by a number of politicians in Europe.[11] The pandemic has led to a certain opportunistic surge in anti-Russia and anti-China rhetoric. However, it works far better on the European Union's less blinkered view of the world than it does on neoliberal apologetics, which in many ways perverts the legacy of liberal thought.

References

1. Allison, G. 2017) *Destined for War: Can America and China Escape Thucydides's Trap?* Boston and New York: Houghton Mifflin Harcourt. https://www.hks.harvard.edu/publications/destined-war-can-america-and-China-escape-thucydidess-trap

---

[10] Pence M. Remarks by Vice President Pence on the Administration's Policy Toward China. The Hudson Institute. 04.10.2018., Perlez J. Pence's China Speech Seen as Portent of "New Cold War". The New York Times. 05.10.2018., Rogin J. Pence: "It is Up to China to Avoid a Cold War." Washington Post. November 13, 2018.

[11] Monaghan [4].

2. Campbell, K.M., and J. Sullivan. 2019. *Competition Without Catastrophe. How America Can Both Challenge and Coexist with China.* Foreign Affairs. https://www.foreignaffairs.com/articles/china/competition-with-china-without-catastrophe
3. Campbell, K.M. 2016. The Pivot: The Future of American Statecraft in Asia. *Canada's Journal of Global Policy Analysis.* https://doi.org/10.1177/0020702018754546
4. Monaghan, A. 2019. *Dealing with the Russians.* Global Politics.

China–Russia–US Trilateral Relations Amid Global Governance in the New Era

Dapeng Pang

As the world moves into a brand-new era with a changing global landscape, China puts its diplomatic focus on proactively broadening global partnerships and establishing a novel type of international relations with win–win cooperation as its core. When considering its foreign policies and showing its proposal for global governance, China attaches great importance to promoting coordination and cooperation among major countries, as well as to building a framework for major-country relations with shared stability and balanced development. Trilateral relations among China, Russia, and the United States, as a new type of major power relations among major countries in the world, are particularly critical, therefore ranking high on China's diplomatic agenda. China always prioritizes the management of its relations with major powers, particularly with Russia, based on *the China–Russia Comprehensive Strategic Partnership of Coordination in a New Era*, and with the United States, in a spirit of coordination, cooperation, and stability in accordance with the consensus reached by Chinese and US leaders to establish and consolidate a framework for major-country relations with shared stability and balanced development.

Recent Updates on China–Russia–US Trilateral Relations

Bilateral Relations Between China and Russia

After the disintegration of the Soviet Union, China–Russia relations have been moving on a comparatively sound and stable track. The current China–Russia partner-

---

D. Pang (✉)
Institute of Russian, Eastern European and Central Asian Studies, Chinese Academy of Social Sciences, Beijing, China

© China Social Sciences Press 2023
Institute of Russian, Eastern European and Central Asian Studies, CASS and Russian International Affairs Council, *Global Governance in the New Era*, https://doi.org/10.1007/978-981-19-4332-4_11

ship is positioned as the *China–Russia Comprehensive Strategic Partnership of Coordination in a New Era*, a proposal announced by Chinese and Russian leaders during President Xi Jinping's state visit to Russia in June 2019. According to the official discourse from both sides, China–Russia relations are *at the best level ever in history*, therefore serving as *a leading example for major-country relations*. This indicates that there are three underpinning characteristics of China–Russia relations, all beginning with *not*: not an alliance, not for confrontation, and not targeting any third parties. The connotation of these three principles is that China and Russia have completely eliminated the traditional philosophies of major power interaction in the old times and with Cold War mentalities. They no longer follow the old style of arms races or military alliances but establish a new outlook on security with mutual trust, mutual benefit, equality, and cooperation as its cornerstones, therefore bringing shared and equal security through disarmament and trust enhancement. Mutual respect and equality are important manifestations of the China–Russia Strategic Partnership for Coordination and are the keys to rendering this kind of bilateral relation a leading example of its kind. Moreover, the *China–Russia Strategic Partnership of Coordination* does not target any third party or pose a threat to any other country, a lesson drawn from the historical experience of China–Soviet relations.

The COVID-19 pandemic has tested China–Russia relations since it suddenly came in 2020. Nevertheless, the pandemic did not have many adverse effects on the development of China–Russia relations. As an old Chinese saying goes, *you cannot choose your neighbors:* China and Russia are neighbors who rely on each other for strategic considerations. Russia needs both China's support and a stable political climate on its eastern front, while this logic is also true with China's case: Good relations with Russia will help China build a strategic buffer zone and barrier for security in Eurasia, making the broad territory to its northern border a safe and stable strategic backyard. This is the overarching principle of China–Russian relations.

At the same time, the strategic consensus between the two sides is of great importance for establishing a solid development basis for China–Russian relations. The political cornerstone for China–Russia bilateral relations is the commitment not to interfere with each other's internal affairs and the promise of respecting each other's choice of development path. With this prerequisite, China and Russia do not shy away from the problems existing in their bilateral relations but believe that this bilateral partnership is never an ordinary one but a unique case between two neighboring major powers with huge global influence. Therefore, both sides are well conscious of the point that even problems, if there are any, should be handled differently as strategic challenges and ordinary ailments. In regard to the pandemic, in particular, we can see that it is precisely on the basis explained above that China and Russia have taken concrete measures to support each other in response to the changing circumstances to build a healthy partnership. The *China–Russia Comprehensive Strategic Partnership of Coordination in a New Era* would not be changed by any external factor and has huge endogenous power and broad prospects for development.

Bilateral Relations Between China and the US

Since the beginning of the twenty-first century, China–US relations have admittedly made some great progress, and bilateral relations were once generally stable for quite a long time. However, as we entered the second decade of the twenty-first century, something new and challenging has emerged in China–US relations: seeing China's rapid rise, the United States announced its *pivot toward the Asia–Pacific* and the deployment of the *Asia–Pacific Rebalancing Strategy*. After the outbreak of the COVID-19 pandemic, the United States has been so aggressive in demanding some so-called *apology diplomacy* and *compensation diplomacy*. High-level exchanges between the two countries have been further frozen. Affected by this round of the pandemic, the *Track Two Diplomacy*, which once played an essential role in the exchange between China and the US, has almost been stalled in stagnation. It can be argued that the occurrence of COVID-19 has accelerated the existing deterioration of China–US relations. According to the US, China is no longer a *rising power* but a de facto *rival* to the US seeking to maximize its security and global influence against American superiority. China–US relations, based on coordination, cooperation, and stability, now face grave challenges.

The pandemic has pushed China–US relations deeper into rivalry. American political elites have intentionally defined China–US relations as a *Thucydides Trap*, which puts China–US relations almost in a free fall. In the eyes of the American political elites, a fierce and vicious competition between China and the US seems to be inevitable, but as a matter of fact, since the establishment of diplomatic relations between China and the US, bilateral relations in between have generally been in a competitive manner yet with increasing interdependence. However, in a global political landscape featuring increased uncertainty, China–US relations change in dynamics: At present, the relations still run on the wheels of both competition and cooperation, but with competition taking dominance.

The competition between China and the US is a comprehensive and strategic one, which is structured at three levels: On the surface, this is a competition over material strength, particularly manifested by the trade war that involves not only products but also technology and standards; from a mid-level perspective, this is a competition over institutional design and path for development; at the deepest level, or at least in the view of the US, this is combat for global leadership, with US foreign policy toward China changing from a combination of cooperation and containment into one dominated by all-round containment.

Bilateral Relations Between Russia and the US

The changing characters in Russia–US relations after the disintegration of the Soviet Union are actually the corresponding results of Russia's gradual improvement and endogenous evolution on the basis of its historical heritage, cultural traditions, and social development. During this process, Russia's perception of the US and the West has played a particularly important role in bringing changes to their bilateral relations. As an important part of both transformation and development, Russia needs to reshape its relations with the US and the West after the disintegration of the Soviet Union. Actually, the relationship between Russia and the West (the US being its leader) is a historical process with a widening gap between internal shifts and external changes. This process shows close interaction with changes in Russia's internal political order: At initial yet critical historical moments, Russia failed to integrate itself into the West due to factors such as the eastward expansion of NATO, the Bosnian War, different political climates, and the Chechen War. Today, Russia has failed to achieve a balance between integration into the West and independence from this US-led bloc. For Russia, the construction of a geopolitical view, internal, and external alike, fails to find *the other*, in a cognitive sense, that can match its identity as a modern nation. Since the end of the Cold War, a series of internationally influential events between Russia and the US or between Russia and the West have generated great political mistrust in the strategic perception by the two sides, finally driving Russia to choose a *new Cold War* against the West.

The most critical factor influencing the changes in Russia–US relations was the Crimea crisis in 2014, which has changed the international landscape formulated since the end of the Cold War: Ground-shifting changes have been made, not only to Russia–Ukraine relations and Russia–West relations but also that between the East and the West. Although there had already been conflicts on global politics before the Crimea issue, this crisis even served as *the last straw* that finally triggered substantial changes. Russia has thus become an important driver for international changes. Its view on international relations, as well as a high degree of relevance between its internal affairs and its foreign policies, exert an important impact on the intentions, targets, and implementations of Russia's road toward greatness.

Russia–US relations came into a deadlock after the Ukraine crisis. As Russia tried to manage its relations with the US, the country finds it trapped in a dilemma against Putin's *Grand Strategy*, whose content can be summarized into two points: First, Russia must become a world power that ensures its national security, maintains and strengthens its sovereignty and territorial integrity, and establishes its firm, central, and authoritative position in the international community as a great power in today's world; second, Russia's geopolitical advantage must be preserved by establishing a buffer zone of good-neighborliness on its periphery that ensures the elimination of existing sources, as well as the emergence of new ones, of tension and conflict in adjacent areas of the Russian Federation. As a result, geopolitical conflicts between Russia and the West continue to occur in various forms. After the Ukraine crisis, Russia and the West fell into a state of long-term soft confrontation (or, say, mild confrontation) that deepened their structural conflicts.

Trilateral Relations Among China, Russia, and the US

As the US observes, China has surpassed Russia to become the primary strategic competitor that the US must handle in future: China will rival US superiority across the globe and in a comprehensive manner, yet not through a completely hostile approach that may involve the severance of diplomatic ties, vicious competition or even warfare. Now, the US regards China as its main adversary, with Russia relegated to a relatively secondary role.

Russian elites regard 2014 as a turning point in Russia's development, thinking that Russia has ended the *era of the liberal world order* and that against the backdrop of China–US competition, *international political Darwinism*, although the most unfavorable trend, may be the most possible reality. Therefore, Russia can act as a balancing factor in international politics that offers an alternative for the development of the world order.

In fact, scholars in Russia have proposed this idea, both before and after the pandemic, that Russia should adopt a balanced policy between China and the US. This is, without a doubt, understandable. At present, trilateral relations among China, Russia, and the US are no longer a great triangle among China, the US, and the Soviet Union during the Cold War, i.e., a zero-sum game where changes in any bilateral relationship would have a direct impact on the other two bilateral relations while one party's gain can only be obtained at the expense of others. Current trilateral relations among China, Russia, and the US are no longer of a zero-sum nature, with expanding common grounds for national interests among these three countries. No country would try to initiate bilateral confrontation, not to mention hostility, or undermine its relations with the other two.

In addition, in the current China–Russia–US trilateral relations, each pair of bilateral relations has its own focus and agenda, particularly with different third-party factors. For Russia–US relations, this factor lies in the relations between Russia and the EU (European factors); for China–US relations, this pertains to US–Japan relations (Asian factors). Therefore, China, Russia, and the US would independently develop their relations with the other two, so there is evidence for, or the need to worry about, taking sides and initiating a fight.

Major Concerns in Current China–Russia–US Trilateral Relations

At present, the US, through its global strategic adjustment, has regarded China and Russia as its *strategic competitors*. When discussing China–Russia–US trilateral relations, the following key questions need to be answered first: Since the COVID-19 pandemic, what kind of changes in human society have China–Russia–US trilateral relations faced? Are China and Russia jointly challenging the US-led international order? How can China and Russia prepare for the upcoming changes in the worldwide political landscape?

First, trilateral relations among China, Russia, and the US have been facing the most profound socioeconomic and political changes in human society since World War II.

On the economic front, European and American governments have generally taken strong intervention measures in fiscal, monetary, and credit issuance policies based on the need to fight against the pandemic, including providing subsidies for companies and households that have been badly infected by the virus. This is quite the opposite of the main mainstream of prepandemic Western economic ideas that advocates liberalization and control over public expenditure. Keynesian philosophies and measures, on the other hand, have made huge progress during the fight against the COVID-19 pandemic. However, if countries all move toward self-sufficient isolationism, it will be even more difficult for global economic recovery.

On the political front, under the influence of the pandemic, the idea of the *nation-state* has made a comeback. The return to nation-states is especially evident in Europe, where vanished border controls within EU countries have been restored. During this global crisis for public health, nation-states have been proven more capable of mobilization than international organizations in the face of an emergency, a phenomenon that may lead to further trends in protectionism that had already been evident before the COVID-19 crisis. Global protectionism, including those in the West, will further rise during the pandemic.

On the diplomatic front, the pandemic has not stopped previous geopolitical and ideological competition, nor has it changed the fundamental logic behind it. Moreover, COVID-19 has widened existing rifts: The severity and extensiveness of the epidemic have driven the West as a whole to become more cooperative, as US *compensation diplomacy* propaganda has actually provided a public good that integrates the West to act against external factors. China–US competition, especially in technological and ideological spheres, will continue to be a structural determinant of the new global order.

Second, China and Russia will not jointly challenge the current US-led international order.

Russia has made no secret of its aspiration to rebuild the international order. For the first time ever, Russia announced that it would replace the US-style oligarchic order with a new one, believing that there would be two opposing narratives in the world: One is the hegemonic order with the US as its leader, while the other aims to create an alternative without US hegemony. This means that, with chaos inevitably arising, the world would shift from a multipolar one to the bipolar kind, with one pole being the US and the other in Eurasia.

Second, the declining capability of governance by the current framework of international relations has been proven to be a *reality*, and the foundation for a rule-based world order is disintegrating. In a broader sense, the unipolar world order dominated by the US is becoming a thing of the past: This is also the source of massive unrest across the globe due, in large part, to US involvement in regime change in other countries. The chaos in the Middle East, in particular, is the best example of this erroneous pattern.

Third, ground-shaking political changes taking place in many developed countries, the US included, have exacerbated such concerns during this critical period for the adjustment of the international order. Russia will be one of the pillars upholding such a new international order, which is arguably more stable than a world dominated by the US.

China is the defender of, participant in, supporter for and reformer of the current international order, as it has joined almost all intergovernmental international organizations and more than 400 international multilateral treaties with a growing number of Chinese professionals serving important positions in international institutions. Therefore, China has become one of the most important participants in and supporters of today's global order and international system that China has no reason to undermine or overthrow. At the same time, however, the international order and its corresponding mechanisms also need to keep pace with the changing realities through constant reform and improvement to conform to new circumstances in the development and progress of international relations, to reflect the legitimate concerns of developing countries, and to better cope with emerging global challenges of all kinds.

With different understandings of the existing international order, there is no basis for China and Russia to join hands and challenge the current US-led international order.

Third, both China and Russia need to be prepared for possible changes, driven by the US, of the international order.

Although China and Russia will not join hands to challenge the current US-led international order, we must also be alerted that COVID-19 has brought about substantial impacts on the global political climate, particularly by accelerating the evolution of the existing international pattern. This argument is correct, yet the key point is that the *essence* of this evolution is changing: It was subjective confinement[1] before, but now an objective rupture.

Before the pandemic, the US kept a rather subjective idea of confining China at the lower end of the global industrial chain by replanning global trade rules, but this idea has not been fully supported by the transatlantic community. In a stealthy manner, European countries, such as France and Germany, have not joined the US in suppressing China's technological development or other related aspects. However, the COVID-19 pandemic has stimulated the US to launch political attacks and diplomatic crackdowns against China and, through this narrative as a public good, bring Western countries back together. It is difficult to imagine that before the pandemic,

---

[1] *confinement*: first, to use a new set of international rules to regulate or limit China's behavior in the high-tech field; in this way, second, to lock China's position in the global value chain, so that China and the United States can maintain a constant gap as large as possible in terms of technology. Please refer to Zhang Yuyan & Feng Weijiang, *From Engagement to Confinement: US Strategic Intentions toward China and Four Prospects for the China–US Game*, Tsinghua Financial Review, No.7, 2018.

European countries, such as France and Italy, and even developing countries, such as Brazil and India, would openly point to China's affairs. Facing a de facto objective rupture of the industrial chain, the US hopes to achieve a comprehensive decoupling of the industrial chain between China and the West under its own guidance. The external challenges China faces are now unprecedented, and unparalleled are the worldwide competitions between the US and China in both intensity and severity. In future, it is likely that a new form of economic globalization might be established based on different rules and standards, with a market economic system by Europe, Japan, and the US on one side and a socialist market economic system with Chinese characteristics on the other side. If such a scenario becomes a reality, its core feature will be an unbalanced parallel structure.

Under such circumstances, both China and Russia need to be ready for response. At present, China is already the world's second-largest economy, serving as an inseparable part of the global supply chain and industrial network, with 20% of the world's total GDP. The impact of the pandemic on China's economy should be fully assessed to ensure good and early preparation. It is impossible either that Russia stands alone and achieves so-called *strategic self-sufficiency* outside the current system. Due to an imperfect market and its overreliance on energy exports in its economic structure, Russia has long been marginalized in economic globalization. However, in today's world, it is impossible for any single country to completely isolate itself from the world beyond. Escaping from the world economic system may result in an awkward trap with high stability yet no development.

In particular, special attention should be given to the urgency of carefully handling strategic security issues, including nuclear weapons and their projection (missiles). Strategic security is one of the core concerns for Russia–US relations and has a huge bearing on China's national interests as well. However, China should not become involved in this agenda but should remain vigilant and guard against its impact. In today's world, strategic security not only means arms control and strategic stability between Russia and the US but also involves global and regional security, the Eurasian regional order and China's neighboring security. Traditional military security agendas, including nuclear weapons and missiles, should be examined from a holistic approach to security. The termination of *the Intermediate-Range Nuclear Forces Treaty* means the collapse of the bilateral arms control and strategic stability framework between Russia and the US. It seems that the end of the *Intermediate-Range Nuclear Forces Treaty* was a result of Russia and the US accusing each other of violating the treaty and developing short- or medium-range missiles, but in fact was caused by different strategic considerations by Russia and the US. The problem is, however, that the de facto end of the *Double Global Zero* has some major implications for China's national security.

Future Prospects of China–Russia–US Trilateral Relations

Future Diplomatic Strategies of Russia

Some questions should be answered before envisaging Russia's future diplomatic strategies: How can the direction of Russia's foreign policy be predicted when the pandemic is over? Will Russia *return to the West*, continue to *move eastwards,* or adopt a more *balanced layout* with rather different strategic considerations?

Since the end of Russia's Putin-Medvedev tandemocracy and Putin's return to the presidency in 2012, the strategic direction of Russia's foreign policy, focusing on Eurasia, has not changed, i.e., through the establishment of the Eurasian Union, a powerful and complicated supranational structure, Russia aspires to become a pillar in the contemporary world order and work as an influential *link* between Europe and the Asia–Pacific region. Under this overarching strategic outlook, Russia proposed the Greater Eurasian Partnership Program, a general strategy that will not change even when the pandemic is over.

The so-called *moving eastwards* only refers to the economic sector of Russia, not its civilization. The goal of this move is not to leave Europe but to improve Asia's relevance in Russia's diplomacy while continuing to foster relations with Europe. Pursuing its target as a political center and an economic link on the Eurasian continent, Russia hopes to get rid of its historical destiny as a marginalized actor which, in essence, requires balanced strategies from Russian policymakers. The key idea of Russia's strategy is to integrate players in the post-Soviet space and accelerate the development of regional economic integration, particularly with the Commonwealth of Independent States (CIS) as Russia's greatest interest. The degree of balance is a specific question in technical terms and does not affect the strategic direction and diplomatic considerations of Russia.

As an independent and promising civilization, Russia belongs to neither the West nor the East. It is actually a sensible decision by Russia to shift from *Greater Europe* to *Greater Eurasia*, trying to find a balance against the backdrop of turbulent vicissitudes in this world. This move actually reflects a certain national character of Russia, namely *dynamic equilibrium*, which will persist in the post-pandemic era.

Future Diplomatic Strategies of the United States

Similarly, the following questions need to be addressed before examining future US foreign policies: How can the direction of US foreign policies be predicted when the pandemic is over? Between an extreme right-wing move and a swing back toward liberalism, which is more likely to happen?

However, something is certain: When the pandemic is over, the strategic direction of US diplomacy will be based on an *America First* principle. Admittedly, the pandemic will exacerbate isolationist tendencies in the US, but the most pressing goal for US diplomatic strategies remains to prevent any loss of international leadership.

James Jay Carafano, Vice President of the Heritage Foundation, believes that after the pandemic, the vast majority of countries in the world will be divided into three groups: the first for the so-called *free world,* which resists China's interference; the second for the *balancers* who keep contact with China and the US alike while protecting their independence and minimizing the likelihood that they themselves become the battlefield for major power competition; and the third for *regions of competition*, which means the US, China and other countries compete in Latin America, Africa and other regions for dominance in economic, political, security and information spheres. Based on this judgment, the strategic direction of US foreign policy should be set to protect the free world, win over balancers, and compete in regions of competition.

Specifically, first, the United States will rely more on the North American Free Trade Area (now the United States-Mexico-Canada Agreement), i.e., a threefold partnership as the foundation of American strength. Second, the US will pay more attention to the transatlantic community. The US-EU strategic alliance is another cornerstone of US power. After the pandemic, the US will reinvest in the transatlantic community, not only to restart the joint economy by the West but also to minimize the influence of China. Third, the US will pay more attention to its *Indo-Pacific Strategy*. The pandemic has promoted the cooperation of the *Quad-Plus Dialog* in developing responding measures. The US, along with India, Japan, South Korea, Australia and New Zealand, will continue to forge a strong diplomatic framework to address China's influence in the region.

Future Trilateral Interactions Among China, Russia, and the US

Likewise, the following questions need to be answered when predicting the future course of China–Russia–US trilateral relations: How will China, Russia, and the US interact when the pandemic is over? Is there a *vortex* that intensifies the competition among these three major powers? If this *vortex* had already come into existence before the pandemic, does COVID-19 make it even greater?

The current structure of China–Russia–US trilateral relations has some features listed as follows: Russia–US relations have long been in a mild (soft) confrontation, while China–US relations are turning into a comprehensive strategic competition. Indeed, in China–Russia–US trilateral relations, the China–US conflict has become the primary concern for US foreign strategies, but this triangle is not a zero-sum game featuring Cold War mentalities. In other words, each of China–Russia, Russia–US, and China–US bilateral relations has its own major concerns.

First come China–Russia relations. In future, possible friction of interest in China–Russian relations will be concentrated in the central Eurasian region, which has a direct bearing on China's overall diplomacy. First, it relates to the territorial security of China's western frontier. Second, it influences the stability of China–Russia relations and, further, China–Russia–US relations, an important factor for China's strategic period of developmental opportunities. Thus, it is of great value to emphasize diplomacy in Asia. Before the *Belt and Road initiative*, China lacked a general strategy in the Eurasian region. As the first section for the Silk Road Economic Belt, cooperation in Central Asia is of great influence and can serve as an example for further connectivity. As China's largest neighbor, Russia plays a fundamental role in the Silk Road Economic Belt. Therefore, China–Russia relations in the new era require both countries to make compromises and/or even concessions when necessary, acting independently yet with shared growth amid regional integration. China's *Belt and Road initiative* focuses on the economic cooperation of the entire Eurasian continent, which, without Russia's endorsement and participation, will suffer huge losses in its prospects. In this sense, China and Russia should take full advantage of the communicating mechanisms of their *Comprehensive Strategic Partnership of Coordination* to minimize political mistrust and achieve shared growth in a community of common interests.

Second come China–US relations. The worrisome part of China–US relations is that the common interests and logical concepts that previously promoted the development of China–US relations are weakening, if not disappearing. Since the beginning of the twenty-first century, an important reason for the overall stability of China–US relations is that the US held sensible perceptions and judgments of China based on the following points: A China with openness is not a challenger but a partner who will increasingly integrate itself into the existing Western-led international system. Therefore, the US developed both economic cooperation and cultural exchanges with China, who, in turn, has become a stakeholder with the US and the West. However, the perceptions and judgments mentioned above no longer exist at this moment. China–US economic cooperation is now in stagnation and, in the post-pandemic era, would probably suffer further deterioration.

Future Diplomatic Strategies of China

In the changing China–US–Russian trilateral relations, China's foreign strategies should take independence as the primary philosophy. In short, China's diplomacy serves its *own interests* amid trilateral relations between China, Russia, and the US.

In the context of ever-increasing competition between China and the US, the fundamental determinant of China's rise lies in its capacity to address domestic challenges for development, which is also the starting point for all foreign policies. Moreover, China should not base future China–Russia strategic cooperation on the joint struggle against the US, as such a harmonious bilateral relation between China and Russia is already a hard-won result. Furthermore, developmental and historical factors have once and again proven that mutual respect, particularly with regard to each other's choice of path for development, is the basis for the healthy development of China–Russia relations. There are indeed differences between these two countries in terms of both industrial structure and national characteristics, so such differences will inevitably be reflected in the bilateral interactions between them and in the foreign exchanges done by each country separately.

Over 70 years since the founding of the People's Republic of China, major problems and troubles have been emerging in its foreign relations almost every decade. Every time, the international landscape must be reassessed, and correspondingly, foreign policies must be adjusted. Thirty years ago, when the Soviet Union disintegrated, the global socialist movement reached its bottom, and China was further sanctioned by the West for a certain period of time. However, under guidelines such as *calm observation, steady stance, level-headed response, a low profile, protection over weak points and never taking the lead,* and *striving to make achievements,* China's diplomacy quickly walked out of such a passive shadow and correctly handled the dialectic logic between domestic politics and foreign affairs, winning nearly 30 years of strategic opportunities for China's national development. There are many strikingly similar periods in history. At present, we are once again facing severe external challenges that require our calm and thorough observation instead of impulsion, aggression, or isolation. To be specific, China should reach essence through phenomenon and calmly cope with challenges from the US.

The world is complex and ever changing. China needs to accumulate its strength and patiently wait for opportunities, to give full play to its own characteristics and advantages, to strengthen its strategic focus with a clear direction, and to implement effective policies for gradual growth to give the regional climate the global landscape a better future that, in turn, is conducive to its own development.

Conclusion

The rationale of properly handling the trilateral relations among China, Russia, and the US is to comprehensively deepen China's external strategic layout, to adhere to the all-around opening up, to promote the establishment of a new type of international relations, to comprehensively develop friendly cooperation with major powers, to continuously enrich and improve the global partnership network, and to create a more favorable external environment for China's own development. Focusing on the general trend of increasing interdependence among countries, China has been expanding the common ground for interests with all other parties. China is always committed to promoting comprehensive and balanced development of relations with major powers, including Russia and the US, therefore providing a stable foundation and strategic guarantee for world peace and global development. As a faithful advocate for *a community with a shared future for mankind,* China remains true with its aspiration to make a more equitable and reasonable framework of global governance.

As part of its practice in global governance, China's ideas and acts for trilateral relations among China, Russia, and the US have once and again proven that China takes mutual respect and mutual trust as priorities for global governance, attaches great significance to dialog and negotiation, insists on seeking common ground while reserving differences, adheres to expanding common ground to resolve differences, and enhances strategic mutual trust and reduces mutual suspicion through candid and in-depth dialog and communication. China adheres to a justifiable view of being righteous and gaining interest, as it puts righteousness first and takes both into consideration, striving to build partnerships for shared destiny. In future, China will continue to proactively participate in the construction of the global governance system, work hard to contribute its own wisdom to the improvement of global governance, and work with people around the world to promote the development of the international order and global governance system in a more equitable and reasonable direction.

China–Russia–India Cooperation in an Era of Global Transformation

Yi Jiang

Since Chinese, Russian, and Indian foreign ministers held their first round of dialog in 2002, the three influential countries in the Asia–Pacific region have established a framework for strategic dialog and cooperation. Their endeavor to begin strategic cooperation reflects the changing international landscape, where emerging markets and developing countries, including them, now have increasing weight in the international economic and political spheres, and their demands for international governance reforms and international order changes have mounted. Such features of the era are fully in line with the three countries' ambitions of becoming major countries and their advocacy of a multipolar world. At the same time, as dictated by realities, the three countries need to cooperate in a number of areas to address the various complex factors and challenges presented by changes in the international arena. The collaboration among China, Russia, and India on major international and regional issues will undoubtedly have important implications for future trends at both the international and regional levels.

An Era of Global Transformation

The end of the "Cold War" ushered in a new era of global transformation. Compounded by the international financial crisis in 2008, the Crimean Crisis in 2014, and the COVID-19 pandemic in 2020, both the depth and breadth of this transformation have become greater with an accelerated pace, which has thus stood as the theme of the ever-changing international landscape.

Y. Jiang (✉)
Institute of Russian, Eastern European and Central Asian Studies, Chinese Academy of Social Sciences, Beijing, China

© China Social Sciences Press 2023
Institute of Russian, Eastern European and Central Asian Studies, CASS and Russian International Affairs Council, *Global Governance in the New Era*,
https://doi.org/10.1007/978-981-19-4332-4_12

Table 1 Comparison between "the BRICS countries" and the Western bloc[1] (2001–2020)

Year	The Western bloc's GDP (US$ 1billion)	GDP growth rate (%)	Share of global GDP (%)	The BRICS countries' GDP (US$ 1billion)	GDP growth rate (%)	Share of global GDP (%)
2001	22,273	− 0.57	66.59	2812	2.97	8.41
2002	23,101	3.72	66.53	2954	5.05	8.51
2003	25,816	11.75	66.28	3432	16.18	8.81
2004	28,428	10.12	64.78	4153	21.01	9.46
2005	29,698	4.47	62.48	5020	20.88	10.56
2006	31,049	4.55	60.26	6062	20.76	11.77
2007	33,678	8.47	58.01	7763	28.06	13.37
2008	35,988	6.86	56.49	9437	21.56	14.81
2009	34,390	− 4.44	56.90	9629	2.03	15.93
2010	35,234	2.45	53.25	11,872	23.29	17.94
2011	37,439	6.26	50.95	14,453	21.74	19.67
2012	37,033	− 1.08	49.26	15,430	6.76	20.53
2013	37,233	0.54	48.15	16,559	7.32	21.41
2014	38,009	2.08	47.83	17,381	4.96	21.87
2015	36,172	− 4.83	48.08	16,648	− 4.22	22.13
2016	37,551	3.81	49.14	16,897	1.50	22.11
2017	39,138	4.23	48.12	18,949	12.14	23.30
2018	41,523	6.09	48.09	20,538	8.39	23.79
2019	42,132	1.47	48.09	21,067	2.58	24.05
2020	36,129	− 14.25	42.65	20,576	− 2.33	24.29

Data source World Bank[2]

It is undoubted that comprehensive national strength remains a prerequisite for the power struggle in an anarchic international system, and what stands behind the aforementioned transformation in today's world reflects the changing international balance of power over the last two decades. As the global economic power structure changes, world power is being redistributed, and countries' respective influence and aspirations are shifting, which means that the international power structure and the international order have to be reshaped and upgraded. Such a structural transformation is driven by the redistribution of power, which is an objective and historical trend that is independent of the will of any country or any individual (Table 1).

With the rapid rise of emerging countries, including China, Russia, and India, the global agenda for a multipolar world order has been pushed forward, and non-Western countries have become more involved in international affairs with gradually

---

[1] Western bloc: including the US, Japan, and the EU.

[2] https://databank.shihang.org/source/world-development-indicators/preview/on.

increasing voices and influence on a range of international issues. Driven by such changes, the international order has shifted from its previous state dominated by Western countries to one that is more balanced and democratic, with a number of centers of political and economic power gradually emerging in this process. Those powerful states can no longer exert absolute power, and the means they historically adopted by dint of their superior strength to simply subdue, coerce, and restrain other countries have largely failed now. At the same time, due to power shifts, increasingly complex international affairs with correspondingly diversified solutions and closer ties between countries and regions, countries, in a relatively balanced state of power distribution, have to face the reality of interdependence even if they are still working to constrain each other as they traditionally did. In this sense, cooperation has become a necessity rather than an option.

That being said, it is axiomatic that the progressing of any transformation will not be plain sailing but rather accompanied by a variety of severe challenges. First, although the dominance of Western countries led by the US over the international community is on the wane, it will not collapse overnight. The transformation might lead to Western countries' instinctive reaction by taking countermeasures or reminding them of the historical trend and the necessity to revise their policies. In any case, Western countries will do whatever it takes to foil any attempt to challenge their hegemony, and how hard they will try depends on how prevailing the trend is. Given the reality that the West still enjoys great advantages in many areas, we must be sober-minded that for that change to happen, it will take a long time, and the process must be fraught with trials and tribulations.

Second, there are always both positive and negative factors in any transformation. As the traditional hegemony declines, constraints previously put in place have less influence, and some rules are being reshaped, a process that provides opportunities for various actors to fill the "vacuum". Depending on their needs and corresponding issues, these actors would choose to champion, follow, or abandon the existing international norms and rules or just accept the ones that favor them. Countries might accuse some powers of coercing others or undermining stability in a way of defending their own interests, and we have seen the frequent emergence of the phenomenon in the history of international relations where countries compete with each other for how unscrupulous they could be. Some countries have leveraged the chaos to gain a special position for themselves in the region, adding to the messy and complex situation, and many incidents have amply demonstrated the mutual distrust and antagonism among countries. These are all indications that international relations are full of uncertainties in the midst of the transformation, and there is already the danger of anomie and disorder.

Finally, instability in the world economy still looms large as a result of both successive international financial crises and the COVID-19 pandemic. At the same time, adjustments must be made to respond to problems encountered in the middle of globalization, and this is also the case for developing countries. Figure 1 illustrates that even emerging countries, one of the drivers of world economic growth, have reached a stage to transform their development models. They are confronted with the task of capitalizing on new governance models, newly created markets, and

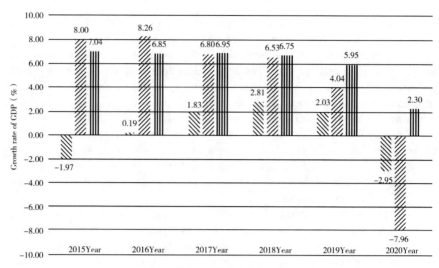

Fig. 1 GDP growth rate of China, Russia and India (2015–2020)

new technological revolutions to bring about economic restructuring and industrial upgrading.

It is clear that in this era of historic changes, it is imperative that China, Russia, and India strengthen cooperation because they share the need to respond to challenges and adapt to these historic trends, fight for their own rights and interests amid the transformation, make the international system fairer and more reasonable, and further develop themselves to bring more changes in their own interests.

China, Russia, and India together account for more than 40% of the world's population and 22.5% of the world's land area. As influential members of the BRICS club, the G20, the East Asia Summit, and some other emerging international platforms, the three countries are all major countries with considerable GDP, and they share the ambition for rejuvenation and the expectation for an increasingly multipolar world (Fig. 2). In fact, in the early 1990s, when Russian Prime Minister Primakov advocated the building of a multipolar world, he showed his great insight and foresight by proposing an initiative to strengthen trilateral cooperation among China, Russia, and India. Since the turn of the century, bilateral relations between China and Russia, Russia and India, and China and India have experienced steady development, laying a solid foundation for the initiation of trilateral dialog and cooperation.

Faced with the ever-changing international environment, all three countries have grown aware of the need for such dialogs. Foreign ministers from the three countries held several informal meetings while attending international conferences, and in 2002, they established a mechanism for their formal meetings, an institutionalized platform that has served as an important means for the three countries to enhance mutual political trust, strengthen strategic communication, coordinate their positions on major issues, and seek consensus and cooperation. Furthermore, the joint

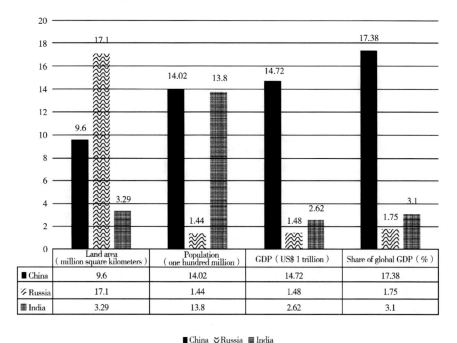

Fig. 2 Statistics about China, Russia and India in 2020

communique issued after each Foreign Ministers' Meeting has become a channel for the three countries to build consensus, express their views about international and regional issues, and declare their propositions of emerging countries. As a complementary part of this platform, the three countries have also conducted exchanges on regional affairs and track two dialogs attended by experts in various fields. It is worth noting that the track two dialog platform attended by scholars from the three countries has played an important role in expanding the areas of dialog and exploring new topics for cooperation. For example, strengthening cooperation in the energy sector among the three countries was first proposed and discussed at the scholars' forum.[3] It was subsequently confirmed as a priority issue for cooperation among the three countries during the Foreign Ministers' Meeting in 2009.[4] In addition, the Shanghai Cooperation Organization, BRICS, and the G20 have served to create more dialog and cooperation opportunities among the three countries in various fields, thus forming a multichannel, multifield, multiperiod, and multidimension system of their cooperation (Table 2).

As the three countries strengthen strategic coordination and cooperation in areas of interest to them, their overall influence will be enhanced, and they will be better

---

[3] Xia [1].

[4] See: "Joint Communiqué of the Meeting of the Foreign Ministers of the People's Republic of China, the Russian Federation, and the Republic of India", October 28, 2009.

Table 2 Foreign Ministers' Meeting of China, Russia and India

	Time	Location
The first time	September 1, 2002	New York, the US
The second time	September 1, 2003	New York, the US
The third time	October 1, 2004	Alma-Ata, Kazakhstan
The fourth time	June 2, 2005	Vladivostok, Russia
The fifth time	September 1, 2005	New York, the US
The sixth time	February 14, 2007	New Delhi, India
The seventh time	October 24, 2007	Harbin, China
The eighth time	May 15, 2008	Ekaterinburg, Russia
The ninth time	October 27, 2009	Bangalore, India
The tenth time	November 15, 2010	Wuhan, China
The eleventh time	April 13, 2012	Moscow, Russia
The twelfth time	November 10, 2013	New Delhi, India
The thirteenth time	February 2, 2015	Beijing, China
The fourteenth time	April 18, 2016	Moscow, Russia
The fifteenth time	December 11, 2017	New Delhi, India
The sixteenth time	February 27, 2019	Wuzhen, China
The seventeenth time	June 23, 2020	Video conference

placed to help build a multipolar and democratic world and explore how to build a new type of international relations with win–win cooperation at its core.

What is the International System We Need

After 1914, the international landscape went through dramatic changes three times. On the one hand, countries have learned lessons from the two world wars and have tried to establish international organizations and norms to build a world order aimed at helping countries avoid vicious competition. In particular, in the aftermath of World War II, more international organizations, international rules, and international law gradually emerged, dealing with issues in political, security, economic, and cultural fields, and even natural persons themselves were covered through the concept of "human rights". On the other hand, mankind has been repeating the old same mistakes: 21 years after the end of World War I, a new, larger, and more brutal war, World War II, began, which was followed only two years later by the "Cold War". Despite a different form, the unchanging theme was still power competition, and due to technological advances, the dangers presented could be worse than those in the previous two wars. The "Cold War", which lasted for a total of 42 years, was accompanied by a paradox where on the one hand, no country would like to engage in a war, and on the other hand, they are all preparing for winning one because they have the firm belief that only by actively preparing for a war could they actually prevent it from happening. The theories of nuclear deterrence and mutual assured destruction are all products of such a paradox.

The end of the bipolar world marked the start of new changes with the process of system building, and again two different perceptions and approaches appeared. One is based on liberalism, promoting political democratization and market-based economic systems by the globalization of production. Western countries (not only governments but also financial groups, industrial giants, emerging industries, cultural communities, and other social sectors) believe that the victory of the Cold War has proven the success of the abovementioned thought and the way of governance. Against this backdrop, as Western countries work to defend their interests in the era of globalization and embrace the characteristics of the times, they are inclined to dominate the world with their vision and experience. The other demand is that more non-Western elements should be embedded in the current international system, more rights should be given to non-Western countries, more non-Western governance in national practices should be regarded as legitimate, and the principles of equality and joint contribution should be enhanced in the international community. As the debate continues over the future of the world, there is a growing trend of acute antagonism, and policies among different groups of countries are becoming increasingly confrontational, which has evolved into conflicts regarding general principles of nationalism, values, and political stances.

Once again, we are at a moment described by Thomas Hobbes, where the disorder in recent years is both a product of the transformation and the fuel for increased uncertainties and the noncooperation of such a drastic change. Disagreements have led to cooperation among countries as a game without rules and order. As for what rules are allowed and forbidden in international relations, major countries do not see eye to eye with each other, and sometimes their views are even poles apart.

It should be noted that, while under the traditional hegemonic system, the interests of the vast majority of countries were indeed infringed, and the disorder brought about by the transformation to a new order will also do no good to world countries. More importantly, once the "law of the jungle" becomes a preferred option in this process, the practice of dividing the world into spheres of influence will be on the rise. Accordingly, Western countries, which are in a favorable position in the existing international system, act more arbitrarily, and other countries or blocs might just follow suit. The only results will be larger-scale anomie in international society, a more complicated international security landscape and a more chaotic international order. This will directly undermine the fundamental interests of developing countries and might bring multipolarity into question among many countries and, in turn, offer Western countries opportunities to consolidate the hegemonic system.

In this connection, emerging countries such as China, Russia, and India, which play an important role in the international landscape and are opposed to the hegemonic system, should work together to build a fairer and more rational global governance system amid the transformation. It is important that in this process, they must become increasingly aware of what the international order and rules are expected.

For many years, virtually, all Meetings of China–Russia–India Foreign Ministers have been focused on important issues centering around the international system and the global order, and a consensus on basic principles has gradually been reached in this regard. In the last decade in particular, the three countries have more frequently issued joint statements addressing international issues, and such statements have become more systematic.[5]

Concerning the international situation, the three countries hold the view that it is undergoing complex and profound changes, the progress toward a multipolar world is irreversible, and emerging markets and developing countries are playing an increasingly vital role in international affairs, reflecting the features and trends of the world's diversity in cultures and civilizations.

In terms of the basic principles of international relations, the three countries have stated that they will make efforts to build a new type of international relations with win–win cooperation at its core, promote democracy in international relations, and remain committed to common, comprehensive, cooperative, sustainable, indivisible, and equal security. The three countries have stressed in particular that the purposes and principles of the Charter of the United Nations and other universally recognized norms are the basis for building such a new type of international relations; sovereignty, independence, national unity, and territorial integrity shall be respected; and all countries' independent choice of development paths and social systems must also be valued.

With regard to global governance reforms, the three countries on the one hand support the United Nations in playing a pivotal role in international affairs and on the other hand are aware that it is necessary to reform multilateral institutions, for example, to carry out comprehensive reforms of the United Nations and its Security Council, which will make the whole UN more representative, efficient, and enhance the voice for developing countries. As two permanent members of the Security Council, China and Russia attach importance to India's status in international affairs and support India's desire to play a more influential role in the UN. The three countries emphasize the necessity of maintaining a rule-based, transparent, nondiscriminatory, open, and inclusive multilateral trading system with the World Trade Organization at its core and support the further enhancement of the global financial safety net with the International Monetary Fund at its core. They are calling for more efforts to improve global economic governance and increase the voice and representation for developing countries, which includes increasing their quota shares, in reforms of the IMF to better reflect the relative weight of emerging markets and developing countries, as well as ensuring that the voices of the least developed countries are heard.

These joint statements indicate that the three countries have taken the same stance that no matter how the international landscape changes, the international system with the United Nations at its core, the international order underpinned by international law

---

[5] For the series of agreements reached by the three countries, please refer to the Joint Communiqués of the 9th, 11th, 13th, and 16th Meetings of the Foreign Ministers of the People's Republic of China, the Russian Federation, and the Republic of India, respectively.

and the basic norms of international relations based on the purposes and principles of the UN Charter must be maintained. At the same time, the three countries are clear that the root cause of the current difficulties and challenges confronting global governance is its failure to meet the requirements of the evolving international pattern and its failure to achieve a pluralistic and well-balanced power structure. The three countries have built a consensus that they should advance reforms while maintaining the aforementioned system, order, and norms.

In the midst of the global transformation, the theme of competition is which country leads the process of reestablishing international rules. As the most important players in this transformation, emerging countries' voices and solutions must be emphasized. However, such an attitude or principle is just too broad to suffice, and much-detailed research is still needed in practice. How can we translate emerging countries' demands into a stable and predictable international order, and how can we ensure such demands are met in a legitimate, reasonable, and feasible manner?

Practices in the past have shown that the United Nations, as well as many other international organizations, have often become the battleground for various views and interests. Some countries have chosen to withdraw from these organizations, create new ones, or stand in the way of reaching a consensus. Even for plans where no fundamental conflicts among major countries can be found, it is still difficult to implement them. What is the approach by which we can uphold the authority of the UN? Emerging countries and developing countries are demanding more legitimate rights, which will mean increased responsibility falling on them, and what is the approach we can take to determine how much responsibility these countries should bear?

After World War II, sovereignty and international attention were enshrined in the UN Charter and many other documents. However, in practice, what we often see is a rather divided picture, where some countries place greater emphasis on the free and open nature of the international order, while others are more concerned about sovereignty and equality in that order. How can we reconcile these two broad principles?

Multiple humanitarian crises after the Cold War gave rise to the concept of responsibility to protect, which was endorsed in principle by the 2005 World Summit and has since been written in Libya, Yemen, and Syria-related resolutions. This shows that in the case of an accident in a certain country, people in that country and neighboring countries still hope that the international community can take a collective approach to these crises and uncertainties. However, Western countries tend to take the opportunity to interfere, intensifying the fears of other countries that such "responsibility to protect" will be abused and even become a pretext for selective and arbitrary interference by powerful countries. Amidst the transformation, efforts should be made to address the root causes of the lack of trust, to strike a balance between safeguarding sovereignty and accomplishing international governance when necessary and to clarify the boundaries between foreign interference and the imposition of external pressure.

Surely, system building is a holistic process involving concept, policy, and practice. In this connection, specific issues covered in this course are neither possible to form a rather complete and systematic plan soon nor to be completed by any single country. According to multilateralism, an international order that is in line with the wishes and interests of the majority of countries must be the result of mutual consultation, joint contribution and shared benefits, requiring emerging countries, including China, Russia, and India, to carry out extensive and in-depth exchanges and discussions through all channels. Building on the consensus they have reached and similar positions they take, the three countries should further study how to put their values and broad statements into practice and how to make it easier for other countries to accept and uphold them, as a way of ensuring that efforts in transforming the international order are not only focused on criticizing the current system's injustice but also on the building of the future one.

The Competition and Cooperation Among China, Russia, and India

Taking into account the current international environment and the international status of China, Russia, and India, there are great possibilities and sufficient space for their cooperation, for their similar positions on many international issues, their expectations for the future world and their need for practical cooperation in many fields. That said, all multilateral processes proceed around intertwined and conflicting interests, and the same is true of the trilateral cooperation among China, Russia, and India. The fact that the consensus among three countries does not mean no competing interests, but rather the agreement based on the assurance and anticipation of interests. More importantly, their cooperation covers many areas, which is mainly carried out in Central Asia–South Asia and places full of competition among major countries inside and outside the region, making trilateral cooperation even more complex and inexplicable. In terms of actual progress, the three countries have still been trying to adapt themselves and get along with each other, and it is true that their cooperation, to a large extent, is focused on superficial formalities rather than in-depth efforts; thus, many agreements have failed to translate into real action.

First, their trilateral dialog and partnership are characterized by seriously unbalanced development and are beset by the weak ability to advance real cooperation in specific fields. Although each of the three countries has established strategic bilateral cooperative partnerships with the other two partners, it is very evident that the comprehensive and strategic partnership between China and Russia and their cooperation in various fields outclass those of the China–India and Russia–India relations. Furthermore, compared with China–India relations, the Special and Privileged Strategic Partnership between Russia and India has been much deeper and broader and has delivered more tangible benefits. China and India established a "Strategic and Cooperative Partnership for Peace and Prosperity" in 2005 and expressed their willingness to expand friendly and mutually beneficial cooperation in all areas. However, many declarations made by the two governments are just empty words on a page, as no significant progress has been made in many areas covered by this partnership, such as clarifying the political positioning of their bilateral relationship, carrying out more coordination in international and regional affairs, deepening economic and trade ties, expanding people-to-people exchanges, building mutual trust in security, and advancing border demarcation negotiations. Plagued by traditional security issues and propelled by nationalist sentiments, it is not that easy to turn theoretical possibilities into realities.

In recent years, as the two countries' overall strength has increased, China and India have become increasingly vocal about their own security and interests, and relatively serious traditional security tensions between them have emerged from time to time. Despite repeated efforts made by China, the political basis for this bilateral relationship is still not solid, and mutual trust between them is not sufficient to manage their differences. India's attitude toward China, especially in regard to dealing with historical issues, clearly reflects the impatient political mindset and strategic anxiety of this rising nation, and as a result, we cannot expect India's policy toward China to be stable.

Cannikin's law indicates that China–India relations are the shortest stave in the trilateral cooperation among China, Russia, and India, which also determines, to a large extent, how much space is left for their trilateral cooperation and how successful it could be.

Second, troubled by traditional security concerns between China and India, the three countries' cooperation and its stability will undoubtedly be in the grip of external factors. In recent years, with the resurgence of the "great power strategic competition", the United States started to regard China and Russia as its main rivals that threaten its hegemony, and it has thus become an inevitable choice of the US to win India over to its side and turn China, Russia, and India against each other. Driven by its own strategic plans and intentions, India has been championing the US Indo-Pacific strategy by adopting assertive security policies toward its main source of threat, China, and deliberately weakening its cooperation with Russia to a certain extent.

Be it on bilateral historical issues or in multilateral mechanisms, India has clearly embraced an attitude of competing with China, as it tries to guard against any possible attempt by China to dominate the construction of the regional order and win new bargaining chips for India's international ambitions. India is the only country in the SCO that does not endorse China's Belt and Road Initiative, and it has even proposed the Asia-Africa Growth Corridor as a counterweight to the Belt and Road Initiative and its growing influence.

India's active interactions with the US and other Western countries and its participation in the Quad, in particular, have also led to increasing concern in Moscow, with senior officials such as Sergey Lavrov explicitly criticizing India's policy of "pulling chestnuts out of the fire" for the US on many occasions. The India–Russia Annual Summit, which had taken place for 20 years in a row, was canceled in 2020 because of the COVID-19 pandemic, which is a clear indication of the strategic difference between the two countries. If we liken those historical issues between China and India to a "weakness" in China–Russia–India cooperation, which has weighed on the process of their trilateral cooperation, then India's policy preference in recent years has become a short stave, which has caused them great difficulties and thus undermined their cooperation.

India's foreign policy reflects its desire to highlight its status in the new international landscape, to gain a favorable position in the game of great powers, and to increase its influence over regional affairs, all serving its purpose of becoming a great power. In addition, it also reveals the two-sided nature of both competition and cooperation in its foreign strategy and its attempt to profit from the hedging policy: On the one hand, by cooperating with China and Russia and participating in the Shanghai Cooperation Organization and the BRICS mechanism, India is placed to engage in global and regional affairs and create new platforms for expanding its international influence and implementing its "Connect Central Asia" policy; on the other hand, India wishes to increase its bargaining power with the US and other Western countries as a member of emerging countries and counterbalance China and Russia's endeavor to shape regional and international agendas with the "Indo-Pacific concept" and the "quadrilateral security dialog" (Quad).[6]

Clearly, the fundamental motives behind India's policy are distinctly opportunistic, undoubtedly adding to the cost and difficulty of strategic coordination among China, Russia, and India. It is also important to note that many of the agreements India has reached with China and Russia under the trilateral framework of China, Russia, and India, within the Shanghai Cooperation Organization and through BRICS and the G20 platforms are not empty ones. A number of important principles, such as building a multipolar world, reforming the system of global governance and strengthening cooperation in an equal manner, are more or less in tandem with India's wishes and do not conflict with its strategic intentions and demands. Moreover, in many areas where pragmatic cooperation is needed, such as the regional counterterrorism endeavor and economic development, India also has the need and willingness to deepen cooperation with China and Russia.

It should also be noted that India has carried out more interactions with the US, Japan, and Australia after 2020 for two reasons: First, India has chosen to distance itself from emerging countries according to the hedging approach; and second, India reacted to some temporary China–India border incidents. Clearly, creating a new military bloc with the United States and other countries would not only undermine India's desired status as a major power but would also overturn the policy of nonalignment that India has maintained since its independence and lose its diplomatic independence. When speaking at the 2018 Shangri-La Dialog, Indian Prime Minister Narendra Modi said that India believes there should be no return to traditional great power rivalry and that India's friendships with other countries are not alliances of containment. At the same time, India is also dependent on Russia for important defense equipment and expects new sources of energy and its access to Central Asia. In this sense, further engagement with the US would undoubtedly lead to estrangement with other key partners, which would in turn be detrimental to India's

---

[6] Shovan Sinha Ray: Quad: An Opportunity for India to Counterbalance China, https://diplomatist.com/2020/08/06/quad-an-opportunity-for-india-to-counterbalance-China/.

China–Russia–India Cooperation in an Era of Global Transformation

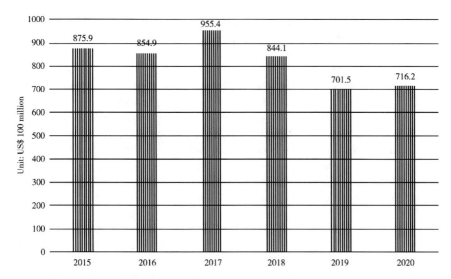

Fig. 3 China-India trade volume (2015–2020)

interests in the region, not to mention the fact that India can hardly afford full-scale competition with China.

Therefore, in the long run, a "one-sided" foreign policy is not sustainable for India, which means that temporary adventurism must be followed by rational adjustments. For China's part, despite the difficulties it faces, it remains that its relations with India do not pose a threat to each other and are actually opportunities for mutual development and holds the belief that China and India are partners, not adversaries, let alone enemies. In its National Security Strategy 2021, Russia has also made clear its intention to develop a special strategic partnership with India and to enhance the China–Russia–India mechanism.[7] Indian Minister of Foreign Affairs Jaishan Su also stated that India is reluctant to give up its friendly and cooperative relations with China (Fig. 3).

Due to the two-sided nature of India's policy, positive-sum and zero-sum games among China, Russia, and India coexist. Hence, the three countries should make efforts to prevent bilateral conflicts from escalating and affecting trilateral cooperation and shield their trilateral as well as other multilateral cooperation processes from bilateral differences, although they are somehow linked—at least in India's policy. At the same time, China and Russia should be better equipped with more wisdom to take advantage of India's hedging strategy and reduce or avoid the negative influence of India's policies. They should also take the initiative to shape the global agenda and conduct cooperation in specific areas, find the 'highest common denominator' in consensus building, increase mutual dependence while promoting cooperation, highlight cooperation and downplay conflicts, and push India into playing a positive role in cooperation by dint of their consensus, common interests, and collective

---

[7] http://www.scrf.gov.ru/security/docs/document133/.

will. In particular, the two countries should capitalize on the changing landscape in Afghanistan to enhance India's integration and deepen cooperation among the three parties in countering terrorism and maintaining regional stability.

While continuing to maintain strategic communication, the three parties can also focus on practical cooperation, boosting their respective growth and ensuring that all three countries can feel some tangible benefits and gains brought by their cooperation. To this end, they should, in the wake of the COVID-19 pandemic, strive to explore cooperation in areas such as economic recovery, industrial restructuring, infrastructure construction, and energy cooperation, as well as ensure that the three countries' development with the world can become more mutually reinforcing and interdependent. In their current trilateral interaction, China–India cultural exchanges lag significantly behind, which means that there is still much untapped potential for them to build mutual understanding, enhance people-to-people ties to lay a more solid foundation for future cooperation, and promote mutual learning among civilizations. It must be stressed that the mainstream media on all sides is supposed to make sure that their reports and cultural communication will become more accurate, rational, and objective, instead of being exaggerated, subjective, and speculative.

Against the background of major international changes, trilateral cooperation among China, Russia, and India will go a long way toward international and regional stability, the reshaping of the international system and pattern, and the three countries' efforts in growing their economy and advancing their diplomatic agenda. Trilateral cooperation is not only riding on the tide of our times but also meets their own needs and interests. However, they must also be well aware that the twists and turns while pressing ahead with these processes. For three different civilizations with different modes of governance and respective ambitions to become global powers, building a new type of relationship featuring equality, mutual benefits, and nonalignment and new cooperation frameworks is still a new topic. The two-sided nature of India's foreign policy has brought great instability to its relations with China in recent years, which means there are still many issues to be discussed and addressed, and there will only be more challenges as the sensitivity and complexity of China–India relations overlap with Western factors such as the US. In other words, while the three countries are working with each other to explore their way forward for high-quality cooperation, India, taking varied stances aimed at securing the best position in the game of great powers, is bound to have inconsistent policies, which will doom trilateral cooperation among China, Russia, and India to more setbacks.

Reference

1. Xia, Y. 1997. Possibilities and prospects for trilateral energy cooperation among China, Russia, and India. *Peace and Development* 4: 35.

Transport Corridors, Belt and Road Initiative, Eurasian Economic Union, and Economic Prosperity Across the Eurasian Continent

Evgeny Vinokurov

Introduction

Developing efficient transportation links is a straightforward means to advance sustainable economic growth. It is particularly so in the context of the Eurasian landmass that, due to its sheer size, it has always been chronically underserved by transportation both along the East–West and North–South axes. The paper argues in favor of the current window of opportunity to advance the East–West land-based transportation corridors and to supplement them with the North–South corridor. In essence, these two transportation axes combined would amount to the infrastructure "skeleton" of the Eurasian continent. In other words, I will discuss the practical economic foundations of Greater Eurasia.

I do so in the context of the Chinese Belt and Road Initiative (BRI) as well as infrastructure development in the Eurasian Economic Union (EAEU). With the BRI, China effectively developed an all-compassing foreign economic policy, which would be attractive for other countries. China made a critical and sustainable political commitment to the BRI and provided a heavy financial impetus for the development of the economies of Greater Eurasia countries.[1] From the EAEU point of view, the BRI concept is generally favorable for the national interests of the EAEU member states—most importantly, since such cooperation should eventually lead to much better internal connectivity between inner-Eurasian regions as well as open new business opportunities (Central Asia, Siberia, the Urals, and the Caucasus).[2]

---

[1] Wang [1], Yu [2], Liu and Dunford [3], Kohli et al. [4].

[2] Nag et al. [5], Vinokurov [6].

E. Vinokurov (✉)
Russian International Affairs Council, Moscow, Russia

© China Social Sciences Press 2023
Institute of Russian, Eastern European and Central Asian Studies, CASS and Russian International Affairs Council, *Global Governance in the New Era*, https://doi.org/10.1007/978-981-19-4332-4_13

The structure of the paper is as follows. Starting with the map of the trans-Eurasian corridors traversing Russia, Central Asia, and the South Caucasus and the estimates of the container freight flows, I quickly move to dissecting the EAEU member states' interests and perceptions on the issue. Then, the paper introduces a new dimension of the North–South transport corridor and argues for the synergy of the East–West and North–South connections. The next section of the paper contains policy recommendations. The conclusion follows.

East–West and North–South: Overview of the Major Trans-Eurasian Corridors Through Russia, Central Asia, and the South Caucasus

There has been a stellar increase in railway container traffic along the China–EAEU–EU axis from 3500 FEU (40-foot equivalent unit) in 2010. As of 2020, the volume of China-to-Europe and Europe-to-China transits container traffic crossing the EAEU reached more than 270,000 FEU. Analysis shows that the annual average doubling of the number of container trains along China–EAEU–EU routes was largely attributable to the subsidization of export-oriented railway freight traffic by the Chinese authorities.[3] A paper by [8][4] further reinforces this view and hints at higher levels of subsidies than previously assumed—up to $6,000 per FEU.

The growth of the volume of transit container traffic continued even in the face of the 2020 COVID-19 pandemic, which has even sped up and increased by 64% y/y. For the first six months of 2021, the volume of container traffic amounted to more than 165,000 FEU, which is 50% higher year-on-year. The East–West trans-Eurasian container traffic through the EAEU continues to grow.

With balanced container loads (containers traveling both ways fully loaded with optimal cargoes; no empty containers), we estimate total container traffic that may be attracted by the EAEU railway networks at 500–650,000 FEU. Finally, our optimistic scenario assumes growth up to 1 million FEU in the time horizon of 2030 if the rate or cargo containerization in the west–east direction (i.e., from the EU, Russia, and Central Asia to China) would continuously grow.[5]

---

[3] Vinokurov et al. [7].

[4] Feng et al. [8].

[5] Vinokurov [6].

EAEU Countries' Interests Concerning the Development of East–West Connections and the BRI

For the EAEU countries, the East–West transportation axis is not only about transcontinental transit. It is primarily about boosting interregional connectivity within the Eurasian landmass and unlocking new economic opportunities. The future of regions—the Russian Urals, Siberia and the Far East, and the totality of Central Asia—critically depends on improved access to markets. These developments will help capitalize on growing inland industrial centers and incorporate innovative industrial and agrarian clusters into the larger international economy. The BRI will be most beneficial for Russia if it will help develop innovative and competitive production centers, create opportunities for small and medium-sized businesses, and boost regional development.

Russia, Kazakhstan, and other EAEU countries appreciated the potential positive implications of the BRI very early on. In summary, they see the following positive implications:

- A good business opportunity on its own. We estimate that the yearly transit revenue in the 2019 split between Belarus, Kazakhstan, and Russia amounted to approximately $2 billion yearly. However, a caveat is that it is a relatively low-margin business. Hence, transit revenues alone do not justify the level of interest to the BRI that we currently witness.
- We perceive BRI within the priority task of raising the economic efficiency of the national economy through raising the level of containerization. The Russian and EAEU transport complex are still undercontainerized.
- Generally, the BRI is a political and economic means to improve Russia's position in the world. As the BRI makes the world more multipolar, Russia appears to be a beneficiary. The BRI in this regard can be viewed through the lens of the nascent Greater Eurasia framework,[6] which also corresponds well to the Russian foreign policy strategy.
- The BRI is a means to advance the economic prosperity of Central Asian states. Just as the future of Russian regions critically depends on improved access to markets, so—to even greater extent—the economic future of all five Central Asian states hangs on the very same thing.

The North–South Axis Will Supplement the East–West Axis and Help Achieve Substantial Synergies

I will now consider supplementing the East–West transportation corridors with the North–South axis. Under the North–South connection, I primarily understand the International North–South Transport Corridor (ITC North–South) that foresees three

---

[6] Vinokurov and Libman [9].

routes—to the west of the Caspian Sea, across the sea (multimodal), and to the east of the sea.

Linking the ITC North–South with the East–West connections, Eurasian transport corridors lay the groundwork for transforming Central Asia into Eurasian transport and logistics crossroads. The unique route of the North–South transport corridor creates opportunities to connect it with other global and regional transport corridors in the East–West direction. The interlinking of these corridors will increase the freight traffic on the main routes. We see significant synergies from interlinking the East–West and North–South trans-Eurasian routes. For example, our estimates imply that developing the North–South transportation corridor in conjunction with the East–West routes would lead to doubling container traffic at the North–South axis compared to the isolated development (ca. 100 and 50 thousand FEU, respectively, in the mid-terms).[7] For example, it would provide access to the North–South transport corridor for the central regions of Russia, as well as the Volga region, the Urals, and rapidly developing Southern Russia.

The ITC North–South ensures continuous trade between Asia and Europe. Cargo owners, freight forwarders, and logistics companies may consider the development of the North–South transport corridor as a way to secure smooth trade between Asia and Europe in case any disruptions occur in the Suez Canal operation, such as the one that took place in March 2021 when the container ship "Ever Given" blocked the canal. Some countries in the region, primarily Iran and Turkmenistan, present the North–South transport corridor, particularly as an alternative to the deep-sea route via Suez.

Notable reduction in duration while offering competitive tariffs is the main advantage of the North–South transport corridor. The key advantage of the North–South transport corridor over other routes, including the sea route via the Suez Canal, is a significant reduction in the duration of freight transport. For example, in 2014, pilot freight transport along the Mumbai-Moscow route of the North–South transport corridor took 19 days, while maritime transport took 32–37 days. A more recent Finland-India pilot trip took 30 days of which 12 days accounted for waiting for the ship to come. The land-based routes' advantage is on average 18–20 days. The development of the global e-commerce market may also give an additional impetus to the freight traffic increase, as this sector aims, among other things, at short delivery times.

Western and Eastern routes of the International North–South transport corridor are the most promising. They have the highest potential to develop in the medium term. This is primarily the case because railway transport is the most developed and provides for seamless monomodal connections with the EU, Russia, Central Asia, etc.[8] In the meantime, there are certain bottlenecks in the maritime transport infrastructure, which result in delays in the Caspian Sea ports and higher shipping costs. International intergovernmental and nongovernmental organizations, as well

---

[7] Vinokurov E., Ahunbaev A., Zaboev A., Shashkenov M. (2021) The North–South International Transport Corridor.

[8] Ibid.

as international development banks, play an important role in "debottlenecking" transport infrastructure and financing needed infrastructure that is currently lacking.

The North–South transport corridor can become a "development corridor" for the EAEU and for Greater Eurasia as a whole. The construction of industrial parks and the establishment of special economic zones along the transit route, creating new production and logistics chains among the EAEU member states and major developing countries of the Persian Gulf and Indian Ocean, including Iran, India, and Pakistan, will ensure new job opportunities, economic growth, and improved well-being of the region's population.

Interlinking North–South and East–West transport corridors would create substantial synergies. It would also lay the groundwork for transforming Central Asia into Eurasian transport and logistics crossroads and effectively benefit the EAEU countries, Middle East, South Asia, the EU, and China. It is a rare case of a win–win policy for all parties involved—except, perhaps, for the maritime logistics companies that will lose a part of their business to the land-based corridors.

Policy Recommendations

Developing the trans-Eurasian infrastructure, including within the realm of the BRI, is a long-term and a truly strategic initiative. To build basic infrastructure in a consistent and efficient mode, one has to stick to a long-term vision that can weather multiple crises along the way. The Belt and Road has a chance to become a classic initiative of this sort. It intends to qualitatively raise the level of infrastructure, connecting the Greater Eurasian landmass in a way it has never been connected before. This view is particularly pertinent for cross-border infrastructure. Apart from long-term financing, it entails a shared strategic vision of international economic cooperation, which is difficult to formulate and very difficult to negotiate.

I will further formulate several general policy recommendations for the medium term, which would make the coordination more effective and the country's interaction more durable in the long term.

First, BRI partner countries and partnering institutions should pay great attention to the issues of debt and fiscal sustainability. In fact, the 2020 crisis has contributed to enhancing the stress on sovereign debt sustainability around the globe. In some BRI partner countries, 40–45% of their external public debt is accounted for by BRI-related financing, much of which comes on concessional terms and in most cases alleviates sustainability concerns. We applaud the 2019 decision, announced at the 2nd BRI Forum in Beijing, to improve debt sustainability analysis in cooperation with multilateral financial organizations.

Second, in the postcrisis years, the BRI success story for trans-Eurasian container transit will largely be determined by China's continued export-related railway subsidies. The spectacular growth in freight traffic along the China–EAEU–EU axis is based on the interplay of three factors: Chinese subsidies for outbound container trains from central provinces; serious efforts by Kazakhstani, Russian, and Belarusian railways and authorities to streamline procedures and eliminate bottlenecks; and realization of the land-based routes' advantage of delivering goods from central China to Central Europe. The first factor was probably the decisive one, at least to jump-start the trans-Eurasian routes. It would be advisable to start reducing subsidy levels as the economies recover. In the longer term, my recommendation would be to at least partially retain export subsidies and, importantly, to provide more transparency about their level.

Third, further growth of trans-Eurasian freight traffic will be contingent upon investments to remove physical bottlenecks in the EAEU railway infrastructure. No mega-projects are required to expand the transport capacity of land corridors along the China–EAEU–EU axis and boost their competitiveness vis-à-vis sea routes. What is truly needed is not a "second Trans-Siberian Railway" but the selective elimination of transport infrastructure bottlenecks, which can be managed with limited financial outlay: constructing and expanding transport logistics centers, construction of additional railways, electrification of new railway sections, upgrade and modernization of locomotives, acquisition of special rolling stock, improvement of border crossing infrastructure, etc.

Fourth, the involvement of Chinese direct investors will make BRI projects more attractive for European investors. In the opinion of potential European investors, direct investments by companies from China (rather than credits extended by Chinese banks) may increase the investment appeal of BRI projects, signaling the emergence of a favorable and stable investment environment in the target area.[9]

Conclusion

The East–West land-based trans-Eurasian corridor along the China–EAEU–EU routes is a major success. Starting from a very modest point a decade ago, it grew to a substantial business. It still keeps on growing, even facing the COVID-crisis. In terms of policy, a key area of common interest for countries and regions across the Eurasian continent—China, EAEU, all of Central Asia, South Asia, and the EU—is the development of efficient cross-border infrastructure in Greater Eurasia. This means, in particular, modern railway and automobile road transport corridors. If the physical connectivity of Russia, Central Asian countries and China were greatly enhanced, and it would unlock the potential of inland regions: Xinjiang, Qinghai, Gansu, and Inner Mongolia for China; the Urals and Siberia for Russia; and all five Central Asian countries. This goal is worth pursuing to ensure and advance sustainable economic growth in the huge regions that were historically underserved by efficient transportation links.

It is in the vital shared interest of these states and regions to simultaneously develop the North–South transport corridor to the west and east of the Caspian Sea.

---

[9] IIASA [10].

It would effectively complement the East–West ones, raising the total efficiency of investment and unlocking the economic potential of the inner-Eurasian regions and countries. In essence, these two transportation axes combined would amount to the infrastructure "skeleton" of the Eurasian continent.

References

1. Wang, Y. 2016. Offensive for defensive: The belt and road initiative and China's new grand strategy. *The Pacific Review* 29 (3): 455–463.
2. Yu, H. 2016. Motivation behind China's "one belt, one road" initiatives and establishment of the Asian infrastructure investment bank. *Journal of Contemporary China* 26 (105): 353–368.
3. Liu, W., and M. Dunford. 2016. Inclusive globalization: Unpacking China's belt and road initiative. *Area Development and Policy* 1 (3): 323–340.
4. Kohli, H., J. Linn, and L. Zucker, eds. 2019. *China's Belt and Road Initiative: Potential Transformation of Central Asia and the South Caucasus*. Los Angeles, New Dehli, Melbourne: Sage.
5. Nag, R.M., J.F. Linn, and H.S. Kohli, eds. 2016. *Central Asia 2050: Unleashing the Region's Potential*. New Delhi: SAGE Publications.
6. Vinokurov, E. 2018. *Introduction to the Eurasian Economic Union*. London and New York: Palgrave Macmillan.
7. Vinokurov, E., V. Lobyrev, A. Tikhomirov, and T. Tsukarev. 2018. Silk Road Transport Corridors: Assessment of Trans-EAEU Freight Traffic Growth Potential. EDB Center for Integration Studies' Report No. 49. St. Petersburg: Eurasian Development Bank. Available at https://eabr.org/en/analytics/integration-research/cii-reports/silk-road-transport-corrid ors-assessment-of-trans-eaeu-freight-traffic-growth-potential-/
8. Feng, F., T. Zhang, C. Liu, and L. Fan. 2020. China railway express subsidy model based on game theory under "the belt and road" initiative. *Sustainability* 12: 2083.
9. Vinokurov, E., and A. Libman. 2012. *Eurasian Integration: Challenges of Transcontinental Regionalism*. London and New York: Palgrave Macmillan.
10. IIASA. 2018. *Trans-Eurasian Land Transport Corridors: Assessment of Prospects and Barriers*. Laxenburg, Austria.

China–Russia–Europe Relations in a New Era of Global Governance

Yonghui Li

Compared with the Cold War and the 20 years afterward, a new picture has emerged in the international system marked by some major changes unseen in a century. Protectionism and unilateralism are on the rise, and the world economy remains sluggish. The global industrial and supply chains are confronted with shocks brought about by noneconomic factors, and the international economic, technological, cultural, security, and political landscapes are experiencing profound adjustments, plunging the world into a period of turbulence and transformation. In this connection, COVID-19 has served to accelerate such changes. Despite the prevailing theme of peace and development, the international system has been running with increasingly complex factors such as the world structure and order, relations between major countries, and the rise of emerging countries, with instabilities and uncertainties significantly compounded. In such an international environment, to ensure world peace and development, the international community has in recent years been fighting populism and extreme nationalism and opposing unilateralism and neo-hegemonism. It is incumbent on these major countries to explore how to better manage global affairs and strike a balance in global governance that can both reflect the national interests of those major countries and encourage multilateral cooperation in a fair and just manner. In addition, it is also imperative for them to jointly drive a new round of globalization, bring about global governance reforms, and champion the vision of building a community with a shared future. This paper analyzes the features, reasons, and trends of the evolution of China–Russia–Europe relations in such a context.

Y. Li (✉)
Institute of Russian, Eastern European and Central Asian Studies, Chinese Academy of Social Sciences, Beijing, China

© China Social Sciences Press 2023
Institute of Russian, Eastern European and Central Asian Studies, CASS and Russian International Affairs Council, *Global Governance in the New Era*,
https://doi.org/10.1007/978-981-19-4332-4_14

The China–Russia Strategic Partnership of Coordination is a Fine Example of a New Type of Relationship Between Major Countries and a Major Force in Building a Multipolar World

Both China and Russia are major countries in the world, and Russia stands as the largest neighbor of China. Despite the fact that international relations are becoming increasingly complex with profound changes, major countries are experiencing the waxing and waning of power, and all countries are pursuing their own national interests in a fiercely competitive environment. The China–Russia strategic partnership has been gaining momentum, as the two sides have gradually built up mutual trust at the bilateral level and reached a broader consensus on cooperation in international affairs as a way of upgrading China–Russia relations. Today, the development of China–Russia relations features stability, maturity, and strategic inclusiveness.

First, China–Russia relations are stable. Since Russia's independence, China–Russia relations have witnessed three stages of development from mutual recognition as friendly countries (1991–1994) to constructive partnership (1994–1996) and strategic partnership (1996-present). Since the establishment of a strategic partnership featuring equality and mutual trust oriented toward the twenty-first century in April 1996 between China and Russia, the two countries' strategic cooperation has been gathering momentum steadily. The Ukrainian crisis erupted at the end of 2013 and led to diplomatic isolation and severe sanctions by the West against Russia and a tense standoff between Russia and NATO on Russia's western borders. The deterioration of geopolitical conditions pushed Russia to adopt an aggressive "Look East" policy, and China thus became a key country as it implemented. In June 2019, the heads of state of China and Russia jointly repositioned their bilateral relations and upgraded them to a comprehensive strategic partnership of coordination for a new era, which has been given new connotations and tasks to China–Russia relations and has thus become more comprehensive, stable, and strategic. "There is no limit, no forbidden zone, and no ceiling to how far China–Russia cooperation can go", "the sky is the limit for Sino-Russian cooperation, and we must continue to make the relationship even better than it already is". China–Russia relations serve as a shining model of a new type of major country relations in today's world where the two countries seek partnership rather than alliance, dialog rather than confrontation, and close cooperation.

Second, China–Russia relations are mature. Such maturity is mainly demonstrated by personal contributions, mutual emphasis, and joint support by the two heads of state. China established diplomatic relations with Russia after its independence, defying all ideological interference. Even after the outbreak of the Ukraineian crisis, the two heads of state met approximately 30 times from 2013 to June 2019, which is the highest ever seen in China's diplomacy and has worked to deepen mutual political trust between the two sides. As a result, China and Russia have continued to upgrade the level and positioning of their bilateral relations, and the strategic partnership is meant for all-round cooperation. In July 2017, China and Russia issued a joint statement announcing that they mutually regard each other as a priority in diplomacy, mutually support each other in safeguarding their respective core interests, such as sovereignty, security, and territorial integrity, and support each other's efforts in following a development path in line with their national realities, pursuing their own development and revitalization, and addressing domestic affairs in an independent approach. The two countries have not only written in their bilateral documents the status of each other as a priority in their respective foreign policies but have also reached a mutual consensus on governance issues based on their governance practices, including a high degree of agreement on core interests such as the leadership of the ruling party and the prevention of color revolutions.

In 2020, while face-to-face meetings between the two heads of state were canceled due to the COVID-19 pandemic, interactions between senior leaders of the two countries did not decrease, as demonstrated by the fact that the two heads of state contacted each other six times via encrypted telephone calls. Russian Foreign Minister Sergei Lavrov visited China in March 2021, and the two foreign ministers met with each other on multilateral diplomatic occasions such as the Shanghai Cooperation Organization (SCO) summit. As the two countries worked together during the COVID-19 pandemic to fight the US efforts in politicizing the coronavirus, their political ties have grown closer, and mutual trust has been consolidated and that is how China–Russia relations weather the pandemic.

The two countries have established the most comprehensive cooperation mechanism that functions as institutional safeguards for bilateral cooperation. Backed by various mechanisms, China–Russia trade and economic relations have been steadily improving, underpinning, and boosting their bilateral relations. China stands as Russia's largest trading partner for eight consecutive years, as well as the largest trading partner in the Far East. 2018 saw a record-high trade volume between the two countries, topping US$100 billion. In June 2019, the two heads of state elevated China–Russia relations to a higher level designated the China–Russia comprehensive strategic partnership of coordination for a new era. Bilateral trade has since exceeded US$100 billion for three years in a row: in 2019 trade volume between the two countries stood at US$110.757 billion; in 2020 despite the COVID-19 pandemic, the total volume of trade in goods between China and Russia totaled US$107.77 billion; from January to August 2021 trade between them grew by 30.3% year on year, reaching US$85.854 billion, and it is estimated that the number will reach US$120 billion by the end of this year. Furthermore, the two countries' trade structure continues to be optimized, as high-tech cooperation, trade in agricultural products, and cross-border e-commerce develop rapidly and have thus become new engines for practical cooperation between the two countries. The development of investment cooperation is also impressive, as embodied by approximately 90 large-scale projects in the Intergovernmental Committee's investment portfolio, with their value amounting to US$150 billion in 2021.

China and Russia have strengthened the docking of development strategies. After the signing of the "Joint Declaration on Construction of the Silk Road Economic Belt and Construction of the Eurasian Economic Union" in May 2015, the docking of the two countries' national development strategies accelerated. On May 17, 2018, China and the Eurasian Economic Union signed an agreement on economic and trade cooperation, which represents the first important institutional arrangement between the two sides on economic and trade matters, marking a shift from project-driven economic and trade cooperation between China and the Union and its member states to a new stage where institutions will play a leading role in their cooperation. This is a milestone in promoting the docking between the implementation of the "Belt and Road" and the construction of the Eurasian Economic Union with greater cooperation.

The two countries have promoted cooperation at the local level. More than 140 Chinese and Russian cities have become sister cities, expanding the scope of their reciprocal cooperation. 2018–2019 marked the "Year of China–Russia Local Cooperation and Exchange", under the framework of which local contacts have become closer, especially in the "Yangtze River-Volga River" region, as well as between Northeast China and the Russian Far East and in other border port areas. To tap into the full potential of cooperation between China and the Russian Far East, the two sides signed a "Plan on China–Russia Cooperation and Development in the Russia Far East Region (2018–2024)" at the Eastern Economic Forum in September 2018, which was then formally approved during the 23rd regular meeting between the Chinese Premier and the Russian Prime Minister in November 2018. In general, the plan fully reflects the industrial advantages, market conditions, and policy environments of both sides. It clearly identifies seven priority areas for China–Russia cooperation in the Russian Far East, including natural gas and petrochemical industries, solid minerals, transport and logistics, agriculture, forestry, aquaculture, and tourism, and specifies the project list under the "One Zone One Port" arrangement between China and Russia. Implementing and deepening the plan will be the main content of bilateral cooperation in future. It is safe to say that there is great potential for cooperation between China and the Russian Far East.

China and Russia have expanded and deepened their people-to-people exchanges. Cultural exchanges and friendship have been enhanced due to related mechanisms, and the ties between them are gaining more popularity in both societies with a significantly better public opinion environment. In recent years, China and Russia have jointly organized many large-scale activities at the national level, such as the "National Year", "Year of Language", "Tourism Year", "Youth Friendly Exchange Year", "Media Exchange Year", and "Local Cooperation Year", which served to forge closer people-to-people ties and then promote the development of bilateral relationships. China and Russia have become some of the most friendly countries in the eyes of each other's population. More than 3 million visits are made each year between Chinese and Russian people. The number of exchange students and personnel exceeded 80,000 annually, reaching 100,000 in 2019.

Finally, China–Russia relations are strategically inclusive. In terms of international strategies, the two countries have closely cooperated with each other, and their strategic collaboration on major international and regional issues usually goes beyond bilateral relations. As a result, they have become major partners and important strategic supporters in international affairs. With regard to strategic balance, despite some differences in the past, the two sides now share the same positions; for example, China and Russia jointly oppose the deployment of Terminal High Altitude Area Defense (THAAD) by the US in South Korea. The two countries also stood together on the North Korean nuclear crisis. As for geopolitical and economic reconfiguration, Russia announced the Greater Eurasian Partnership, where China is seen as a major partner and an indispensable source of support for Russia in its pursuit of global status as a major power and geopolitical security. Concerning the issue of building a multipolar world, Russia stands as China's most important partner in containing US hegemony, and China and Russia have been jointly promoting the SCO, BRICS, and China–India–Russia cooperation mechanisms.

In 2021, China and Russia extended the 20-year-old Treaty of Good-Neighborliness and Friendly Cooperation, which further demonstrates the two's common stand of nonalignment, nonconfrontation, nontargeting a third country, and nonideologization. The two sides have decided to develop their relations based on such basic principles, reflecting their mutual respect for each other's national sovereignty and national interests and showcasing the inclusiveness of this bilateral relationship.

The Political and Economic Separation of Russia–Europe Relations Highlight the Special Nature of Their Interdependence and Mutual Antagonism

Russia's relations with Europe are characterized by political and economic separation and entanglement of compromise and struggle. Russia–Europe relations feature huge security and economic interests, which are qualitatively different from Russia–US relations. The Ukraine crisis has strained political relations between Russia and Europe because Europe views Russia with Western values, concluding that Russia has violated international law by occupying Crimea. Europe has been suppressing Russia on human rights-related issues with the Alexei Navalny poisoning case and the previous poisoning case of the Russian spy Sergei Skripa and has been working with the US to impose uninterrupted economic sanctions on Russia. Against this backdrop, Russia and Europe have adopted a policy of separating politics from the economy in an unspoken manner, reflecting the autonomy of Europe.

The EU stands as Russia's most important economic partner, accounting for more than half of Russia's total trade, and has always been one of the largest investors in Russia. The economic sanctions imposed on Russia by the EU after the outbreak of the Ukraine crisis have only led to a lose–lose scenario. Russia needs to better its relations with Europe to ease the sanctions it faces and restore economic ties, but the outbreak of the Ukraine crisis has highlighted the security dilemma from which both Russia and Europe cannot escape. Russia's attempt to reduce tensions with Europe was also disrupted by the "spy poisoning" case in the UK in March 2018, which quickly festered and then grew from a single case to a coalescing Western movement against Russia. More than 20 Western countries expelled all together over 150 Russian diplomats, representing the largest expulsion of diplomats since the end of the Cold War. Russian scholar Lukyanov believes that such a move means the start of an all-out diplomatic war between the West and Russia, and the outbreak of it has been the most crisis moment in Russia's relations with the West since the 1980s. Even the Ukraine crisis and the annexation of Crimea did not lead to such a shock in the international community, with such drastic retaliatory measures. These are measures that countries would normally take before the outbreak of a war or during the war. However, now while the conflict is not in sight, Western countries have automatically behaved in a way that only allies would do.

In the absence of political rapprochement, Russia is using energy as a door opener and again knocking at the doors of European countries by dint of "pipelines" and "shipping lanes". First, Russia has established itself as an influential energy player in Europe with the "Nord Stream-2" gas pipeline. The construction of the "Nord Stream-2" pipeline suffices as a "ballast" project to improve Russia's relations with Germany and an example of how Russia–Europe relations have gone against the tide and maintained cooperation despite severe US sanctions since the outbreak of the Ukraine crisis. The EU is dependent on Russia for its energy supplies, with 1/3 of EU's energy demand coming from Russia. Russia has capitalized on Germany's strategic plan to cooperate with Russia on "Nord Stream-2" projects and has doubled its efforts to make a breakthrough in its relations with Germany and then beyond, facilitating a visit by the German Chancellor to Russia in May 2018, with their talks mainly focused on the construction of "Nord Stream-2". Austria also favored the use of Russian energy and expressed its sympathy for Russia under severe sanctions, so Vladimir Putin attended the Austrian Foreign Minister's wedding in a high profile. All these moves were aimed at making the EU and the US divided and ensuring that the EU can take different political and economic policies toward Russia. However, Europe is under enormous pressure from the US, which has expressed its strong opposition to energy cooperation between European countries and Russia while trying more to contain Russia with NATO. The Kerch Strait Crisis that broke out in November 2018 dealt another blow to Russia's efforts in easing tensions with the EU, which extended sanctions against Russia, and the "Nord Stream-2" negotiations were thus temporarily suspended. Late in the Trump administration, even more severe sanctions were directed at "Nord Stream-2", resulting in the suspension of this nearly 94% completed project. In the wake of the poisoning case of Russian opposition leader Alexei Navalny, the US and Europe jointly deployed other sanctions on the project.

Since Biden took office in early 2021, relations between Europe and Russia have been tumultuous and fraught with danger. Biden then imposed some additional sanctions and tried to prevent Germany from continuing to support the "Nord Stream-2" project in the hope that the project would be totally shut down. However, that ran counter to Germany's wishes. On 23 February 2021, the US State Department announced extra sanctions on the "Nord Stream-2" pipeline project in accordance with the Protecting Europe's Energy Security Act, and the main target was the Russian barge "Fortuna" (responsible for laying shallow submarine pipelines) and the company it belongs to. Since the Biden administration wants to repair relations with the EU that have been damaged by the Trump administration and step up policy coordination to deal with Russia, Germany also holds out hope that the US will not impose more sanctions on "Nord Stream-2".

The US and Europe have very different interests around the "Nord Stream-2" project. First, a constant source of energy is crucial to supporting Germany's continued economic development in future, which makes the energy supply from Russia's direct pipelines important. If Germany's energy supply from Russia is reduced and even worse if the Strait of Hormuz is blocked after some conflict between the US and Iran, the German economy might just collapse. Second, the US covets the European energy market. The US wants Europe to be a stable market for its massive extraction of liquefied natural gas. Third, natural gas is a political tool for Europe and the US. The US sanctions against "Nord Stream-2" have divided the EU and turned the project from an energy cooperation program into a geopolitical and international interest dispute. The US fears that the EU will increasingly rely on Russia if the gas pipeline project continues, while the EU, and Germany in particular, believes that the gas pipeline will in turn become a tool to influence and restrain Russia. The Russian gas pipeline has become a bone of contention in the game between Europe, the US, and Russia, affecting the geopolitical and energy strategies of each side.

In the second half of 2021, as energy supply shortages were felt around the world, Russian President Vladimir Putin stated that Russia would increase the supply of natural gas to Europe if needed while working to put Nord Stream-2 into operation as soon as possible in the face of energy supply constraints. What is happening now indicates that Nord Stream-2 has become a geopolitical tool for Russia to divide the US and Europe, and its construction process has been pushed forward, come hell or high water, demonstrating the "strategic resilience" of major European countries such as Germany and France. The Trump administration followed the arrogant policy of "America First", and in August 2021, the US suddenly decided to accelerate the complete withdrawal of US troops from Afghanistan in disregarding other NATO countries' arrangements for the aftermath. In September, a trilateral security partnership agreement was signed among the US, the UK, and Australia. The US then torpedoed Australia's submarine contract previously signed with France and signed another contract with Australia. As a result, the close ties between the US and Europe were undermined, and lasting grudges emerged between them. Despite the Biden administration's efforts to repair their relationship, it is still certain that the future of US–Europe relations will be more about Europe seeking autonomy while cooperating with the US rather than the US "guiding" Europe.

The operation of the "Nord Stream-2" will present new opportunities for Russia–Europe business cooperation. Although China–Russia trade is still expected to exceed US$100 billion in 2021, the increase rate in this bilateral trade will be lower than that of Russia's foreign trade, and the growth of Germany–Russia trade outpaces that of China–Russia trade. As a result, China's market share in Russia has fallen by 0.6 percent, which is lost to Germany. After the tensions between Russia and Europe are eased, China–Russia trade will suffer a decline while Russia–Europe trade will grow, and such declines and growth are always coupled. The growth in China–Russia trade is due in part to European sanctions on Russia, but Germany has been the largest investor in Russia since 2018. Even in the face of serious sanctions, Germany tried its level best to stay in the Russian market instead of pulling itself out. Moreover, as Russia defied sanctions and issued government bonds in Europe, France has not withdrawn from the Russian market.

China–Europe Relations Move Forward in Twists and Turns and Join Hands in Multilateral Cooperation for Global Governance

The European Union and China are geographically far away from each other, but strategically speaking, it is China's best choice for the diplomatic vision of befriending distant countries. In recent years, China–Europe relations have gone through some twists and turns because of, on the one hand, the changes in Europe's self-perception and, on the other hand, the changes in China–US relations and Europe–US relations. As Europe further recognizes and strengthens its "strategic autonomy", there is still enormous room to better China–Europe relations.

The political relationship between China and Europe is overshadowed by ideological struggles. As Europe gives priority to democratic and liberal values and upholds the "political correctness" of the US, it considers China as an "opponent to the western system", and that is why it has put a lot of pressure and sanctions on China in the area of human rights and obstructed the China–EU Comprehensive Agreement on Investment. As competition between China and the United States intensifies, Europe does not want to be a playing field for them but rather a competitor. Hence, it will actively participate in the game as a third party and demonstrate its great ability to shape the world as one pole. The EU is interested in distancing itself from the US at the policy level. In regard to the origin of the COVID-19 pandemic, the EU has rejected "stigmatization" by the US and adhered to the official name of the virus announced by the World Health Organization (WHO) and has not blindly followed the US attempt to "hold China accountable for the virus". Although the EU also emphasizes the security and autonomy of the industrial chain, it does not agree with the US policy of "hard decoupling", which it believes will not only divide Europe and the US but may also lead to a new Cold War that does not serve the interests of the world.

China–Europe economic cooperation has been relatively smooth, and under the strategic guidance of the leaders of both sides, China–EU economic and trade cooperation has developed rapidly and fruitfully. In 2020, China–EU trade reached US$649.5 billion, with China leaping forward to become the EU's largest trading partner for the first time. Trade between China and Europe continued to grow rapidly from January to September 2021, with bilateral trade totaling US$599.34 billion, an increase of 30.4%. The EU is also an important source of foreign investment and a destination for direct investment in China. China and Europe should compete in the field of science and technology in a way that can circumvent the US constraints and crave their own paths that feature autonomy and mutual benefits.

The China Railway Express plays an important role in China–EU economic and trade relations. As the situation remains tense in the global maritime transport market, a large number of Chinese and European traders have started to transport their goods by rail through Russia. Russia, surprised by the "unimaginable" surge in demand, has also been working to increase its transport capacity. Russian Railways reports that it has transported a total of 782,000 twenty-foot equivalent units (TEUs) from January to September 2021, and this number is expected to exceed a million by the end of the year. Most of this increases come from the "China–Russia–Europe" route, which jumped by 47% to 568,700 TEUs in the first 9 months this year.

China–Europe economic cooperation works as a long-lasting driving force for the development of bilateral relations. As the COVID-19 pandemic dealt a heavy blow to Europe's economy across the board, the already sluggish economic growth since 2009 further deteriorated. The continued spread of the pandemic is hitting European countries hard, especially those that rely mostly on tourism and services. The EU's gross domestic product (GDP) fell by approximately 10% in 2020, and the prospect for recovery remains bleak in 2021. To drive economic recovery amid the pandemic, the EU has overcome internal obstacles and launched a "recovery fund" totaling €750 billion, but in the process of implementation, internal problems such as the original "East–West and North–South" conflicts will still reemerge, limiting the extent of its implementation and pushing up the cost.

COVID-19 disrupted the political dynamics and policy design of Europe. The newly elected EU institutions were supposed to make a large difference in 2021, which was later characterized by the pandemic. Before its outbreak, the EU rolled out a series of top-level plans and strategies involving industrial development and geopolitics. The pandemic and its negative effects have not only forced the EU to adjust its policies but have also further strained its resources and capacity to implement such strategies and plans, which will further amplify the gap between Europe's political will and its actual capability.

Despite some intractable political differences, Europe will not easily cease to carry out pragmatic cooperation with China in some specific areas, and China–Europe relations will enter a complex period when cooperation and competition go hand in hand as well as consensus and disagreement coexist. In the next four years, the interactions among China, Europe, and the US will also become more complicated and fraught with uncertainties. China's political and diplomatic differences and conflicts with Europe and the US will continue to emerge and even be magnified, but there will also be more room for business cooperation in fields such as going green, going digital, and protecting the environment as well as for multilateral cooperation on issues such as climate change, resulting in an "intertwined" relationship.

Taking a perspective from China, it is clear that China is pursuing a more open dual-circulation development pattern instead of a closed domestic one, which is meant to unleash the potential of China's domestic demand and will provide a broader market with exciting development opportunities for European investment. In recent years, the Chinese government has continued to liberalize market access, encourage

European investors to step into more fields, build more open platforms, improve the environment for foreign investment, and promote trade and investment liberalization and facilitation as a way of building a new economic system featuring a higher level of openness. The reform and opening-up are China's fundamental state policy, and China will keep opening its door wider, creating more opportunities for China–EU economic and trade cooperation.

In short, what stands at the core of Europe's strategic autonomy is deeper European integration. Over the past 70 years, Europe has fully enjoyed the dividends of integration, as it managed to avoid a decline through regional cooperation and safeguard its international status and interests. However, due to the European debt crisis, the refugee crisis, and the COVID-19 pandemic, Europe's economy has been hit hard with growing social inequality and rising populism. These factors have led European leaders to reconstruct their discourse on European integration, and strategic autonomy represents a new story and narrative in this regard. Despite many challenges, China and Europe still share a broad consensus within the framework of multilateralism, and there is ample room for cooperation. Both China and Europe champion multilateralism firmly uphold the international system with the United Nations at its core and the international order based on the purposes and principles of the UN Charter and oppose unilateralism. Both sides should strengthen multilateral cooperation in areas such as climate change, combating the pandemic, and digital governance, convert the spirit and values of multilateralism into concrete diplomatic practice, and jointly build a new type of international relations and a community with a shared future for mankind.

Conclusion

The China–Russia comprehensive strategic partnership of coordination is crucial to the evolution of the international situation, structure, and order. China and Russia should further bring into play the efficiency of the "China–Russia combination", have more communication and coordination in multilateral frameworks such as the United Nations, SCO, and BRICS, stand firmly on the right side of history as well as fairness and justice, and continuously promote democracy in international relations. The two sides should put forward more "China–Russia solutions" and provide more "China–Russia wisdom" to make a greater contribution to the cause of maintaining world peace and stability.

As an important international actor, the EU is instrumental to the transformation of the international system and order by dint of its great international status, the power it possesses and the way it exerts the power. In a world full of uncertainties, whether China and Europe, as two major forces, two major markets, and two major civilizations in the world, will settle for cooperation, competition or confrontation will have immeasurable implications for the future of the international community. At present, China–EU relations are still going through a long period of transition. Their relationship features zero fundamental geopolitical conflicts, deep economic inter-dependence, and common interests in a range of multilateral issues and in addressing many common challenges. In addition, it is worth noting that their bilateral relations are also resilient enough because they have been developing and adapting for a long time.

Promoting global governance that favors multilateral cooperation and jointly building a community with a shared future for mankind can be links between China, Russia, and Europe by promoting interactions among them. However, in the face of an uncertain future, Russia and Europe may also view bilateral relations through the lens of competition and conflict, leading to more strategic suspicion toward China. In any case, more wisdom is needed for the three sides to be better placed to address the asymmetry in bilateral relations and abandon zero-sum thinking. It is hoped that China, Russia, and Europe can leap over ideological barriers, build better China–Russia, China–Europe, and Russia–Europe partnerships, contribute to peace and stability in the region and beyond, and work together to build a community with a shared future for mankind.

Global Governance: Solutions for the Future

Environmental Governance: A Perspective from Industrial Civilization to Ecological Civilization

Yongsheng Zhang

Introduction

Since the Industrial Revolution, the traditional development mode of "resource-intensive, high carbon emission, and high-environmental costs" has drastically increased productivity and advanced industrial civilization at an unprecedented scale. Yet it has led to a global unsustainability crisis, including climate change. Currently, over 130 countries have promised to go carbon neutral or reach net zero carbon emissions by the mid-twenty-first century. Those countries represent some 90% of global carbon emissions and GDP and 85% of global population. More importantly, about 70% of them are developing countries. That is to say, developing countries may skip the traditional "emit first and mitigate later" development path that the industrialized countries took and head for a low-carbon takeoff. The global carbon neutrality consensus and initiatives herald an end to the mode of traditional industrialization and the advent of a new era of ecological civilization and green development.

Traditional environmental governance is rooted in the mode of traditional industrialization and development concepts. Under the traditional mode, not only environmental protection is at odds with economic development, but countries are engaged in a zero-sum game when it comes to global environmental responsibilities, and dilemmas exist in the interests of current and future generations. Accordingly, environmental governance aims to maximize the space of compromise between environment and development to attain a higher level of economic development. Global environmental governance is more concerned with how the burden of environmental protection is shared among countries. In terms of inter-generational responsibilities,

Y. Zhang (✉)
Research Institute for Eco-Civilization (RIEco), CASS, Beijing, China

© China Social Sciences Press 2023

Institute of Russian, Eastern European and Central Asian Studies, CASS and Russian International Affairs Council, *Global Governance in the New Era*, https://doi.org/10.1007/978-981-19-4332-4_15

the current generation should be responsible for the posterity and try to avoid occupying resources or damaging the environment. This approach is reflected in the definition of sustainable development in the Brundtland report, i.e., "sustainable development is a development that meets the needs of the present without compromising the ability of future generations to meet their owns".[1]

As Albert Einstein noted, "we cannot solve problems by using the same kind of thinking when we created them". There is very little space to compromise between the environment and development as long as the two are in conflict. Even if such space can be expanded with better technology and more efficient management practices, this mode will eventually take its toll on the environment. Hence, environmental governance must shift from unsustainable industrial civilization to ecological civilization. The fundamental approach for environmental governance under the concept of ecological civilization is to create benign interactions between the government, enterprises, and consumers, shift the conflicting relationship between the environment and development into a mutually beneficial one, transform development paradigm, and achieve modernization in which man and nature live in harmony, and prosperity is shared globally.

This paper aims to provide a conceptual framework to reveal the fundamental differences of environmental governance under traditional industrialization and ecological civilization, as well as their different mechanisms of realization and policy implications. Part 2 reviews the history and research literature on environmental governance and explains the limitations of existing studies and the importance to shift from traditional industrial civilization to ecological civilization. Part 3 discusses the environmental governance approach and limitations under the traditional concepts of industrial civilization, as well as why sustainability problems cannot be resolved under such concepts. Part 4 employs a conceptual framework to reveal the new environmental governance mechanism under ecological civilization. Part 5 offers discussions on related matters. The final section provides brief concluding remarks.

Transformation of Environmental Governance Approach

Conflict Between the Environment and Development and Governance Approach Under the Traditional Development Mode

Since the mid-twentieth century, the traditional mode of industrialization has led to an environmental crisis of great concern to all nations. In 1972, the United Nations held the Environment and Development Conference for the first time and adopted the *Declaration of the United Nations Conference on the Human Environment*,

---

[1] World Commission on Environment and Development, Our Common Future, Oxford: Oxford University Press, 1987, p. 27.

which called upon governments and peoples to take joint actions to conserve and improve human habitat for the benefit of future generations. Thereafter, the relationship between the environment and development has become a key item on the global agenda. On September 25, 2015, the United Nations Sustainable Development Summit was held at its headquarters in New York, which officially adopted 17 sustainable development goals (SDGs). Nonetheless, the reasons why these goals have not been achieved are not because their importance was not well-understood, but because they conflicted with each other in the traditional industrialization mode. Without fundamental transition of development mode, it is hard to form a mutually beneficial relationship between the 17 SDGs and overcome daunting difficulties for their achievement.

Standard economics, however, has not offered sufficient theoretical insight on how to understand and tackle the relationship between environmental protection and economic development. As the most influential theory, the environmental Kuznets curve (EKC) considers that an inverted U-shaped trend exists between the environment and development, which makes environmental improvement possible after economic development reaches a certain level.[2] This has become a major theoretical basis for the "pollute first, clean up later" policy and global environmental governance. Though this theory is widely accepted, it is far from a law of economic development.[3]

Although environmental issues have increasingly received attention in economics, as reflected in the creation of economics disciplines such as ecology /environment/natural resources economics, environmental issues are far from being incorporated into mainstream economic analysis. According to Polaski et al., most researchers of sustainable development are natural scientists.[4] Take standard economics as an example. Prof. Esther Duflo was awarded Nobel Prize in Economic Sciences in 2019 for her outstanding contributions to development economics, one of which is an important experimental study on incentivizing farmers to use fertilizer.[5] Nonetheless, the excesses use of fertilizer is a major cause for unsustainable "modern" agriculture. In the developing world, agricultural development should avoid the old path of "pollute first, clean up later". Since poverty eradication tops the 17 SDGs, their research is regarded as part of sustainable development research.

Economists tend to treat environmental issues as an application and branch discipline of standard economics. In this regard, the most representative environmental issue is climate change research. A typical approach is to figure out an optimal global level of greenhouse gas emissions (GHGs) through cost and benefit analysis (CBA), and then individual countries negotiate their emissions reduction obligations and pursue international cooperation.[6] The benefit of emissions reduction is defined

---

[2] Grossman and Kruger [1].

[3] UNEP, Toward a Green Economy: Pathways to Sustainable Development and Poverty Eradication, 2011, www.unep.org/greeneconomy; Stern [2].

[4] Polasky et al. [3].

[5] Duflo et al. [4].

[6] Nordhaus [5].

as the reduction of future losses stemming from climate change, i.e., social cost of carbon. This approach is characteristic of the traditional industrial era, i.e., emissions reduction conflicts with economic development, current generation conflicts with future generations, and countries see their interests clash. Under this approach, the optimal global carbon emissions are 3 °C increase in global mean temperature,[7] which is a far cry from the goal set forth in the Paris Agreement and the estimates of mainstream natural scientists, and their research methodology is also broadly controversial.[8] Such debates are not just a simple question about the value of model parameters but involve basic theoretical questions in economics. In fact, emissions reduction can be a process of creative destruction, which may bring the economy to a new and more competitive structure. The benefit of carbon emissions is not just the reduction of future loss, but more importantly, the emergence of new technologies and sunrise industries, as exemplified in the substitution of fossil fuels with new energy and the substitution of gasoline-fueled vehicles with electric vehicles.[9]

Many studies on environmental governance are focused on the aspect of mechanism design. The best-known environmental governance problem is "the tragedy of the commons".[10] According to Hardin, there are two ways to resolve the tragedy of the commons: either to privatize or nationalize the commons.[11] Coase theorem is extensively applied to environmental economics,[12] i.e., in the absence of transaction cost, optimal resource allocation is irrelevant to the initial allocation of property ownership. Considering the cost of defining and enforcing property rights, externalities cannot be truly removed. According to Cheung, the degree of optimal externalities is subject to an efficient trade-off between the cost of externalities and the cost of removing externalities.[13] That is to say, with the passage of time, the optimal environmental choice under the narrow economic perspective will eventually exceed the scientific threshold with disastrous consequences. For instance, even if annual GHGs meet so-called annual optimal level, climate change will accelerate once cumulative emissions exceed a tipping point.

Ostrom suggested that environmental governance goes beyond the above-mentioned two pathways.[14] "Humans have a more complex motivational structure and more capability to solve social dilemmas than posited in earlier rational-choice theory". As she noted, designing institutions to force (or nudge) entirely self-interested individuals to achieve better outcomes has been the major goal posited by policy analysts for governments to accomplish for much of the past half century. Extensive empirical research leads her to argue that instead, a core goal of public policy should be to facilitate the development of institutions that bring out the best

---

[7] Nordhaus [5].

[8] Stern [6], Stern and Stiglitz [7], Weitzman [8].

[9] Zhang and Shi [9], Zhang [10].

[10] Hardin [11].

[11] Hardin [11].

[12] Coase [12].

[13] Cheung [13].

[14] Ostrom [14].

in humans. According to the Institutional Analysis and Development framework put forth by [14], people in those regions tend to self-govern to form an effective governance structure of common pool resources.[15]

Environmental problems essentially stem from development paradigms. Since the development and research paradigms established after the Industrial Revolution largely result from the traditional industrial era, it is hard to addressing the sustainability crises facing the world today by simply applying the existing standard theories to sustainability problems. We must revisit and extend some basic questions in economics, including the value theory and analytical perspective, in light of those crises. Unless the development paradigm is transformed to turn the environment-development relationship from conflicting to mutually reinforcing, it would be hard for effective environmental governance to take hold.

Journey of China's Environmental Governance

China has experienced an arduous path of understanding and dealing the relationship between the environment and development. Environmental problems were initially thought to be non-existent in socialist countries and when they started to appear, were believed to be surmountable with the strengths of socialism. It was not until rapid economic development took its toll on the environment in the post-reform era since 1978 that the conflict between the traditional mode of development and environmental protection became apparent. The 17th CPC National Congress puts forth the concept of ecological civilization, calling for making environmental protection compatible with economic development under the scientific outlook on development. After the 18th CPC National Congress, the concept of ecological civilization took on new implications and became written into the *Constitution of the People's Republic of China* and the *Constitution of the Communist Party of China (CPC)* as a pillar of the "Five-Pronged Strategy". With refreshed understanding comes great change in action. China has made unprecedented efforts to protect the environment with significant achievements in both environmental and economic endeavors, forming a benign cycle where environmental protection begets economic development.[16]

In terms of scale and speed, China is the biggest beneficiary of the mode of traditional industrialization. But why does China take the lead to embrace ecological civilization and pursue green development? An underlying reason is that the traditional mode of polluting and resource-intensive industrial development entails hefty external, implicit, long-term costs, opportunity cost, and welfare costs that render economic growth unsustainable. Meanwhile, upsurge in the green economy led by new energy, electric vehicle and 5G communication have opened up vast opportunities that undergird China's shift toward ecological civilization and green development.

---

[15] Schoon and Cox [15].

[16] Zhang [16].

Modernization of China's governance system and capabilities for ecological civilization is all about establishing a mutually conducive relationship between the environment and development to achieve sustainable development goals, specifically, at three levels. First is at the domestic level. The conflict between the environment and development under the mode of traditional industrialization should be transformed into a mutually conducive one to defy the "modernization paradox" under the industrial civilization, so to follow a path of modernization in which man and nature live in harmony, and pursue sustainable development for the Chinese nation. Second is at the international level. The great rejuvenation of the Chinese nation under this new development philosophy represents an opportunity for the world at large. International environmental obligations can be turned into shared opportunities. Third is at the inter-generational level. A Pareto improvement can be achieved for the welfare of both current and future generations, and the welfare of our posterity may not come at the expense of the current generation.

Environmental Governance in the Lens of Traditional Industrial Civilization

Intrinsic Characteristics and Environmental Governance Dilemmas Under the Traditional Mode of Industrialization

The mode of traditional industrialization, by its nature, puts economic development at odds with ecological environment, and consequently, ecological governance can only broaden the space of compromise between the two. The mode of traditional industrialization is more focused on the mass production and consumption of material wealth and characterized by intensive material resource input, carbon emissions, and environmental costs. Meanwhile, little consideration is given to the environmental, social, and cultural impacts of economic activities, some of which yield handsome returns at the expense of external, implicit, long-term and opportunity costs, and welfare losses. Unlike large-scale and dedicated production for industrialization, social organizations, culture, and ecological environment are more dependent on diversity and symbiosis. Hence, there tends to be an intrinsic conflict between the mode of traditional industrialization and ecological environment.

Assuming that an economy consists of two product categories, i.e., (X, Y). Where X is industrial products based on material resources with a higher environmental intensity, i.e., $e_1 > 0$; Y is service products based on intangible resources, whose production does not damage the ecological environment, $e_2 = 0$. Condition for sustainable development is that actual environmental emissions E does not exceed the environmental capacity $\overline{E}$, i.e., $E < \overline{E}$. The aggregate environmental footprint of both types of products is

$$E = e_1 X + e_2 Y = e_1 X \tag{1}$$

We will reveal that without changing what produce and consume, raising the efficiency of environmental management alone can hardly achieve pollution mitigation. As can be learned from Eq. (1), there are two ways to reduce aggregate environmental footprint E under the mode of traditional industrialization. One is to reduce e_1 through technology progress, i.e., to make X with greener technologies, which tends to raise the cost of production. The other way is to reduce the output of X, which means an economic contraction similar to reaching the limit of growth.[17] Both pathways are seen as a burden of economic development.

The first pathway alone, i.e., to reduce e_1 with new production technologies, may not reduce the aggregate environmental footprint E since X may increase at a faster pace, so that growth in X will cause an environmental footprint that outweighs what decreasing environmental intensity e_1 helps to reduce. Even if it is the other way around, i.e., decreasing environmental intensity e_1 does more to shrink environmental footprint than the increasing output of X expands it, the cumulative environmental impact will eventually exceed the environmental threshold over time, i.e., $\int_0^t E(s) \cdot ds > \overline{E}$, thus triggering an environmental crisis. The second pathway, i.e., protecting the environment at the expense of economic growth, is hard to be embraced either.

Due to the environment-development conflict under the mode of traditional industrialization, environmental governance relies more on technology progress, management efficiency, or economic slowdown or contraction to postpone the exceedance of environmental threshold. None of these measures may fundamentally resolve environmental problems or avoid the Malthusian trap. If development is based on the production and consumption of material wealth, the limitation of resources, e.g., space for further global carbon emissions, presents a dilemma in the distribution of limited resources between current and future generations. To realize sustainability, therefore, economic development must be decoupled from environmental degradation and resource consumption as much as possible, i.e., to move from the traditional economy (X, Y) to the green economy (X', Y'). Where $X' < X, Y' > Y$. Only in this manner will the sustainability condition $E < \overline{E}$ be satisfied, and economic growth occurs at the same time.

Dilemma Facing Global Environmental Governance Under the Traditional Mode of Development

Lack of sustainability due to the environment-development conflict will present a dilemma between nations. The mode of traditional industrialization highly dependent on the input of material resources and fossil fuels since the Industrial Revolution has brought material abundance to a minority of people in certain parts of the world, but once this mode is scaled up on a global scale or a longer timeframe, a crisis of unsustainable development will ensue.

---

[17] Meadows et al. [17].

We assume that two types of countries exist, i.e., developed and developing countries. Condition for global sustainability is $E_{\text{global}} = e_1 x_1 M_1 + e_2 x_2 M_2 < \overline{E}_{\text{global}}$, where e_i, x_i, M_i, $i = 1, 2$ which, respectively, denote the environmental intensity of unit output from developed and developing countries, per capita output and population size; E_{global} is the degree of global environmental degradation; $\overline{E}_{\text{global}}$ is global environmental capacity, e.g., total global carbon emissions that correspond to an increase in global mean temperature by 1.5 °C. When the gap between the global North and South is large enough, and the per capita output x_2 of developing countries is sufficiently below x_1 of developed countries, the condition for global environmental crisis $E_{\text{global}} = e_1 x_1 M_1 + e_2 x_2 M_2 < \overline{E}_{\text{global}}$ can be satisfied to the extent that no major global environmental crisis will occur. At this moment, the mode of modernization in the developed world appears replicable in the rest of the world, and its intrinsic attribute of environmental unsustainability becomes concealed due to the global North–South divide.

As such, the modernization mode of the developed world is seen as a template for modernization in the developing world. The concept of modernization accepted by most countries is modernization based on the production and consumption of material wealth with industrialized countries as the benchmark. In exploring their own paths to modernization, late-moving countries are obsessed with how to achieve the sort of modernization in the developed world based on their national conditions, i.e., how to raise per capita output from x_2 to x_1, without questioning what modernization should be, i.e., whether X is sustainable and may improve people's welfare. When emerging countries attain rapid development following the trail of industrialized nations, the global environmental crisis led by climate change will erupt, and the unsustainability of such a path to modernization is laid bare.[18]

How to deal with the global environmental crisis? Under the mode of traditional industrialization, environmental protection is in conflict with economic development, and a typical approach to solving global environmental problems is for all countries to "fairly" share their environmental responsibilities. Take climate change as an example. A typical practice is to first estimate the volume of carbon emissions that needs to be cut to keep global warming within 2 or 1.5 °C, and then bringing countries to the negotiation table to divide the burden. This old approach of sharing the burden has made it hard to find a real solution to global environmental problems.[19] A new approach should be to view emissions reduction as an opportunity for green development and create and share such an opportunity through international cooperation.

---

[18] Zhang [18].

[19] Zhang and Shi [9], Zhang [10].

Environmental Governance Trap Under the Mode of Traditional Industrialization

Coming back to [11] tragedy of the commons, this section will reveal why the mode of traditional industrialization cannot achieve sustainable development goals at the microscopic level of institutional design. In the lens of ecological civilization, the so-called tragedy of the commons or development trap falls into three categories.[20]

The first type of development trap is the tragedy of the commons such as overfishing and overgrazing. According to [14] research, stakeholders may form effective incentives through cheap talk to avoid overfishing and overgrazing and control output X within a certain range, i.e., $X < \overline{X}$, to avoid overfishing or overgrazing and satisfy the sustainability condition $E = e\overline{X} < \overline{E}$. While the avoidance of overfishing or overgrazing may sustain output at a level above overfishing or overgrazing, such "sustainability" remains at a low level, and the upper limit of sustainable fishing or grazing $\overline{X}$ becomes the ceiling of development.

The second type of development trap is environmental degradation under the mode of traditional industrialization. Although overfishing can be disincentivized, fish farmers are tempted to use excessive fertilizers that pollute lakes. Even if chemical fishing is abandoned, pollution from chemical agriculture and industrial activities in surrounding areas will still pollute lakes. Environmental damages wrought by human activity have already penetrated into uninhabited areas including deep oceans through the Earth's complex circulatory systems. Without transforming the mode of economic development on a broader scale, microscopic design to avoid the tragedy of the commons is of limited effects to achieving global sustainability.

The third type of development trap is that the economy is locked-in the mode of traditional industrialization and cannot leap to a more competitive green development structure, i.e., from (X, Y) to (X', Y'). Green transition is similar to the structural leap from 0 to 1. This leap is similar to the chicken or egg paradox. Risk-averse decision-makers refrain from taking emissions reduction initiatives unless enough green evidences are seen; but in the absence of emissions reduction initiatives, green evidences will not appear anyway. To break through this "evidence-action" dilemma, it takes new theories to foresee new outcomes that would appear under certain circumstances.[21] Without a fundamental transformation of the development model, the economy will be locked-in a traditional structure due to path dependence and cannot unlock the potential benefits of green transition.

The global unsustainability crisis facing mankind is not just an externality problem of the tragedy of the commons but involves a paradigm shift of values, the matter and mode of development, and systems and institutions. Only by extricating ourselves from the traditional mode of industrialization and embracing the concept of

---

[20] Zhang [19].

[21] Zhang and Shi [9].

ecological civilization will we establish a mutually conducive relationship between environment and development.[22]

Environmental Governance Under Ecological Civilization: A Conceptual Framework

President Xi Jinping called for "two win–win results" at the Paris Climate Conference in 2015, which underpin China's approach for environmental governance under the concept of ecological civilization. First, win–win results between the environment and development; second, win–win results between countries. As discussed before, it is hard to achieve sustainable development goals under the mode of traditional industrialization. Next, we will focus on ecological governance under the concept of ecological civilization and how those win–win results could be achieved.

Mechanism of Behavior for Environmental Governance Stakeholders

The fundamental solution to environmental problems is to ditch the traditional mentality of industrial civilization and decouple economic development from environmental degradation under the concept of ecological civilization. That is to say, we should try to reduce the production and consumption of high-environmental footprint product X and increase the production and consumption of green product Y to transform the economy from (X, Y) to (X', Y'). Where $X' < X, Y' > Y$.

The question is how to realize such a transition? Here, we use a simple general equilibrium model to reveal the interactions between the environmental governance stakeholders of the government, enterprises, and consumers, as well as how they change their behaviors under the new concepts and constraints and embrace green transition.

It is assumed that consumers consume two types of products X and Y, whose utility functions and constraints are

$$\max U = x^\alpha y^{1-a} \tag{2}$$

$$\text{s.t.} p_x x + p_y y = I \tag{3}$$

where U is utility, and α and $(1 - \alpha)$ are the preference parameters of X and Y, respectively. I is income (wage), and P_x and P_y are the prices of X and Y, respectively. Demand functions of the two types of products are solved as

---

[22] Zhang [20].

Environmental Governance: A Perspective from Industrial Civilization … 177

$$x = \frac{\alpha I}{P_x}, y = \frac{(1-\alpha)I}{P_y}. \tag{4}$$

For the simplicity of analysis, it is assumed that only labor input exists for Firm X and Firm Y. It can be understood that the production of X requires the application of labor to material resources, while the production of Y is more dependent on intangible resources such as knowledge, culture, and environment, and the production functions are $X = AL_x, Y = BL_y$. Where A and B are technical parameters, and L_x and L_y are labor inputs. In most cases since the 1970s, there has been only input of labor in the production functions of the new trade theory, the new growth theory, and industrialization and new economic geography models based on Dixit and Stiglitz's (1977) model.

We introduce a new environmental constraint into the firm decision-making system to assess its impact on firm behaviors and general equilibrium result. The objective function for the profit maximization of firm X is $\pi_x = k P_x X - \omega L_x$. Where $0 < k < 1$ is the effective output coefficient. Since the government follows a "polluter pays" principle, the firm must consume $(1 - k)$ of its output for the treatment of environmental pollution for the emissions of its products to stay below environmental standard e_x (compliance with environmental standard does not mean zero pollution). The firm's net revenue after deducting the cost of environmental treatment is $k P_x X$, and ω is wage. Due to market competition and free entry, firms X and Y offer equal wages. For the simplicity of analysis, we make wage ω a price numeraire and have $\omega = 1$, and all prices in the model are relative prices. Green product Y has no environmental cleaning-up problem, and the objective function of its profit maximization is $\pi_y = P_y Y - \omega L_y$.

The results of general equilibrium are

$$\text{Price: } p_x = \frac{1}{kA}, p_y = \frac{1}{B} \tag{5}$$

$$\text{Per capita consumption: } x = akA, y = (1 - \alpha)B \tag{6}$$

$$\text{Labor allocation: } L_x = akM, L_y = (1 - ak)M \tag{7}$$

$$\text{Total output: } X = aAkM, Y = (1 - ak)BM \tag{8}$$

$$\text{Utility: } U = (akA)^{\alpha}[(1 - \alpha)B]^{1-\alpha} \tag{9}$$

How to transform the economy from a traditional economy (X, Y) into a green economy (X', Y'), where $X' < X, Y' > Y$, to reduce the environmental impact of the economy as a whole? This requires a step change in the behaviors of government, businesses, and consumers. In performing a comparative static analysis of $X = aAkM$ and $Y = (1 - ak)BM$, we have

$$\frac{\partial X}{\partial k} > 0, \frac{\partial Y}{\partial k} < 0, \frac{\partial X}{\partial \alpha} > 0, \frac{\partial Y}{\partial \alpha} < 0 \tag{10}$$

As can be learned from Eq. (10), there are two basic pathways for the economy to transform from traditional economy (X, Y) into a green economy (X', Y'):

The first pathway is to enforce stricter environmental constraints upon firms to change the relative prices of green and non-green products, i.e., raise p_x and decrease p_y. As can be learned from $p_x = \frac{1}{kA}$, $x = \alpha kA$ and $X = aAkM$, the relative prices of X and Y will change with their costs of environmental regulation. The more environmental cost $(1 - k)$ polluting firms pay, the higher the relative price p_x of polluting product X becomes, and the more the market will reduce demand for X and raise demand for Y. The share of X in the economy decreases, and the share of green product Y increases. In the absence of environmental constraint, i.e., if $k = 1$ or $1 - k = 0$, it becomes difficult to raise the relative price of non-green products p_x, and it is hard for the green transition to occur.

The second pathway is the transformation of consumption mode. The first pathway primarily deals with the internalization of external cost in standard economics, which alone cannot solve environmental problems without transforming the underlying value system and development mode. As can be learned from $x = \alpha kA$ and $y = (1 - \alpha)B$, when α decreases, there will be less demand for X and more demand for green product Y. Notably, standard economics has a different attitude from other disciplines on the change of consumer preferences. In such disciplines as psychology, marketing, anthropology, and sociology, changing preferences are a normalcy, but standard economics is more concerned with resource allocation analysis under given preferences. The reason is that changing preferences will present numerous difficulties to "science-based analysis" and affect the scientificity of economics.[23] Yet many challenges facing economics derive from problems arising from such an assumption. Without evolving preferences, many changes in economic structure may not even occur. Judging by economic history and behavioral and experimental economics, people's preferences are not constant as assumed in standard economics. On the contrary, preferences keep evolving.[24] Massive changes in social psychology and consumer habits form the premise of transition from agricultural to industrial society.[25] High productivity in the modern industrial society needs to transform "frugal men" into "hungry consumers" to create market demand.[26]

---

[23] Bruni and Sugden [21].

[24] Stern and Stiglitz [7]; Grune-Yanoff and Hansson, S.O., "Preference Change: An Introduction", in Preference Change: Approaches from Philosophy, Economics and Psychology, Theory and Decision Library A42, 2009; Becker [22].

[25] Rostow [23].

[26] Atkisson, A., "Life beyond growth: Alternatives and complements to GDP-measured growth as a framing concept for social progress" (2012 Annual Survey Report), Tokyo: Institute for Studies in Happiness, Economy and Society, 2012.

Green Transition and Ecological Civilization

The above basic pathways correspond to two core concepts of ecological civilization, i.e., man and nature living in harmony and "green is gold", while the former has to do with constraints under different analytical perspective, the latter has to do with the concept of values.[27]

The first represents a broader perspective of "man and nature". The mode of traditional industrialization is confined to the narrow perspective of man and goods and cares little about the environmental impact of human activity. In various standard economics textbook models, ecology and environment play a marginal role.[28] So-called optimal human behavior of single-mindedly maximizing material wealth production and consumption inevitably brings destruction to the relationship between man and nature. A broader perspective of "man and nature" corresponds to the increasing environmental cleaning-up cost of $(1 - K)$ for firm X in the model. Such a new constraint will change relative product price and push up demand for green goods while reducing demand for non-green goods.

The second is the concepts that "green is gold", and "a beautiful environment is the most inclusive well-being". Such new development concepts mean new preferences and redefinition of a good life. It corresponds to change in consumer preference parameter α in the utility function, as well as such factors as intangible ecology and environment in the standard utility function. Since standard utility function $U = x^\alpha y^{1-a}$ does not consider the adverse impact of intangible factors such as environmental degradation, real consumer utility is not as high as what the nominal goods consumption reveals, i.e., "high GDP and low well-being". This has been extensively verified by happiness economics.[29] Once the social well-being loss from environmental degradation $(1 - k_s)$ is taken into account, the real utility function would become $U = k_s x^\alpha y^{1-a}$, where $0 < k_s \leq 1$. As the preference parameter α for product X decreases and environmental cleaning-up intensifies, environmental quality would improve and so would k_s in the utility function and real utility. For instance, consumption of goods worth 1000 yuan would create different well-being in a clean environment as opposed to a heavily polluted one. Just like that the transition from an agrarian society to an industrial society is conditioned upon a mass transformation of social psyche and consumer habits, the shift from unsustainable mode of traditional industrialization to green development also entails a systematic and profound transformation of social psyche, consumer mentality, and lifestyle. Otherwise, the green transition could not be achieved with technology progress alone.

The intrinsic difference between traditional industrial civilization and ecological civilization means different definitions of cost, benefit, well-being, and optimality, as well as different implications to ecology, environment, society, and culture. Under the mode of traditional industrialization, economic development somehow conflicts with

---

[27] Zhang [24].

[28] Smith [25].

[29] Easterlin [26].

ecology, environment, society, and culture; the green development mode of ecological civilization offers the prospect for a mutually conducive relationship between economic development and ecological environment, society, and culture.[30]

Discussions on Relevant Matters and Policy Implications

Shift in the Role of Ecological Governance Stakeholders

Environmental governance is the result of joint actions by the government, enterprises, and consumers. As can be seen from the changing constraints of consumer and producer decision-making system, transition from the traditionally economy (X, Y) to the green economy (X', Y') involves change in key parameters such as preference α, environmental regulation k, and technologies A and B. Among them, the most critical is government support.

First, transition in development philosophy and strategy. As far as governance is concerned, the key to the green transition is to refresh development concepts and replace the GDP-oriented development objectives with well-being-centric ones. New strategic development concepts and objectives are self-fulfilling and will transform development pattern, business model, and institutional systems and policymaking.

Second, changing role of the government. According to Stern and Stiglitz, environmental crisis is a typical market failure.[31] In establishing the governance system for ecological civilization, some fundamental questions need to be revisited, including the redefinition of market and government functions. From the supreme ruler in *Leviathan* to the contractual relationship between the government and citizens in *The Social Contract*, the night-watchman state in the *Wealth of Nations* [25], and new government functions of the modern market economy, the perception of government functions has experienced a substantive evolution. The Third Plenum of the 18th CPC Central Committee called for "fully leveraging the decisive role of the market in allocating resources and giving better play to the role of government", and the Fourth Plenum of the 19th CPC Central Committee made a decision on the modernization of national governance system and capabilities. These policy initiatives will redefine market and government functions. For instance, tight environmental regulation will change the relative price of products, and government support to green technology will lower the price of green products.

Third, change in the role of enterprises. In the past, the goal of firms was to maximize shareholder profits with little consideration over externalities. Under the mode of traditional industrialization, corporate governance puts shareholder interests above everything else. Under the principles of ecological civilization, considerations

---

[30] Zhang [20, 24].

[31] Stern and Stiglitz [7].

should be given to the social, environmental, and cultural impacts of economic activities, and shareholder's profit can only be maximized subject to the condition with the key stakeholders to be included into corporate governance in various forms. The objective function of firm X is then transformed from $\pi_x = P_x X - \omega L_x$ in the past to $\pi_x = k P_x X - \omega L_x$ at the present.

Fourth, change in consumer behaviors. Aside from the factor of relative price, consumer preferences are a key impetus of economic transition. Change in consumer behaviors can be driven by (i) perception of how environmental pollution affects their own interests; (ii) deepening experience of the benefits of environmental improvement; and (iii) education and public awareness. According to Zhang and Ilan, "green knowledge" is vital to changing consumer preferences and behaviors, and education is an important way to increase such knowledge.[32] Notably, the government should create a negative list of unsustainable consumer behaviors so the consumer can have freedom of choice, rather than imposing certain preferences upon consumers.

Implications of Green Transition to Productivity, Well-Being, and Sustainability

It should be noted that X and Y mentioned above refer to a set of products of two types, which, respectively, contain a series of products, i.e., $X = (x_1, x_2, ..., x_n)$, $Y = (y_1, y_2, ..., y_n)$. In this manner, change in the relative share of X and Y may be construed as a process in which non-green sunset industries vanish and green industries emerge. Such a green transition is a Schumpeterian creative destruction process. As Zhang and Shi revealed, emissions reduction may drive economic structure to a more competitive one, so that emissions reduction turns into an impetus rather than a burden of economic development.[33] For instance, strict emissions reduction policy propels the transition of economic structure from "gasoline-fueled vehicles and gasoline stations" to a more competitive one featuring "electric vehicles and charging points", as well as increasingly deepened division of labor and lowering costs. China's booming new energy vehicle industry is a vivid reflection of creative destruction.

Green transition will not impede economic growth as some fear. Instead, it may serve as a path to better and faster growth. The whole sentence can be changed into this one: The key point of green transition is a shift from GDP-centric development to a focus on people's well-being. Under the model of green economy, category-Y goods and services are based more on non-rivalrous intangible resources such as knowledge, ecological environment, and culture, and compared with category-X goods dependent on the input of material resources, category-Y production has higher increasing returns since the marginal costs of knowledge, ecological environment, and culture, once formed, are extremely low and even zero. Unlike traditional

---

[32] Zhang and Chabay [27].

[33] Zhang and Shi [9].

economy (X, Y) dependent on exhaustible material resources with damaging effects on the ecology and environment, the new green economy (X', Y') is largely based on intangible resources that are inexhaustible. The key problem is that those products and services based on intangible resources often require new business models for the realization of their value. Admittedly, it is a tall order to transform existing business models that took hold in the traditional industrial era.

Take the management of common pool resources, under the traditional concept of industrialization, the function of lakes or forests is to farm fishes or graze cattle, which is a standard definition in traditional development economics centered around material wealth production and consumption. But apart from fish farming, lakes also have various ecological and cultural functions such as ecotourism, sports, recreation, culture, and education. Intangible ecological resources like lakes are non-rivalrous and offer value (such as landscapes) to the masses. Those functions of lakes, if fully utilized, will endow the ecological protection of lakes with new implications to development, so that polluting fish farming is no longer the only way to make more profits. Once development is redefined, [14] IAD framework will take on new development implications, and the development traps discussed before will vanish.

Furthermore, a plausible illusion needs to be clarified. A key reason that the mode of traditional industrialization appears more efficient than the green economy is the non-inclusion of its exorbitant social costs into the economic analysis and evaluation systems. For instance, if the medical cost $C_{medical}$ of environmental pollution is taken into account, the budget constraint of consumers will decrease, i.e., from $p_x x + p_y y = I$ to $p_x x + p_y y = I - C_{medical}$. For the simplicity of analysis, we can introduce a coefficient of social cost k_s into the utility function to transform it from $U = x^\alpha y^{1-a}$ to $U = k_s x^\alpha y^{1-a}$, where $0 < k_s \leq 1$. When polluting enterprises step up environmental control, the society as a whole will benefit from non-rivalrous environmental improvement, and at this moment, k_s in the utility function will increase for everyone. In this sense, tight environmental regulation will enhance society-wide real well-being level.

Brief Concluding Remarks

Since the Industrial Revolution, the mode of traditional industrialization has vastly increased productivity but has also led to unsustainability crises globally. Not only is the environment conflicted with economic development, but dilemmas exist between the present and future generations and between countries. This paper reveals that environmental governance in the traditional industrial era could only expand the space of compromise for those dilemmas by advancing technology progress and raising governance efficiency. At the fundamental level, it cannot harmonize the conflicting relationship between environmental protection and economic development. Under ecological civilization, the goal of environmental governance is to foster a mutually conducive relationship between environmental protection and economic development, so that countries will share the opportunities rather than burden of environmental protection, and it can benefit both the current and future generations.

The transition from traditional industrial civilization to ecological civilization represents a systematic change of development and research paradigms. Consideration of environmental governance under this paradigm requires redefining such concepts as the objective function, cost, benefit, well-being and optimization, as well as changes in the behavior and modes of government, enterprises, and consumers with different environmental consequences. Put forth at the Fourth Plenum of the 19th CPC Central Committee, ecological civilization underscores environmental protection, resource utilization, ecological conservation, and restoration, as well as environmental accountability. Under the concept of ecological civilization, those priorities assume different policy implications compared with the traditional industrial era. Once we free ourselves from the mindset of the industrial era, some firmly believed theories may have to be revisited.

References

1. Grossman, G., and A.B. Kruger. 1995. Economic growth and the environment. *Quarterly Journal of Economics* 110 (2): 353–377.
2. Stern, D. 2010. Between estimates of the emissions-income elasticity. *Ecological Economics* 69 (11): 2173–2182.
3. Polasky, S., C.L. Kling, S.A. Levin, et al. 2019. Role of economics in analyzing the environment and sustainable development. *PNAS* 116 (12): 5233–5238.
4. Duflo, E., M. Kremer, and J. Robinson. 2011. Nudging farmers to use fertilizer: Theory and experimental evidence from Kenya. *American Economic Review* 101 (6): 2350–2390.
5. Nordhaus, W. 2019. Climate change: The ultimate challenge for economics. *American Economic Review* 109 (6): 1991–2014.
6. Stern, N. 2016. Current climate models are grossly misleading. *Nature* 530: 407.
7. Stern, N., and J.E. Stiglitz. 2021. The social cost of carbon, risk, distribution, market failure: an alternative approach. NBER Working Paper 28472, 2021. http://www.nber.org/papers/w28472.
8. Weitzman, M.L. 2011. Fat-tailed uncertainty in the economics of catastrophic climate change. *Review of Environmental Economics and Policy* 5 (2): 275–292.
9. Zhang, Y.S., and H.-L. Shi. 2014. From burden-sharing to opportunity-sharing: Unlocking the deadlock of global climate change negotiation. *Climate Policy* 14 (1): 63–81.
10. Zhang, Y.S. 2014. Climate change and green growth: A perspective of division of labor. *China & World Economy* 22 (5).
11. Hardin, Garrett. 1968. The tragedy of the commons. *Science* 162 (3859): 1243–1248.
12. Coase, Ronald. 1960. The problem of social cost. *Journal of Law and Economics, The University of Chicago Press* 3: 1–44.
13. Cheung, S. 1970. The structure of a contract and the theory of a non-exclusive resource. *The Journal of Law and Economics* 13 (1).
14. Ostrom, Elinor. 2009. Beyond markets and states: Polycentric governance of complex economic systems. *American Economic Review* 100 (3): 641–672.
15. Schoon, M., and M.E. Cox. 2018. Collaboration, adaptation, and scaling: Perspectives on environmental governance for sustainability. *Sustainability* 10: 679.
16. Zhang, Y. 2020. Ecological civilization system reform. In *China's Reform and Opening Up: Practical Process and Theoretical Exploration*, ed. Xie Fuzhan. China Social Sciences Press.

17. Meadows, D.H., D.L. Meadows, J. Randers, and W.W. Behrens III. 1972. *The Limits to Growth: A Report for the Club of Rome's Project on the Predicament of Mankind*. New York: Universe Books.
18. Zhang, Y. 2020. Building a modernization of harmonious coexistence between man and nature. *Finance & Trade Economics* 12.
19. Zhang, Y. 2021. The paradox of modernization and the modernization of ecological civilization. In *Promoting the Modernization of National Governance*, eds. Gao, Peiyong, and Zhang Yi. China Social Sciences Press.
20. Zhang, Y. 2019. Ecological civilization is not equal to green industrial civilization. In *Beautiful China: 70 Years Since 1949 and 70 People's Views on Eco-civilization Construction*, ed. Pan Jiahua. China Environmental Science Press.
21. Bruni, L., and R. Sugden. 2007. The road not taken: How psychology was removed from economics, and how it might be brought back. *The Economic Journal* 117 (516): 146–173.
22. Becker, G.S. 1996. *Accounting for Tastes*. Cambridge, MA: Harvard University Press.
23. Rostow, W.W. 1960. *Stages of Economic Growth: A non-communist manifesto*. Cambridge: Cambridge University Press.
24. Zhang, Y. 2021. Why Carbon neutrality must be incorporated into the overall layout of ecological civilization construction—Theoretical explanation and its policy implications. *China Population, Resources, and Environment* 9.
25. Smith, A. 1776. *An Inquiry into the Nature and Causes of the Wealth of Nations*. London: W. Strahan and T. Cadell.
26. Easterlin, R. 1974. Does economic growth improve the human lot? Some empirical evidence. In *Nations and Households in Economic Growth*, ed. P.A. David and M.W. Reder, 89–125. Academic Press.
27. Zhang, Y.S., and Chabay, I. 2020. How "green knowledge" influences sustainability through behavior change: Theory and policy implications. *Sustainability* 12: 6448.

Challenges for the Environmental Restructuring of the Global Economy

Natalia Piskulova

"Greening" Processes of Global Economy

In recent decades, environmental issues have taken the center stage among other global challenges. The World Economic Forum singles out environmental concerns as one of today's most serious issues—in 2019, they were named third out of five most likely long-term risks for humankind and fourth out of five biggest problems in terms of their potential impact on the world. Currently, the most pressing problems are air, water, and soil pollution, resource depletion, lack of pure drinking water, deforestation, and its repercussions for biodiversity. None of the issues caused by progressing air pollution is more challenging and more difficult to solve than climate change.

It is this awareness that solving environmental problems is urgent and has led the world to formulate a development strategy focused on the environment.[1] Among the factors driving this strategy, along with rapid environmental deterioration, are resource constraints, energy security issues, growing environmental costs for the economy, public pressure, and the emergence of the "environmental factor" as a means of increasing the competitive advantages of countries and companies. The strategy is now being implemented at the global, state, private, nongovernmental, and individual levels.

As a result, we are witnessing deep restructuring of the global economy, expansion of its environmental component under the influence of increasing conservation policies, transformation of business activities, and innovation, investment, and information growth in this area. Almost all branches of science are engaged in solving environmental problems. The total capitalization of green markets—renewable energy,

---

[1] A collective term, the elements of which are present in the strategy of sustainable development, green economy, circular economy, etc.

N. Piskulova (✉)
Russian International Affairs Council, Moscow, Russia

© China Social Sciences Press 2023
Institute of Russian, Eastern European and Central Asian Studies, CASS and Russian International Affairs Council, *Global Governance in the New Era*,
https://doi.org/10.1007/978-981-19-4332-4_16

energy conservation, clean water supply, sustainable forestry, fisheries, plastic and solid waste recycling, green infrastructure, and sustainable cities—is higher today than that of many traditional sectors.

Experts insist that this restructuring can, in addition to improving the environment, facilitate economic growth, boost the labor market, and improve living standards. According to the International Renewable Energy Agency, "the energy transformation would provide a 2.5% improvement in GDP and a 0.2% increase in global employment" in 2019–2050, with GDP gains adding up to $99 trillion.[2]

That said, environmental initiatives are progressing at a much slower pace than the environmental degradation of the planet due to the unprecedented challenges that we must tackle in the coming years. They encompass not only transforming the economic structure (or at least its key sectors—energy, manufacturing, agriculture, and transport) but also the very way of life. This requires fundamental changes in innovation, investment, and trade. The main obstacles are of a financial, technological, managerial, and psychological nature.

The main reason why economic restructuring is so expensive is the very cost of green technologies. According to various estimates, anywhere from 2 to 25% of global GDP, or even more, are needed for the transition to a green economy, says the United Nations Environment Program. The World Economic Forum has gone on record as saying that $5.7 trillion need to be invested in global infrastructure alone (mainly in developing countries),[3] while a report published by the United Nations Department of Economic and Social Affairs sets global replacement costs of existing fossil fuel and nuclear power infrastructure at $15–20 trillion.[4] The International Renewable Energy Agency estimates that $110 trillion will have been invested in carbon-free energy by 2050, or 2% of global GDP.[5] What makes matters worse is that we are unlikely to see the benefits of green investment in the short-term perspective.

Technological aspects should be taken into account when discussing green initiatives. The technologies needed to build a green economy exist and are, in fact, quite widespread: wind and solar energy, energy storage and distribution systems, carbon dioxide capture technology, biodegradable materials, etc. In addition, these technologies are becoming cheaper and more effective, which stimulates their further development. For example, the cost of photovoltaics and wind power for electricity generation has decreased by an average of 73 and 22%, respectively, since 2010, and this trend is expected to continue. In the United States, wind and solar energy production costs are approaching 2–3 cents per kilowatt-hour. In Europe, offshore wind energy is a viable alternative to traditional energy costwise. Making the most of new opportunities, such as a combination of smart grids, digital systems, the Internet of things, big data, artificial intelligence, and other technologies that can significantly improve energy demand and trade management, as well as the introduction of new

---

[2] Global energy transformation: A roadmap to 2050. IRENA. April, 2019. URL: https://www.irena.org/publications/2019/Apr/Global-energy-transformation-A-roadmap-to-2050-2019Edition.

[3] The Green Investment Report [1].

[4] World Economic and Social Survey 2011 [2].

[5] See Footnote 2.

business models, can completely transform the energy sector. In the long run, next-generation renewable biofuels and bioenergy will play a role in sectors that are hard to electrify, such as aviation, shipping, and certain industrial processes.[6]

Renewable energy has grown at an unprecedented rate over the past decade, faster than all other energy sources. According to the latest projections, the share of renewable energy in the primary energy supply could grow from approximately one-sixth today to two-thirds by 2050.[7] This, together with improved energy efficiency, will allow for a global restructuring of the energy sector.

At the same time, given the increasing speed with which traditional technologies are replaced with renewable alternatives, there is still a lot to be done to increase the efficiency of renewable energy while reducing its cost (particularly in energy conservation), as well as to make sure it is adopted in key sectors of the economy. Additional incentives to switch to renewables are also needed, which could come, for example, in the form of maintaining sufficiently high prices for traditional energy sources. Due to the complexity of making changes to the energy infrastructure, it takes a long time for significant transformations to occur in the global energy sector.

The implications of new technologies are still highly uncertain. For example, most green technologies use large amounts of plastic in their production. Oil (a nonrenewable energy source) is also consumed, and dioxins are emitted (this happens when using green technologies as well). The production of solar panels produces fluorine, chlorine, nitrates, carbon dioxide, sulfur dioxide, and other hazardous substances.[8] It is difficult to predict what new technologies will be developed in future. Recent years have demonstrated that the situation can change very quickly. One example of rapid changes in the markets is the accelerated growth in shale oil and gas production, which has impacted energy markets and reduced incentives to develop alternative sources.

The gravity of the environmental situation is such that we are in a race against time to create and disseminate green technologies. All signs point to a revolution in green technologies taking place within the next two to three decades. Scientists warn to quickly rebuild the global energy system to prevent a climate catastrophe. This is an exceedingly difficult task given the time it takes to develop, introduce, and disseminate new technologies. The previous technological revolutions unfolded over a much longer period, over the course of 70 or more years. Moreover, energy efficiency gains are "offset" by population growth and increased consumption.

It is not impossible to accumulate money and technology, however. According to international organizations, the money needed for green investments is there, and most of the technologies for transitioning to a new economy are already available. Thus, accelerating the process of economic restructuring also relies on other, equally important factors. They primarily concern changing the way of thinking and policy at all levels.

---

[6] See Footnote 2.

[7] Ibid.

[8] Phylipsen and Alsema [3].

Environmental strategies and policies are constantly delayed by the indecisiveness, lack of awareness, and focus on short-term goals of leaders, companies, and the general population. Despite political claims, green strategies in most countries are not sufficiently focused on the preservation of natural capital. Government policies are often inconsistent: Incentives for cleaner manufacturing often exist alongside significant subsidies for fossil fuels and agriculture, both of which increase the environmental burden. In 2018 alone, fossil fuel subsidies exceeded $400 billion.[9]

There are also other reasons for these difficulties, namely a high degree of uncertainty regarding the rate of environmental degradation. Research shows that the environment is degrading in certain areas at a pace faster than previously thought—faster than countries are apparently able to respond to. As scientists warn, this process could further accelerate sharply. Geopolitical factors also have a role to play.

One obstacle is the inherent contradiction between the primary goal of any business, which is profit, and the task of building a green economy. Despite the new opportunities, many companies, including Russian ones, continue to negatively look at "greening" their activities, seeing environmental measures as additional costs. Green investments do not typically provide immediate returns, and the benefits are not always obvious.

The "greening" of the global economy is uneven. Currently, the environmental sector is concentrated in a small number of predominantly developed (the European Union, the United States, and Japan) and rapidly developing (China, India, and Brazil) countries. This is, among other things, due to the level of development of states and the structure of their economies. Environmental initiatives can have long-term negative consequences for countries that rely on energy exports, as well as for traditional energy companies. The resource dependence of a large number of countries in Africa, the Middle East, and Latin America may lead to loss of markets as a result of deterioration of trade conditions.

In addition, a significant number of developing countries see the idea of "greening" economies as having a limited profit, fearing that it will divert resources and attention away from development issues and the issue of inequality. There are also concerns that all natural resources—as well as other aspects of human life—will be commercialized, resulting in increased profits for companies but a further destruction of the natural environment against public interests. For example, mining companies continue seriously damaging the environment, offering financial aid as a means of "compensation."

Developed countries can use environmentally friendly strategies to justify unilateral protectionist measures, which might further exacerbate inequality. The pushback on the part of developing countries has to do with the potential acceleration of the liberalization of trade in environmental goods and services, where developed countries have a competitive advantage.

---

[9] Energy subsidies. Tracking the impact of fossil-fuel subsidies. International Energy Agency. URL: https://www.iea.org/topics/energy-subsidies.

Challenges for the Environmental Restructuring of the Global Economy 189

There are other obstacles to the "greening" of the global economy. Some problems can be solved through integrating the concept of eco-friendly growth into government strategies; strengthening the role of the state in promoting and investing in green innovations; expanding the number of economic tools available for state environmental policies—including financial incentives for specific economic activities; drawing people's attention to the cultural, informational, and educational component of environmental policy; enhancing international interaction in this area, taking the interests of countries that do not receive immediate benefits from developing a green economy into account; and overcoming political distrust among states.

How Governments and Business Can Tackle the Problem

Despite numerous problems, environmental policy results in "greening" processes in several areas. Climate change is just one important issue to tackle as part of this policy, alongside biodiversity conservation and ecosystem health.

Human impact on the environment has resulted in biodiversity declining at an unprecedented rate, which is only getting faster. Approximately, two-thirds of ecosystem services are degraded or unsustainably used, even though they form the basis of the economy and are estimated to be $125 trillion worth. Some one million species of animals and plants are on the verge of extinction—something that has never been observed in the history of humankind. Over 40% of the world's population is affected by land degradation, which in turn affects food security.[10]

A number of international agreements have been concluded to tackle this problem, including the Convention on Biological Diversity, the Convention on the Conservation of Migratory Species of Wild Animals, and the Convention on International Trade in Endangered Species of Wild Fauna and Flora, among others. In 2010, the Parties to the Convention on Biological Diversity adopted the Strategic Plan for Biodiversity 2011–2020. Significant headway has been made around the world toward achieving a number of the Plan's goals, particularly with regard to the identification of invasive species, the expansion of protected areas, and the development of national strategies and plans for the conservation of biodiversity.

A number of countries have stepped up their activities in this area, including through informational, educational and other kinds of work. The result is a high level of public awareness (as high as 90%) of environmental issues in countries such as France, Mexico, Brazil, Peru, China, and Vietnam. Tourism activities in national parks and at World Heritage sites are expanding, which helps raise awareness of the values of biodiversity. Local communities undergo training to boost their participation in park management, thus increasing their role in biodiversity conservation activities. Many countries have introduced agricultural development

---

[10] Summary for policymakers of the global assessment report on biodiversity and ecosystem services of the Intergovernmental Science-Policy Platform on Biodiversity and Ecosystem Services. IPBES. 2019. URL: https://ipbes.net/global-assessment.

schemes in environmentally sensitive areas, where farmers receive allowances to implement biodiversity-friendly practices. Biodiversity-relevant taxes have also been introduced in a number of states. Market instruments, such as the Marine Stewardship Council certification, are used with increasing frequency. Governments and local consumers are adopting participatory management practices to achieve more sustainable fisheries, such as setting catch limits to conserve resources.

Economic instruments such as taxes, levies, tradable permits, payments for the use of ecosystem services, environmental subsidies, and other measures to encourage manufacturers and consumers to behave in an environmentally responsible manner are increasingly being used. Direct payments are collected, for example, for the protection of water basins. Tradable permits allow companies to purchase environmental permits from companies that have restored their natural habitat in a different area.

Businesses are increasingly starting to understand the need to properly manage ecosystems to maintain profitability. There is growing demand for products by companies that show concern for the environment. These companies are doing their part for biodiversity conservation, introducing voluntary eco-certification and eco-labeling programs, instituting new business models for obtaining environmental benefits, exploring opportunities to participate in ecosystem markets, etc.

According to the Global Assessment Report on Biodiversity and Ecosystem Services, the situation could be far worse if such initiatives were not in place.[11] Even so, more proactive programs are needed since, despite all efforts, extinction risk trends for animals and plants are accelerating, and the natural habitat continues to deteriorate.

Public–Private Partnership: Transition to Environmentally Friendly Development

The transition to environmentally friendly development requires different stakeholders to participate. Specifically, partnerships between the state, private, and public organizations—which have existed for several decades at various levels—could be effective. There are approximately 4000 public–private partnerships around the world geared toward achieving the UN Sustainable Development Goals. New types of partnerships use a combination of government and voluntary instruments for business regulation.[12]

The Digital Impact Alliance, a public–private partnership bringing together scientists, investors, and government officials to ensure food security in Africa using big data in agriculture, is a good example. For example, farmers in Malawi have access to information concerning fertilizers, appropriate to local conditions.[13]

---

[11] Ibid.

[12] Ibid.

[13] Ibid.

Such partnerships can work well under certain conditions, such as the common goals of participants and professional management. The 2011 partnership between Marks and Spencer and Somerset County Council to increase the recycling of roadside reusable waste, including plastic bottles, can provide a good example. For Marks and Spencer, the benefit was the reduction in landfill volumes and costs.

Innovative Solutions for Ecosystem Preservation

The rapid development of new increasingly affordable technologies expands the possibilities for biodiversity preservation and "greening" in general. Modern solar-powered cameras allow observing wildlife remotely and storing and transmitting large amounts of data, which helps to achieve the former. For example, the use of drones has facilitated studies of the natural environment in the Caribbean. In the United States, drones are used to monitor water quality in streams and swamps. Farmers in Japan use "precision" farming as a way to reduce resource consumption. Using combined technologies, including drones, computers, and state-of-the-art sensors, farmers are able to determine how much water, fertilizers, and other materials are needed for each square meter.[14] In the fishing industry, mobile apps are used on ships and in ports to record how much fish has been caught and monitor fish populations.

Russia is also witnessing a gradual increase in the use of various environmental policy instruments. Dozens of environmental laws have been adopted over the past few years... The Ecology national project has been launched. A number of companies have started to implement resource-efficient technologies, recycle waste, and use environmental certification and eco-labeling. Despite these efforts, the environmental situation in the country continues to deteriorate. Thus, more proactive measures are needed, including innovative methods based on artificial intelligence, big data, the Internet of things, and other cutting-edge technologies that are becoming increasingly prevalent in countries that are more advanced in these areas.

References

1. The Green Investment Report. The ways and means to unlock private finance for green growth. *World Economic Forum.* https://www3.weforum.org/docs/WEF_GreenInvestment_Rep ort_2013.pdf
2. World Economic and Social Survey 2011. *The Great Green Technological Transformation.* UN. https://www.un.org/en/development/desa/policy/wess/wess_current/2011wess.pdf

---

[14] Mader et al. [4].

3. Phylipsen, G.J.M., and E.A. Alsema. 1995. Environmental life-cycle assessment of multicrystalline silicon solar cell modules. Available at: http://seeds4green.org/sites/default/files/10.1.1.126.292.pdf
4. Mader, A., A. Ralevski, A. Fischer, and J. Lim. 2019. *Biodiversity—A Key Source of Technological Innovation*. G20 2019 Japan. https://t20japan.org/wp-content/uploads/2019/03/t20-japan-tf3-3-biodiversity-source-technological-innovation.pdf

Role, Competition and Cooperation: China, Russia and the United States in Global Climate Governance and Low-Carbon Green Growth

Hongfeng Xu

Thermometer readings around the world have been significantly rising since the Industrial Revolution, and the decade since 2011 has been confirmed as the warmest 10 years in more than 170 years. According to the IPCC assessment report, greenhouse gases from human activities have become the most significant driver of observed climate change since the year 1750, and the largest source of carbon emissions is from activities in the fields of energy, transportation, construction and manufacturing. Developed countries such as the US and European countries are historically the main contributors to cumulative global greenhouse gas emissions, while countries such as China, Russia and India have become major carbon emitters since the Kyoto Protocol. Global warming will bring physical and transition risks that will spill over from the real economy to the financial sector. In response to various impacts of climate change, related international conventions have evolved with intensified actions, and major countries around the world have set their own "carbon peak" and "carbon neutrality" targets.

Global Efforts in Climate Governance

Global Warming is Real and Obvious

Climate warming is one of the major concerns of the international community today and a challenge that all countries, especially the world's major powers, must face together. Over the past 100 years or so, global temperatures have risen more rapidly than at any other time in history. According to estimates of the Met Office Hadley

---

H. Xu (✉)
Institute of Russian, Eastern European and Central Asian Studies, Chinese Academy of Social Sciences, Beijing, China

© China Social Sciences Press 2023
Institute of Russian, Eastern European and Central Asian Studies, CASS and Russian International Affairs Council, *Global Governance in the New Era*,
https://doi.org/10.1007/978-981-19-4332-4_17

Centre (Had), the National Oceanic and Atmospheric Administration (NOAA) and other national and regional organizations, global warming can be divided into three stages: the first stage is before 1900, when global temperatures remained stable and basically equaled to the average temperature. Since the twentieth century, global temperatures have fluctuated in a "hot-cold-hot" but generally upward trend, with temperatures slowly rising in this second phase. Average temperatures rose by a maximum of around 0.5 °C between 1900 and 1950 compared with that in the pre-industrial era (1850–1900), which then declined but was still around 0.2 °C above the baseline for the next two decades. The third stage is after 1975, when global warming became more pronounced as global industrialization and urbanization programs accelerated, with the temperature change compared with the average level reaching between 0.5 and 1.2 °C. In recent years in particular, annual average temperatures have risen at an increasingly faster rate compared to previous periods.[1]

The decade since 2011 has proved to be the Earth's warmest decade in the last 170 years or so, and the global average temperature in 2020 was 1.2 °C higher than the pre-industrial level. Although the appearance of La Niña in the second half of the year 2020 helped reduce temperatures in winter, that year was still the second hottest year since complete climate observations were recorded, which is second only to 2016 and followed by 2019, 2015 and 2017.[2] In February 2020, a high temperature of 20.75 °C was measured in the northern Antarctic, which set a new record since the temperature there had never exceeded 20 °C before. In June of the same year, a high temperature of 38 °C was recorded in the Arctic, representing also a new record in history.

Greenhouse Gases Produced by Human Activities Are Major Drivers of Global Warming

There are a variety of causes behind a warming planet, including both natural factors such as solar activities and volcanic eruptions, and human factors such as urbanization and industrialization, deterioration of marine ecosystems and destruction of soil and vegetation. The observed global warming is, to a great extent, caused by the increased concentration of greenhouse gases due to human activities, and carbon dioxide makes up the vast majority of greenhouse gas emissions, with the largest rise in carbon emissions coming from energy, transport, buildings, and manufacturing related activities. In accordance with the IPCC Fourth Assessment Report, the net effect of human activities since 1750 has become the main reason behind global warming, with a radiative forcing on the climate reaching up to $+1.6$ W/m^2, while changes in solar irradiation have only led to a small radiative forcing of $+0.12$ W/m^2.[3]

---

[1] World Meteorological Organization: https://public.wmo.int/en.

[2] See Footnote 1.

[3] IPCC Climate Change 2007: Synthesis Report, Theme 2. pp. 36–41. https://www.ipcc.ch/report/ar4/syr/.

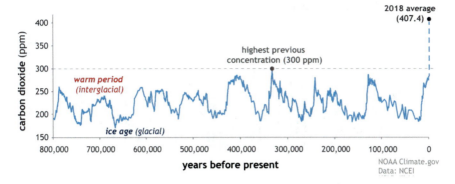

Fig. 1 CO_2 during ice ages and warm periods for the past 8,00,000 years. *Unit* CO_2 concentration (ppm). *Data Source* National Oceanic and Atmospheric Administration, https://www.noaa.gov/

NOAA statistics indicate that global atmospheric CO_2 concentrations have shown a fluctuating upward trend during both glacial and interglacial periods over the last 8,00,000 years, with historical highs of 300 ppm (Fig. 1).[4] If current emission levels remain the same in the coming years, temperatures are likely to rise by 1.5 °C by 2030 at the earliest. In order to ensure that global warming will stay below 2 °C, atmospheric CO_2 concentrations should be below 350 ppm, which already stood at 407.4 ppm in 2018. Similarly, the IPCC Sixth Assessment Report in August 2021 concluded that since 1850, the global average surface temperature has risen by around 1 °C, and if this rate is here to stay, global temperatures will reach or even exceed 1.5 °C within 20 years.[5]

Since the mid-nineteenth century, as the speed of industrialization and urbanization in Western countries picked up, these countries have experienced faster economic growth, and since the twenty-first century, emerging countries such as China and India have also embarked on the "fast track" of economic development. While developed countries including the US and those in Europe stand as main contributors to the world's historical cumulative greenhouse gas emissions, China, Russia, India and other countries have become the main drivers of global carbon emissions since the Kyoto Protocol was signed.

---

[4] National Oceanic and Atmospheric Administration, https://www.noaa.gov.
[5] China Meteorological Administration, http://www.cma.gov.cn.

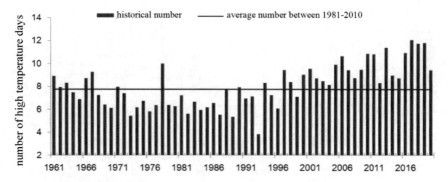

Fig. 2 Average number of days with a temperature of over 35 °C from 1961 to 2020 (days). *Data Source* China Meteorological Administration, *China Climate Bulletin 2020*, P6

Global Warming Will Bring Physical Risks and Transition Risks

The Physical and Transition Risks of Climate Warming Are Becoming Increasingly Evident

According to the G20 Green Finance Study Group (2017), the Task Force on Climate-related Financial Disclosures (TCFD), and the Network of Central Banks and Supervisors for Greening the Financial System (NGFS), the risks arising from climate change include both physical and transition risks.

Physical risks stem from direct losses to micro-economy and macro-economy brought about by extreme or abnormal weather events and ecological degradation, including acute risks such as rainstorms, hurricanes, droughts and hailstorms, as well as chronic risks such as seawater acidification, food security, rising sea levels and biodiversity loss.

Take China as an example, there were 9.4 days in 2020 when the national average maximum daytime temperature exceeded 35 °C, 1.7 days more than the average of the past 30 years, while more than 10 days with a temperature over 35 °C were recorded each year between 2016 and 2019 (Fig. 2). In 2020, the rate of recorded extreme heat in meteorological stations was 0.22, 0.1 higher than the average, and this number even climbed to 0.38 in 2019. In terms of heavy rain, the number of days with daily rainfall equal to or greater than 50 mm recorded by national stations was 7408 and 24.1% more than normal, which ranked second most since 1961.[6]

When considering the bigger picture, it is self-evident that extreme weather events have become much more frequent, subjecting more countries and regions to its adverse impact. In February 2020, locust outbreaks threatened many African countries' food security, leaving tens of thousands of people facing starvation, and the root

---

[6] China Meteorological Administration, *China Climate Bulletin 2020*. http://zwgk.cma.gov.cn/zfx xgk/gknr/qxbg/202104/t20210406_3051288.html.

cause of the plagues was a global warming-induced powerful cyclone off Somalia that resulted in locusts' proliferation. In July 2020, the record-breaking flooding struck the plum rain belt over Japan, which triggered mudslides and resulted in heavy casualties and economic damage. In August 2020, the United States experienced extreme heat and wind storms, causing severe mountain fires. During the same period, Australian wildfires also led to serious ecological destruction and economic losses.

Transition risks are those associated with changes in policy and law, technology substitution, consumer preferences and corporate reputation that generally emerge while countries are responding to climate change and promoting the transition to a low-carbon economy (Table 1).

Physical and Transition Risks May Affect the Real Economy and the Financial System

As both physical and transition risks arising from global warming affect the income and asset values of businesses, households and governments, they will also have a bearing on banks and other financial institutions' asset values through macro and micro channels such as collateral, output and liquidity, resulting in non-performing loans or investment losses.

When physical risks subject the real economy to business disruption, capital scrapping, plant reconstruction and increase in commodity price, they will spill over to the financial system through a series of transmission mechanisms (Fig. 3).

Compared with physical risks' implications, the impact brought about by transition risks on the financial system features more uncertainties. As the world transitions toward a low-carbon economy, carbon-intensive industries will face greater transition risk, which will present transition risks to the financial system through a range of transmission mechanisms (Fig. 4).

Global Governance and National Efforts to Address Climate Change

International Conventions on Climate Change Are Evolving

At the global level, climate governance started with the United Nations Framework Convention on Climate Change (UNFCCC) in 1992, with principles such as "common but differentiated responsibilities", "coordinated efforts", "efficiency", "adaptation" and "cooperation" enshrined in it, and it thus served as the basic framework for international cooperation to combat climate change. Later, Kyoto Protocol, the first international agreement to limit greenhouse gas emissions, was adopted in 1997, requiring developed countries to reduce their greenhouse gas emissions by

Table 1 Classification of climate risks and potential financial implications

Types	Climate-related risks	Potential implications on finance
Physical risks	Acute risks	– Reduced production capacity or interrupted production (e.g., closures, transportation difficulties, supply chain disruptions) – Impact of workforce management and planning (e.g., health, safety, absenteeism) – Write-off and early retirement of existing assets (e.g., property and asset damage in high-risk areas) – Increasing operating costs (e.g., insufficient water supply for hydroelectric power plants or cooling nuclear and fossil fuel plants) – Increasing capital costs (e.g., damage to facilities) – Reducing sales revenue – Increasing insurance premiums and reducing the viability of property insurance in high-risk areas
	Increased severity of extreme weather events (e.g., hurricanes and floods)	
	Chronic risks	
	– Extreme changes of precipitation patterns and weather patterns – Rising average temperatures – Rising sea levels	
Transition risks	Policies and laws	
	– Raising the prices of greenhouse gas emissions – Enhancing emissions reporting obligations – Authorization and regulation of existing products and services – Exposure to risks	– Increased operating costs (e.g., compliance costs) – Write-off and early retirement of existing assets due to policy changes – Damage to assets – Increasing insurance premiums – Fines and judgments

(continued)

Table 1 (continued)

Types	Climate-related risks	Potential implications on finance
	Technology	
	– Replacement of existing products and services by equivalents with lower emissions – Failed investments in new technologies – Early-stage costs of the transition to lower-emission technologies	– Write-off and early retirement of existing assets – Reducing demands for products and services – Early-stage research and development (R&D) expenditures for new and alternative technologies – Early-stage capital investment in technology development – Early-stage costs for adoption/deployment of new practices and processes
	Market	
	– Changing customer behavior – Uncertainty of market signals – Rising raw material costs	– Reduced demands for goods and services due to the shifting of consumer preferences – Raising production costs because of changes in input prices (e.g., energy, water) and output requirements (e.g., waste disposal) – Sudden and unanticipated changes in energy costs – Changes in revenue mix and sources – Asset repricing and the speed of repricing (e.g., fossil fuel reserves, land valuation, securities valuation)
	Reputation	
	– The shifting of consumer preferences – Discrimination in the industry – Increasing attention to stakeholders or feedback about negative stakeholders	– Reduced demands for goods/services – Reduced production capacity or interrupted production (e.g., closures, delays in planning and approvals, supply chain disruptions) – The impact of management and planning on the workforce (e.g., attractiveness to employees and employee retention) – Reduced capital availability

Data Source TCFD (2016)

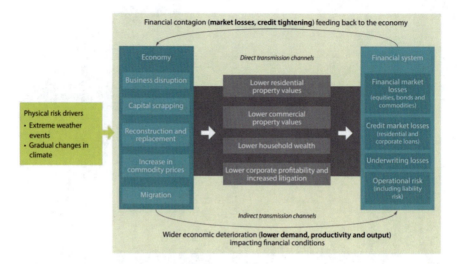

Fig. 3 From physical risks to financial stability risks. *Data Source* A call for action Climate change as a source of financial risk, April 2019, NGFS

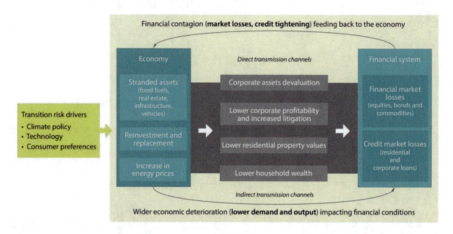

Fig. 4 From transition risk to financial stability risk. *Data Source* A call for action Climate change as a source of financial risk, April 2019, NGFS

5.2% compared with 1990 the level by 2010, and introducing three market-based flexible mechanisms to honor the protocol and encourage cooperation among countries for decarbonization, including Joint Implementation (JI), Clean Development Mechanism (CDM) and Emission Trading (ET). The Bali Road Map in 2007 called for the full, effective and sustained implementation of the UN Framework Convention on Climate Change (UNFCCC) as well as attention given to climate finance related issues. The Copenhagen Accord in 2009 stated that global warming should be limited to below 2.0°C, and specified a quantified and predictable climate finance mechanism. Moreover, the Cancun Agreements in 2010 proposed the establishment of a Green Climate Fund.

The adoption of the Paris Agreement in December 2015 and the Implementation Guidelines for the Paris Agreement in 2018 marked a new phase in global climate governance. The Paris Agreement put forward a more ambitious goal of "holding global warming below 1.5 °C" instead of the previous 2 °C goal, established a global climate change governance system based on "Nationally Determined Contributions", combined "bottom-up" target-setting and "top-down" accounting, transparency and compliance rules, and introduced a new mechanism with a "global stocktake as the core on a five-year cycle" (starting in 2023). It stressed the importance of finance and made "finance flows consistent with a pathway toward low greenhouse gas emissions and climate-resilient development" as one of the three major objectives for addressing climate change, alongside mitigation and adaptation.

Major Countries Have Announced "Carbon Peak" and "Carbon Neutrality" Goals

Currently, 54 countries' carbon emissions have peaked, and among the world, top 15 emitters of carbon dioxide in 2020, the United States, Russia, Japan, Brazil, Indonesia, Germany, Canada, South Korea, the United Kingdom and France have all peaked their carbon emissions. In September 2020, Chinese President Xi Jinping stated at the General Debate of the 75th Session of the United Nations General Assembly that "China aims to have CO_2 emissions peak before 2030 and achieve carbon neutrality before 2060".

In terms of carbon neutrality targets and actions, 126 countries have set carbon neutrality targets, accounting for about 51% of total global carbon emissions. Most European countries have been active in leading the global process of achieving carbon neutrality, such as Iceland, which now boasts carbon-free electricity and heating, and Austria, which is set to achieve 100% clean electricity by 2030. Many European countries' carbon neutrality targets are legally binding, such as France, Germany, the UK, Denmark and Spain, which are obliged by law to achieve carbon neutrality by 2050. At the same time, the European Climate Law sets a legally binding goal of net zero greenhouse gas emissions by 2050. Compared with European countries, Asian countries mostly declare semi-mandatory policies, such as South Korea and Japan, which plan to be carbon neutral by 2050 as stated in their policies. The Americas, on the other hand, have much fewer responses to such targets, and their goals are meant to be achieved in a semi-mandatory and voluntary manner (Fig. 5).

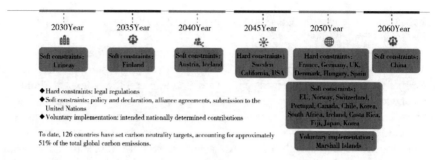

Fig. 5 Carbon neutrality targets of major countries

Big Emitters Such as China, Russia and the United States Must Shoulder Their Responsibility as Major Countries in Global Climate Governance

China, the United States and Russia, as the world's first, second and fourth largest carbon emitters, respectively, and the main leaders of international climate governance under the UN framework, have all put forward their own targets for tackling climate change and taken a series of concrete actions.

"Common but Differentiated Responsibilities" of China, the United States and Russia

Considering that developed countries such as the United States and European countries created most of the planet's cumulative carbon emissions during the period of rapid industrialization and urbanization, the principle of "common but differentiated responsibilities" for both developed and developing countries was established in the United Nations Framework Convention on Climate Change, stipulating that developed countries should take the lead in cutting emissions. After that, in line with such a principle, the Kyoto Protocol required developed countries to take specific measures to limit greenhouse gas emissions, while developing countries, in accordance with the accord, were only obligated to provide national inventories of greenhouse gas sources and sinks, without undertaking legally binding greenhouse gas reduction obligations. At the same time, the Kyoto Protocol also required developed contracting parties to provide necessary financing and technical assistance to developing countries to support them in reducing GHG emissions.[7] The following Paris Agreement decided to include climate finance as the third major goal in addressing climate change, and proposed that developed countries should mobilize at least US$

---

[7] Kyoto Protocol.

Table 2 Carbon dioxide emissions of major global carbon emitters and their share of the global total (%)

Country	Carbon emissions in 2019 (one hundred million tons)	Carbon emissions in 2005 (one hundred million tons)	Share of the global total in 2019 (%)	Change in the country's carbon emissions from 2005 to 2019 (%)
China	116	63.2	30.52	83.5
The US	51.1	59.5	13.45	−14.1
India	26.0	12.2	6.84	113.1
Russia	17.9	17.3	4.71	−3.5
Japan	11.5	12.8	3.03	−10.2
Iran	7.0	4.7	1.84	48.9
Germany	7.0	8.4	1.84	−16.7
South Korea	6.5	5.2	1.71	25.0
Indonesia	6.3	3.6	1.66	75.0
Saudi Arabia	6.1	3.4	1.61	79.4
Canada	5.8	5.8	1.53	0.0

Data Source Trends in Global CO_2 and total greenhouse gas emissions: 2020 Report (The Hague: PBL Netherlands Environmental Assessment Agency; Ispra: Joint Research Centre), p. 66, https://www.pbl.nl/sites/default/files/downloads/pbl-2020-trends-in-global-co2-and_total-greenhouse-gas-emissions-2020-report_4331.pdf

100 billion in climate finance to support developing countries each year after 2020, and the number will continue to rise with new amount to be determined by 2025.

Since the Kyoto Protocol came into force in 1997, developed countries such as the United States have significantly reduced their emissions and thus peaked their emissions one after another, driven out of the slowdown of industrialization and urbanization on the one hand and more carbon emission reduction policies and actions on the other hand. China, as a newcomer with rapid industrialization and urbanization, has replaced the United States as the world's largest carbon emitter since 2005, with its carbon emissions increasing from 6.32 to 11.6 billion tons in 2019.[8] Meanwhile, Russia has become the fourth largest carbon emitter. The US, as the largest contributor to cumulative carbon emissions, and China and Russia, as current top emitters, must play an important role in global climate governance as responsible major countries, complying with the principle of "common but differentiated responsibilities" (Table 2).

---

[8] Trends in Global CO_2 and total greenhouse gas emissions: 2020 Report (The Hague: PBL Netherlands Environmental Assessment Agency; Ispra: Joint Research Centre), p. 66. https://www.pbl.nl/sites/default/files/downloads/pbl-2020-trends-in-global-co2-and_total-greenhouse-gas-emissions-2020-report_4331.pdf.

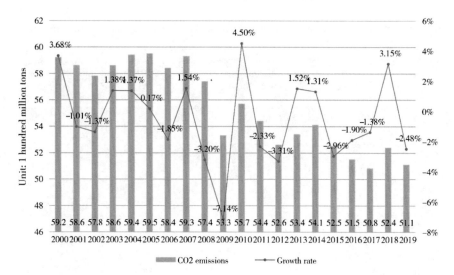

Fig. 6 The US CO$_2$ emissions and trends (2010–2019). *Data Source* Trends in Global CO$_2$ and total greenhouse gas emissions: 2020 Report (The Hague: PBL Netherlands Environmental Assessment Agency; Ispra: Joint Research Centre), p. 66. https://www.pbl.nl/sites/default/files/downloads/pbl-2020-trends-in-global-co2-and_total-greenhouse-gas-emissions-2020-report_4331.pdf

The United States is Historically a Big Emitter of Carbon Emissions

Although the US carbon emissions have fallen year by year in recent years, and its share of carbon emissions in the world has declined from 23% in 2000 to 13.45% in 2019, it still stands as the world's largest emitter in terms of cumulative emissions and should thus bear the main responsibility in global governance so as to address climate change.[9] According to our world in data, before the nineteenth century, virtually all global carbon emissions came from the industrialized European countries, while the United States overtook them and its growth of carbon emissions was relatively fast for more than 200 years since its founding in 1776, with its share of the global total rising from zero to nearly 40% in a period of 150 years from 1800 to 1950.[10] Moreover, the US also has the highest carbon emissions per capita, producing 13.45% of the world's total carbon dioxide emissions in 2019 with about 4.5% of the world's population, reaching 15.5 tons of carbon emissions per capita (Fig. 6).

---

[9] Trends in Global CO$_2$ and total greenhouse gas emissions: 2020 Report (The Hague: PBL Netherlands Environmental Assessment Agency; Ispra: Joint Research Centre), p. 66. https://www.pbl.nl/sites/default/files/downloads/pbl-2020-trends-in-global-co2-and_total-greenhouse-gas-emissions-2020-report_4331.pdf.

[10] Our World in Data, https://ourworldindata.org.

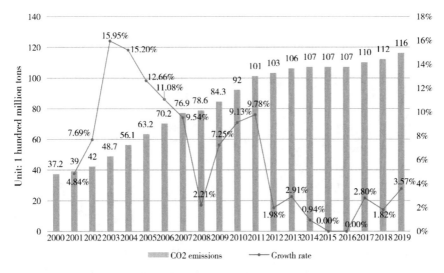

Fig. 7 China's CO_2 emissions and trends (2000–2019). *Data Source* Trends in Global CO_2 and total greenhouse gas emissions: 2020 Report (The Hague: PBL Netherlands Environmental Assessment Agency; Ispra: Joint Research Centre), p. 66. https://www.pbl.nl/sites/default/files/downloads/pbl-2020-trends-in-global-co2-and_total-greenhouse-gas-emissions-2020-report_4331.pdf

China and Russia Are the Current Major Carbon Emitters

Since the twenty-first century, as China makes strides in its industrialization and urbanization endeavors, this emerging country's carbon emissions have been on the rise during the past 20 years, especially during the decade of 2000–2010 when the year-on-year increase of carbon dioxide emissions stood mostly at about 10%. China's carbon dioxide emissions have more than tripled from 3.72 billion tons in 2000 to 11.6 billion tons in 2019, and its share of carbon emissions has increased from 14.47% in 2000 to 30.52% in 2019.[11] Despite the fact that China represents the world's largest carbon emitter now, the growth of its carbon emissions has started to slow down in recent years, with the annual growth standing at below 3% during 2012–2019 (Fig. 7).

As one of the world's largest producers and exporters of hydrocarbons, Russia's energy-related carbon emissions account for a significant share of the global total and are a major source of world CO_2 emissions. Russia's total CO_2 emissions amounted to 1.68 billion tons in 2000, peaked at 1.82 billion tons in 2011, and then started to fall until the year 2016. But its emissions started to grow again in 2017, and totaled 1.81 tons in 2018, second only to the 2011 level. Russia had been the third largest carbon emitter in the world before India surpassed it in 2009. Now, with 1.79 billion tons

---

[11] Trends in Global CO_2 and total greenhouse gas emissions: 2020 Report (The Hague: PBL Netherlands Environmental Assessment Agency; Ispra: Joint Research Centre), p. 66. https://www.pbl.nl/sites/default/files/downloads/pbl-2020-trends-in-global-co2-and_total-greenhouse-gas-emissions-2020-report_4331.pdf.

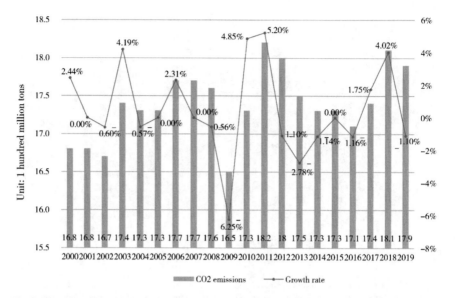

Fig. 8 Russia's CO_2 emissions and trends (2000–2019). *Data Source* Trends in Global CO_2 and total greenhouse gas emissions: 2020 Report (The Hague: PBL Netherlands Environmental Assessment Agency; Ispra: Joint ResearchCentre), p. 66. https://www.pbl.nl/sites/default/files/downloads/pbl-2020-trends-in-global-co2-and_total-greenhouse-gas-emissions-2020-report_4331.pdf

of emissions, Russia accounts for about 4.71% of the global total, ranked only after China, the US and India (Fig. 8).[12]

Policies and Actions of China, Russia, and the United States to Address Climate Change

China, the United States and Russia, as the world's first, second and fourth largest carbon emitters, respectively, and the main leaders of international climate governance under the UN framework, have all put forward their own targets for tackling climate change and taken a series of specific actions.

China's Policies and Actions to Address Climate Change

The Chinese government has always attached great importance to climate change and has put in place a series of policies and plans, as a way of responding to the

---

[12] Trends in Global CO_2 and total greenhouse gas emissions: 2020 Report (The Hague: PBL Netherlands Environmental Assessment Agency; Ispra: Joint Research Centre), p. 66. https://www.pbl.nl/sites/default/files/downloads/pbl-2020-trends-in-global-co2-and_total-greenhouse-gas-emissions-2020-report_4331.pdf.

needs of economic and social development at various stages and shouldering the responsibility of tackling climate change as a major country. During the "Eleventh Five-Year Plan" period, China issued the National Climate Change Program in 2007, including policies with the goal of "lowering energy intensity per unit of GDP by 20% in 2010 compared to that of 2005" so as to mitigate CO_2 emissions.[13] A number of policies have been announced in the 12th Five-Year Plan period, and in 2011, a white paper titled China's Policies and Actions for Addressing Climate Change (2011) was published, stipulating that "by 2015, energy consumption per unit of GDP will be reduced by 16% and carbon dioxide emissions per unit of GDP is set to be slashed by 17% on the basis of 2010".[14] Thereafter, in September 2014, the State Council approved China's National Plan on Climate Change (2014–2020), clearly setting out China's timeline and roadmap for addressing climate change: China is set to lower CO_2 emissions per unit of GDP by 40%–45% by 2020 compared to the 2005 level, while increasing forest stock volume to 40 million hectares and 1.3 billion m^3.[15] "In the 13th Five-Year Plan period, China worked harder on climate change with stricter polices and more ambitious low-carbon targets so that compared with the 2015 level, its energy consumption per unit of GDP would be reduced by 15%, CO_2 emissions per unit of GDP would be reduced by 18%, and non-fossil energy sources would account for 15% of primary energy consumption in the year 2020.[16]

Since September 2020, Chinese President Xi Jinping has announced China's carbon peak and carbon neutrality targets at several international conferences: China aims to have CO_2 emissions peak before 2030 and achieve carbon neutrality before 2060. For this to happen, China has to make sure that by 2030, its carbon dioxide emissions per unit of GDP drop by more than 65% compared with the 2005 level, the share of non-fossil energy in total consumption of primary energy rises to about 25%, and the total installed capacity of wind and solar power reaches more than 1.2 billion kW.[17] In the "14th Five-Year Plan" period, its energy consumption per unit of GDP and carbon dioxide emissions per unit of GDP will be set to fall by 13.5% and 18%, respectively; the installed generating capacity from renewable power will account for over half of China's total, renewable energy will account for about 2/3 of the increase in electricity consumption of the whole society, and renewable energy will take up over 50% of the increase in the primary energy consumption.[18] In addition, the National Strategy for Climate Change Adaptation 2035 formulated by the

---

[13] The full text of China's National Climate Change Program. http://www.gov.cn/gzdt/2007-06/04/content_635590.htm.

[14] China.s Policies and Actions for Addressing Climate Change (2011), http://www.scio.gov.cn/tt/Document/1052047/1052047_7.htm.

[15] China's National Plan on Climate Change (2014–2020), p. 5.

[16] Outline of the 13th Five-Year Plan for National Economic and Social Development of the People's Republic of China, Chap. 3, http://www.gov.cn/xinwen/2016-03/17/content_5054992.htm.

[17] Building on Past Achievements and Launching a New Journey for Global Climate Actions, http://www.chinapower.com.cn/xw/zyxw/20201222/38955.html.

[18] The Outline of the 14th Five-Year Plan (2021–2025) for National Economic and Social Development and Vision 2035 of the People's Republic of China, Chap. 3, http://www.gov.cn/xinwen/2021-03/13/content_5592681.html.

Chinese government was approved on February 18, 2022, and the National Measures for the Administration of Carbon Emission Trading (Trial) has been implemented since February 1, 2021.

On October 24, 2021, the Chinese government released the "Working Guidance For Carbon Dioxide Peaking And Carbon Neutrality In Full And Faithful Implementation Of The New Development Philosophy", in which it proposed three stages of achieving low-carbon targets in the future: First, by 2025, China will have created an initial framework for a green, low-carbon and circular economy. Its energy consumption per unit of GDP will be reduced by 13.5% from the 2020 level, carbon dioxide emissions per unit of GDP will be lowered by 18% from the 2020 level, the share of non-fossil energy consumption in the total will have reached around 20%, the forest coverage rate will have reached 24.1% and the forest stock volume will have risen to 18 billion cubic meters, all laying a solid foundation for carbon dioxide peaking and carbon neutrality. Secondly, by 2030, China will have made major headway in the comprehensive green transformation of the social and economic development, with energy consumption per unit of GDP will have declined significantly, carbon dioxide emissions per unit of GDP will have dropped by more than 65% compared with the 2005 level, and the share of non-fossil fuel consumption will have reached around 25%. Moreover, the total installed capacity of wind power and solar power will have amounted to more than 1.2 billion kW, the forest coverage rate will have reached about 25% and the forest stock volume will have totaled 19 billion cubic meters. As a result, carbon dioxide emissions will reach a peak, remain stable and then gradually decline. Finally, by 2060, China will have fully established a green, low-carbon and circular economy and a clean, low-carbon, safe and efficient energy system. Its energy efficiency will be at the advanced international level, the share of non-fossil fuel consumption will be over 80% and its goal of carbon neutrality will be achieved.[19]

Russia's Policies and Actions to Address Climate Change

After the collapse of the Soviet Union, Russia's carbon emissions are at a relatively lower and slower rate. However, as one of the world's leading producers and exporters of oil and natural gas, Russia has been weighing the impact of climate change on its own for a long time amid global efforts in cutting emissions. First, the low-carbon energy transition in response to climate change will seriously impede Russia's oil and gas production and export; second, Russia is home to rich forest resources, which can absorb a large amount of carbon dioxide and reduce considerable carbon emissions, and these forests have great potential to be tapped as carbon sinks. In addition, since Russia is located at high northern latitudes, the overall ecological impact of global warming on it is not significant, and as the planet gets

---

[19] Working Guidance for Carbon Dioxide Peaking and Carbon Neutrality in Full and Faithful Implementation of the New Development Philosophy jointly released by the CPC Central Committee and the State Council. http://www.qstheory.cn/yaowen/2021-10/24/c_1127990704.htm.

warmer, some of Russia's permafrost regions will become more suitable for living and land development, which, to a certain extent, means that Arctic Sea lanes will be more frequently used. Hence, Moscow in general has paid relatively little attention to climate change and has not yet taken substantive actions in recent years.

However, as the climate crisis continues to worsen, Russia is becoming aware of the potential implications of a warming planet on its economy, society, politics and diplomacy and has gradually attached more importance to climate change with a more positive attitude.

In 2009, led by President Dmitry Medvedev, the federal government approved the "Climate Doctrine of the Russian Federation", which set out Russia's position on climate change and proposed climate-related goals and measures. Subsequently, in order to implement the Doctrine, President Vladimir Putin signed a presidential decree in 2013 to ensure that the country's greenhouse gas emissions would be reduced to no more than 75% of the 1990 level by 2020. At the 2015 Paris Climate Conference, Russia further raised its emission reduction standards and stated that it would cut its CO_2 emissions by 30% by 2030 compared with the 1990 level, higher than the 25% target previously agreed on by most sectors in Russia. Furthermore, the Russian government has pledged to reduce energy consumption per unit of GDP by 25% and electricity consumption per unit of GDP by 12% by 2025. In recent years, Russia has been working to play a prominent role as a major country in global climate governance. In November 2020, President Vladimir Putin signed another presidential decree to ensure that Russia's greenhouse gas emissions will be reduced to 70% of the 1990 level by 2030 and adopted the Strategy for the Socio-Economic Development of the Russian Federation with a low level of greenhouse gas emissions until 2050. This strategy, as the guiding policy in Russia's response to climate change, requires the world's fourth largest emitter to cut its greenhouse emissions by 60% compared with the 2019 level and 80% compared with the 1990 level by 2050, and achieves carbon neutrality by 2060.[20]

The US Policies and Actions to Address Climate Change

The US government started to focus on climate issues earlier than many other countries, but has repeatedly backtracked on its policies. As early as the Bill Clinton administration, the US announced a national emission cut target to gradually lower greenhouse gases to the 1990 level by 2000.[21] However, when George Bush took office, the US government took a negative attitude toward climate change and even withdrew from the Kyoto Protocol in 2001. In 2009, Barack Obama entered the White House and he stood for a stronger response to climate change. As a result, in 2013, President Obama's Climate Action Plan was launched, which stood out as the most

---

[20] Russia unveiled its low-carbon development strategy by 2050. Xinhuanet, http://www.xinhuanet.com/energy/20211103/f607e3e5de974e9bbe5fd6129a4b7abd/c.html.

[21] Remarks on Earth Day, https://www.govinfo.gov/content/pkg/WCPD-1993-04-26/pdf/WCPD-1993-04-26-Pg630.pdf.

comprehensive domestic action plan to address climate change in the United States at that time. Internationally, the US actively participated in global climate governance, provided climate finance to developing countries and took the lead in ratifying and promoting the implementation of the Paris Agreement. However, after Obama left office, the Donald Trump administration continued the Bush administration's policy, doubting the authenticity and science of climate change, and eventually pulling the US out of the Paris Agreement in June 2020.

Contrary to Trump's negative attitude toward climate change, the Joe Biden administration again made climate change one of its top priorities with the fundamental goal of "America First", and put in place a series of concrete measures to strengthen its leadership on climate issues.

First, the Biden administration has given priority to climate change. When serving as the vice president, Biden was already one of the major advocates of the Paris Agreement and has been critical of Trump's withdrawal decision. During his presidential campaign in July 2020, the Biden team unveiled a $2 trillion climate plan, in a bid to build up America's clean energy infrastructure, reduce its dependence on fossil fuels and achieve carbon-free power generation by 2035. When he took office in January 2021, Biden signed an executive order announcing that the US would rejoin the Paris Agreement and the "Keystone XL" oil pipeline project between the United States and Canada would be canceled. This was followed by a series of executive orders on climate change-related issues, as a way of increasing investment in clean energy, pushing for the shift to zero-emission vehicles for both federal and state governments, suspending the issuing of oil and gas leasing permits on federal lands and waters, as well as phasing out federal subsidies for fossil fuels. In March 2021, the Biden administration unveiled the US Economic Recovery Plan, with great emphasis on climate change-related issues. Such measures have fully demonstrated that the Biden administration has placed the response to climate change at the core of its foreign policy and national security.

Second, the Biden administration has set up organizations and a core working team dedicated to climate governance. In January 2021, Biden signed a presidential executive order on climate change, making clear that the federal government must give priority to the climate crisis, and established a coordination mechanism for cooperation among various federal executive departments as part of its efforts to address climate change. A first-ever US National Climate Task Force was created, headed by former EPA (Environmental Protection Agency) Administrator Gina McCarthy, serving the purpose of coordinating different departments' reactions to the crisis. At the same time, in order to implement its climate policies, Biden appointed John Kerry as the Special Presidential Envoy for Climate, in the hope that his extensive experience in diplomatic negotiation would help the US regain its leadership on the world stage of climate governance; he appointed Michael Reagan as the EPA Administrator, hoping that he, with rich experience in environment improvement in government, the businesses circle and non-governmental organizations, could help the US government better deal with challenges brought about by climate change; he appointed Jennifer Granholm, a strong advocate of clean energy, as the Secretary of Energy, who would work to promote the shift toward a low-carbon energy system; he also appointed Pete Buttigieg as the Secretary of Transportation, who was expected to leverage his innovative practices in urban management and make transportation a low-carbon sector which is now the largest carbon emitter in the US. Last but not the least, in the American Rescue Plan released in March 2021, a new National Laboratory for Climate was proposed and $50 billion would be provided for the National Science Foundation.

Third, the Biden administration has been actively engaged in "climate diplomacy". While paying great attention to climate issues domestically, the Biden administration has also been active to promote "climate diplomacy" internationally. For example, on March 23, 2021, Kerry attended the Fifth Ministerial Conference on Climate Action co-hosted by China, the European Union and Canada, which marked the return of the United States to the negotiating table on climate-related matters. Kerry also participated in a climate dialog for the Middle East and North Africa in April 2021. In March 2021, China–US high-level strategic dialog in anchorage announced the establishment of a joint working group on climate change. Whenever attending the EU summits, Biden speaks about addressing climate change repeatedly, which serves as a means of drawing more allies over to its side and reflects the need to strengthen its leadership on climate issues. In April 2021, Global Climate Summit was held and attended by leaders from China, the US and Russia, as well as the President of the European Commission and the President of the European Council, during which the US announced its emission reduction targets by 2030 and made it the "Nationally Determined Contribution (NDC)" under the Paris Agreement. In order to renew its leadership in global climate governance, the Biden administration has attached more importance to "climate diplomacy" since taking office.

Cooperation Among China, Russia and the United States in Global Climate Governance and Low-Carbon Green Growth

As permanent members of the UN Security Council, China, Russia and the United States have a strong voice and leadership in the global governance of climate change and are the main leaders and representatives of the international community in addressing climate change under the UN framework.

First, as the United States reentered the Paris Agreement, the international agenda to address climate change under the UN framework would be restarted with substantive progress in sight. As three major carbon emitters, China, the US and Russia combined account for more than one-third of the global total, which means that the attitudes and actions of the three countries will, to a large extent, determine the success or failure of the international community's joint efforts to cope with climate change. There are salient differences in the UN Framework Convention on climate change regarding the responsibilities and contribution requirements for global countries in addressing climate change, and such differences have a direct bearing on these countries' economic costs while reducing carbon emissions and their corresponding contributions. In this sense, China, the United States, Russia and other major countries all aspire to gain an important voice in the relevant rule-making process and play a significant role in global climate governance, so as to maximize their own interests and minimize their risks and losses.

Second, combating climate change does not simply mean seeking solutions to climate and environmental problems, but rather a long-term global competition heralding a new era in the international economic and political landscape. The approach to climate change will be ultimately boiled down to specific key areas of carbon emission reductions: clean energy, green transportation, low-carbon green buildings, green manufacturing, green consumption and low-carbon lifestyle. Such transitions will give rise to new low-carbon green technologies, products, services, supply chains and trade. Propelled by such changes with the support of green finance, the future will witness a holistic transformation from a traditional economy to a new low-carbon green economy globally.

Different from the traditional economy, all countries are about on the same starting line when it comes to the low-carbon green growth. And countries that traditionally lagged behind might have the chance to leap ahead in developing the new low-carbon green economy. As the trends toward low-carbon economic development continue, the economic competitiveness and overall economic strength of countries will undergo great changes, which will spill over to the geopolitical dimension and then reshape the international political landscape. Taking Russia as an example, the immediate consequence of a global fight against climate change is reduced production and consumption of fossil fuels. This will seriously affect the oil and gas export revenues and fiscal revenues of Russia as a big exporter of oil and gas, weakening Russia's economic and overall national strength and thus directly undermining the weight of "oil and gas resources" in geopolitics. As a result of the above-mentioned factors, Russia's international status and influence may further decline in the future, changing the international political landscape in a profound manner.

Third, in the short term, the COVID-19 pandemic is expected to increase the willingness and speed of global economic transformation to a low-carbon green future as well as accelerate the rearrangement of global economic and political landscapes. The pandemic hits traditional developed countries hard, which reported negative growth in 2020. China is the only country that registered positive growth, showing that the economic gap between China and developed countries such as the United States and European countries has narrowed and the international economic landscape has been experiencing faster changes. In addition, before the pandemic broke out and after that, China has been working steadily to transform its economy toward a low-carbon and green form in various fields, and the rapid and stable growth of China's economy is driven to some extent by low-carbon green technology, low-carbon green products and services, low-carbon green production and low-carbon green consumption. China is now capable of competing with other major players in the international arena in clean energy such as photovoltaic and wind power, in green transportation such as electric vehicles and high-speed railroads and in fields of building-integrated photovoltaics, energy-efficient buildings and green buildings. China and the US, one emerging country that has benefited greatly from the low-carbon economy and the other developed country benefiting from the traditional economy, will have to cooperate and compete with each other in their efforts to seize more opportunities for growth in low-carbon and green field.

Global climate change governance is not only a process for China, Russia and the United States to seek common ground while shelving differences and compete for more gains, but also an opportunity for global cooperation to keep global warming below 1.5 °C, for green economic recovery and for long-term low-carbon sustainable growth after the COVID-19 pandemic. China, Russia and the United States shall shoulder their responsibilities commensurate with their status as major countries, by seeking common ground, exploring new fields where win–win cooperation can be achieved, and playing a leading role in global climate governance and low-carbon green economy. Specifically, the three major carbon emitters, namely China, Russia and the US, can strengthen cooperation in three main areas: improving global climate governance, promoting the transition to green and low-carbon energy sources, as well as increasing green finance to provide financial support for climate governance and low-carbon economic transition.

Improving Global Climate Governance

China and Russia have already carried out extensive cooperation to fight climate change. As early as the twentieth century, the two countries launched a series of projects for cooperation on technologies and services such as meteorological monitoring and meteorological satellites. In 1993, the two countries signed a Memorandum of Understanding on China–Russia Cooperation in Meteorological Science and Technology and set up a national liaison group dedicated to development and climate change with annual meetings held, which paved the way for deeper cooperation between the two countries on climate.

In recent years, since China and Russia paid more attention to climate and environmental issues and elevated their bilateral relations, their cooperation on climate issues has become deeper and gradually moved from policy adoption to implementation. In September 2017, the China–Russia Joint Research Center on Oceans and Climate was founded in Vladivostok, Russia, aiming at establishing a new platform and mechanism for maritime cooperation between the two countries, and strengthening the capacity to address climate risks through joint research by scientists from both countries.[22] Subsequently, the two countries signed the Joint Statement of the People's Republic of China and the Russian Federation on the Development of a Comprehensive Strategic Partnership of Coordination for the New Era (hereinafter referred to as the Statement) when the 70th anniversary of the establishment of diplomatic relations between China and Russia arrived in 2019. The statement announced that the two countries will strengthen cooperation to deal with global environmental

---

[22] China Daily, http://cn.chinadaily.com.cn/2017-09/28/content_32599007.htm.

issues such as climate change and biodiversity.[23] Later, in June 2021, the China–Russia Joint Statement on the 20th anniversary of the signing of the China–Russia Treaty of Good-Neighborliness and Friendly Cooperation again made mention of climate change-related issues, stating that the two countries would further enhance ecological and environmental collaboration, as well as expand exchanges and cooperation for combating climate change within the framework of the United Nations, BRICS and the Shanghai Cooperation Organization.[24]

Both China–US and Russia–US cooperation on climate issues are mainly multilateral under the framework of the UN. At the 2015 Paris Climate Conference, China and the US took the lead in ratifying the Paris Agreement on the same day, setting an example to the international community and demonstrating a consistent attitude of the two countries on climate change. Subsequently, in March 2021, the China–US anchorage talks announced the establishment of a joint working group to address climate change; and on April 22, American President Biden hosted the Leaders Summit on Climate with leaders from China, Russia and other major carbon emitting countries invited. At the summit, Chinese President Xi Jinping delivered a speech, stating that China is willing to work with the US to make its due contribution and then Russian President Putin also made remarks that Russia stands ready to implement international initiatives while actively participating in the research and development of low-carbon technologies.

As leading players in global climate governance, there are both cooperation and competition between China, the United States and Russia. On April 13, 2021, the US Intelligence Community released the *2021 Annual Threat Assessment*, considering both China and Russia as threats and concluding that China stands as a "peer competitor" of the United States in many areas including climate change, and its multi-faceted cooperation with Russia.[25] Recently, developed countries such as the US and the EU have on many occasions opposed the principle of "common but differentiated responsibilities" and require China to bear the same responsibility for carbon emission reduction as developed countries. China and Russia have similar positions on this note: Compared with the United States and European countries, which are among the largest emitters that have already finished their industrialization, China, as the biggest developing country, is still experiencing rapid industrialization and urbanization and its carbon emissions have thus been on the rise. Considering this, China's decision to prioritize carbon emission intensity and energy intensity in its response to climate change during the 14th Five-Year Plan period is made in light of China's realities. Russia's situation is not looking any better, because as a big producer and exporter of oil and gas, energy-related emissions account for a large

---

[23] Joint Statement of the People's Republic of China and the Russian Federation on the Development of a Comprehensive Strategic Partnership of Coordination for the New Era (full text), http://www.gov.cn/xinwen/2019-06/06/content_5397865.htm.

[24] The China-Russia Joint Statement on the 20th Anniversary of the Signing of the China-Russia Treaty of Good-Neighborliness and Friendly Cooperation (Full text) http://www.gov.cn/xinwen/2021-06/28/content_5621323.htm

[25] 2021 Annual Threat Assessment of the US Intelligence Community. pdf. April 9, 2021.

chunk of its total. Taking its energy endowment and industrial structure into consideration, there is good reason for Russia to tailor its emission reduction arrangements according to specific national conditions. As a result, cooperation and competition coexist between China and the US as well as between Russia and the US in the struggle to increase their voice and rule-making power in global climate governance.

Promote the Transition to Green, Low-Carbon Energy Sources

Since 2014, the global energy landscape has undergone a qualitative change amid global efforts in fighting climate change and the significant increase in US shale oil production.

First, the world has begun to enter a buyer's market in the oil and gas industry featuring potential oversupply in the long run. During nearly 40 years after the three oil crises in the Middle East started in the 1970s, the global oil and gas market were chronically over-demanded. Since the second half of 2021, international oil prices climbed higher as OPEC countries reduced their output, the world economy was expected to recover with increased vaccination coverage, and China and many countries in Europe experienced energy shortages, coupled with the current Russia–Ukraine conflict. However, the international oil and gas market has started to see changes since 2014, and now, it has been transformed into a buyer's market of oversupply, which will remain unchanged for a long time due to the following reasons: First, the US shale oil and gas production has increased substantially in the past decade or so, and currently more than 50% of all the increase in global crude oil production comes from the US; second, as the international community works to fight climate change, countries have worked fast to replace fossil fuels by clean energy, significantly reducing global oil and gas demand; third, propelled by technological progress, energy efficiency has continued to increase, leading to much less demand for oil and gas.

Second, as the world responds to climate change, the transition to low-carbon energy sources has been accelerated. Since energy-related carbon emissions account for more than 60% of the global total, it is imperative that countries speed up the transition to low-carbon energy sources and most countries around the world have set their own goals for clean energy development in this regard. It is predicted in the World and China Energy Outlook 2060 of the CNPC Economics and Technology Research Institute that by 2060, non-fossil fuels will account for 74.3% of the energy mix and 58.6% of global primary energy will come from non-water renewables.[26] Renewable energy will gradually replace fossil fuels as the dominant energy source for social and economic development.

These two fundamental changes in the global energy landscape will have far-reaching implications, reshaping global energy politics and directly affecting the

---

[26] World and China Energy Outlook 2060 (2021 version), CNPC Economics and Technology Research Institute, http://seatone.net.cn/uploads/tan/372.pdf.

energy interests and status of the three major energy countries: China, the United States and Russia.

On the one hand, in the traditional oil and gas industry, since the world entered a long-term buyer's market, China, as one of the world's largest oil and gas importers, might be gradually transformed from a previous weak position at the negotiation table to a strong buyer. Russia, on the contrary, as one of the world's largest oil and gas exporters, will consider more about how to find stable and reliable partners for its oil and gas exports, which might gradually turn Russia from a strong seller to a weak seller. The United States, with a massive increase in its shale oil and gas production, will change its status from one of the world's largest oil and gas importers previously to one of the world's largest oil and gas producers, and may even become one of the world's largest oil and gas exporters in the near future, which will have to find major importers for its massive increase in shale oil and gas production. In this sense, the US and Russia, as two major oil and gas producers, might try to reach China for oil and gas cooperation in an oversupplied buyer's market.

On the other hand, in the clean energy industry, with more than ten years of continuous growth, China has topped the world in terms of photovoltaic and wind power's research and development, production, sales and applications, as well as ranked first globally in multiple segmented markets of the new energy industry. The rapid development of China's power generation application market has served to wean China off its heavy reliance on the US and European markets in the photovoltaic, wind power and other renewable energy manufacturing industries. China has also shifted its focus of exporting photovoltaic and wind power products to the Asia–Pacific and African countries, with such products gaining great popularity in these markets. As for the US, during the Trump administration, its policies regarding climate change and transition to low-carbon energy sources regressed. As a result, it lost its first-mover advantages and was overtaken by China in new energy fields. Russia, with its abundant oil and gas resources, has been slow to restructure its economy with heavy dependence on oil and gas exports, has done little to promote its transition to a low-carbon economy, and as a result, few progress in developing the new energy industry has been seen yet. Comparatively speaking, China is placed, to a certain degree, in a favorable position to export to Russia and the US in the fields of renewable energy technologies' research and development, product manufacturing and power generation application.

Promoting the transition to low-carbon energy sources and vigorously developing clean energy instead of traditional fossil fuels are crucial to all countries' climate action. On this note, energy cooperation between China and Russia is complementary, and their cooperation in the fields of nuclear power, wind power, hydropower and photovoltaics has thus been steadily increasing in recent years. In terms of hydropower cooperation, large hydropower enterprises of the two countries have signed a number of agreements to develop such resources in the Russian Far East and Siberia; in the field of wind power, in 2017, China and Russia worked together to build the first large-scale wind farm in Russia, namely the Ulyanovsk Wind Farm; as for photovoltaic cooperation, although Russia is a late starter in photovoltaic power generation, China is still gradually participating in the construction of Russian photo-voltaic power plants, such as the 75 MW photovoltaic power plant in Samara Oblast in southwest Russia; speaking of nuclear power, in May 2021, Chinese President Xi Jinping and his Russian counterpart Vladimir Putin witnessed the groundbreaking ceremony of the largest nuclear energy cooperation project, Tianwan nuclear power plant and Xudapu nuclear power plant. When completed and put into operation, the annual power generation will reach 37.6 billion kWh, which is equivalent to reducing carbon dioxide emissions by 30.68 million tons per year.[27]

While China–Russia cooperation becomes more fruitful and effective in the clean energy sector, there is uncertainty about China–US and Russia–US cooperation in this field, and the US policy for climate and the energy transition is subject to changes in the US administration. During the Obama administration, the US government included clean energy in the high-level US–China strategic and economic dialog, and then the two countries established a series of cooperation mechanisms and plat-forms, such as the China–US Renewable Energy Partnership and the China–US Clean Energy Research Center, while during the Trump administration, clean energy cooperation between the two sides was frozen. Subsequently, the Biden administra-tion has rejoined the Paris Agreement and has issued the China–US Joint statement addressing the climate crisis with the Chinese government and established several dialog mechanisms, restarting the China–US clean energy cooperation.

Increasing Green Finance to Provide Funding Support for Climate Governance and the Low-Carbon Economic Transition

Global climate governance and the transition to a green and low-carbon economy would just be empty words without the support of finance. During the Copenhagen Climate Change Conference in 2009, developed countries were committed to a collective goal of mobilizing USD 100 billion per year by 2020 for climate action in developing countries. The Paris Agreement made clear that developed countries should continue their existing collective goal to mobilize USD 100 billion per year, the lower limit for such finance, by 2020 and extend this until 2025. A new and higher goal will be set for after this period.

However, the UNFCCC statistics show that the public climate finance provided by developed countries to developing countries is far away from the "USD 100 billion" funding target, and even if private sector finance is included, the number still fails to reach USD 100 billion. According to the World Bank data in 2010, the annual adaptation costs in developing countries were estimated at USD 70–100 billion between 2010 and 2015, while the UNEP predicted that this number

---

[27] "Chinese President Xi Jinping and Russian President Vladimir Putin jointly attending the groundbreaking ceremony of the Sino-Russian nuclear energy cooperation project," Construction Machinery Technology and Management, Issue 3, 2021, pp. 12–13.

would reach USD 140–300 billion in 2030, and USD 280–500 billion in 2050.[28] The Global Green Growth Institute (GGGI) estimated that the funding gap on global climate would amount to \$2.5–\$4.8 trillion over the period of 2016–2030.[29]

In response to the financial needs in global climate governance and the transition to a low-carbon economy, the international community has decided to focus on green finance, as an important way of mobilizing investment and finance. At the 2016 G20 Hangzhou Summit, an initiative dedicated to promoting green finance was written in the G20 Leaders' Communique Hangzhou Summit and the G20 Hamburg Action Plan, and the G20 Green Finance Study Group was established, co-chaired by the People's Bank of China (PBC) and the Bank of the England (BOE), which since then has proposed different green finance initiatives every year. In 2021, the G20 Summit in Italy re-established the Sustainable Finance Study Group, co-chaired by the People's Bank of China and the US Treasury Department, demonstrating China and the US began to jointly play the leading role in global green finance. At the bilateral level, during the Obama administration, the US and Chinese governments started to promote green finance cooperation and set up the China–US Green Fund in 2016. With the implementation of the "Green New Deal" after Biden took office, China–US green finance cooperation is expected to be further promoted.

China–Russia green finance cooperation has achieved some results albeit from a late start. As the Russian government pays more attention to climate and environmental issues, it has realized its demands for developing green finance. As a leader in global green finance, China had been the world's largest green credit market and the world's second largest green bond market by the end of 2020, and Russia has thus been learning from China's experience in green finance and actively promoting green finance cooperation with China in recent years. On September 21, 2020, Russian VTB bank organized a large-scale conference with the participation of 32 Russian and Chinese banks and financial institutions. During the conference, they focused on the topic of green finance, and the Russian side expressed its intention to learn from China's experience and build Russia's own system of green finance.[30] At the local level, the Heilongjiang (in China) Provincial Government released the "The Implementation Plan for Green Finance Work in Heilongjiang Province", stating that it would actively carry out green finance cooperation with Russia, leverage preferential policies for the construction of the Heilongjiang Free Trade Zone and the special financial center in Harbin New District, and turn Harbin New District into a demonstration area for China-Russia green finance exchanges and cooperation.[31]

---

[28] Xinhuanet, UNDP: the fund gap in helping developing countries' respond to climate change far exceeds our expectation. 2016–05-16. http://www.xinhuanet.com/world/2016-05/16/c_128984983. htm.

[29] The necessity of and suggestions for developing climate investment and financing to respond to public health events amid the pandemic, Hong Ruichen, http://iigf.cufe.edu.cn/info/1012/1376. htm.

[30] China Council for the Promotion of International Trade (CCPIT) Russian representative office, http://www.ccpit.org/Contents/Channel_3974/2020/0924/1294449/content_1294449.htm

[31] The Implementation Plan for Green Finance Work in Heilongjiang Province, https://zwgk.hlj. gov.cn/zwgk/publicInfo/detail?id=449784.

Conclusion

China, as a responsible major country, has proposed and is fully committed to its carbon peak and carbon neutrality targets. However, as mentioned above, how the international community responds to climate change will inevitably create a scenario where the three major countries, namely China, the US and Russia, are expected to experience changes in their relative economic strength and geopolitical influence, leading to profound rearrangements of the international economic and political landscape. In this connection, China might as well take targeted measures in the following fields:

Climate Governance

China and Russia have similar positions on mandatory targets of emission reduction as the United States and European countries, the largest emitters that have already finished their industrialization, call on the two countries to follow their practice and assume such responsibilities. China, as the biggest developing country, is still experiencing rapid industrialization and urbanization and its carbon emissions have thus been on the rise. Considering this, China's decision to emphasize carbon emission intensity and energy intensity in its response to climate change during the 14th Five-Year Plan period is made in view of China's realities and also demonstrates its commitment to the "common but differentiated responsibilities" principle. Russia is confronted with a similar problem, because as a big producer and exporter of oil and gas, energy-related emissions take the lion's share of its total. Taking its energy endowment and industrial structure into account, it is reasonable for Russia to design an emission reduction regime that reflects its real conditions. Due to such common ground, China can work with Russia in the efforts to increase voice and rule-making power in climate governance.

Energy

On the one hand, in the field of fossil fuels:
First, both the United States and Russia are in demand to export large amounts of oil and gas to China. This means that China is in a position to change its long-term practice of relying mainly on traditional oil and gas exporting countries such as Russia and the Middle East. Rather, by diversifying its oil and gas imports like importing more liquefied natural gas from the United States, China is more likely to import oil and gas at a lower price and with preferential trade arrangements.

Second, as a major importer of oil and gas, China is well-placed to request the United States to stop imposing trade sanctions on China and isolating the technology-based industry, support China's participation in its upstream exploration and development of oil and gas as well as drop its threshold for market access of China's oil and gas equipment, technology and services; China can promote the use of RMB as the valuation and settlement currency in other countries' oil and gas exports, and gradually make "Petro-RMB" a reality; China can call for the entry into its trading partners' markets of oil and gas refining products in the downstream as well as their consumer markets; China can require any trade of oil and gas to be conducted at the Shanghai Futures Exchange, so as to increase China's discourse power and influence in the international oil and gas market, etc.

Third, as the United States is well under way to become one of the world's largest oil and gas producers and even exporters, the long-standing OPEC and OPEC+ mechanisms will be put to severe tests. Any global attempt to limit crude oil production and stabilize its price without the participation of the United States is predestined to achieve little and the US and Russia, as the emerging producer and the traditional exporter in oil and gas field, will be stuck in direct competition and conflicts of interest. In this context, China, as one of the world's largest oil and gas importers, has more leverage to strike a balance between the US and Russia.

Fourth, when in a sellers' market where oil and gas are over-demanded, countries such as Russia and Saudi Arabia tend to use oil and gas exports as weapons to pursue more geopolitical interests, and China can just follow suit in a buyer's market which favors it. For example, China, using its imports of LNG from the US as a bargaining chip, can start negotiations with the US to make sure that the US side would keep its hands off China's Taiwan, Hong Kong and Xinjiang, refrain from interfering in the South China Sea disputes, and cease to stigmatize and isolate China on issues such as the COVID-19 pandemic. Likewise, it is also possible for China to gain Russia's support for synergizing China's Belt and Road Initiative and Russia's Eurasian Economic Union, for China's participation in the development of East Siberia, and for further cooperation as a counterbalance to the US hegemony.

On the other hand, in the field of clean energy:

First, China and the United States have their respective advantages in the field of clean energy technology, and there are both competition and complementarity between them. China has achieved corner overtaking in terms of photovoltaic power and wind power technology and leaped ahead of the US endowed with a first-mover advantage, but it still lags behind its counterpart when it comes to energy storage, electric vehicle manufacturing, hydrogen energy, as well as carbon capture and storage technology. China has become the world's largest manufacturer of photovoltaic products and wind power products. Besides, while satisfying domestic needs for clean energy products, China has climbed to be one of the world's largest exporters of photovoltaic and wind power products, and promises to compete with the US in this field.

Targeted measures can be taken accordingly. China is supposed to strengthen technology cooperation with the US and enhance its technology capabilities so as to make up for its shortcomings in some segments; as for product manufacturing, investing in the US to build factories might be an option for China to circumvent its trade barriers; in terms of international trade of clean energy products, China stands to compete with the US in the global market by virtue of its low prices, advanced technology and good services, while giving priority to maintaining and expanding market in Southeast Asia, East Asia and Eurasia that are geographically speaking more accessible, and in Africa that has traditionally kept good diplomatic relations and economic cooperation with China.

Secondly, with less attention paid to climate change and richness in oil and gas, Russia's economy is still underpinned by oil and gas exports despite its efforts over the years to restructure its economy. The direct consequence is that Russia is not at the forefront in this round of global trends where clean energy serves as a new economic pattern and a driving force for growth and has been left far behind China and the US in terms of clean energy technology research and development, product manufacturing, export trade and foreign investment. Therefore, in every field of clean energy, Russia needs to cooperate with China and the United States, which are now global leaders in this field. Given this, China can fully leverage its sound strategic collaboration and diplomatic relations with Russia to promote the entry of Chinese clean energy technology, products, services and investment into Russia, and carry out negotiations to make sure that import of oil and gas from Russia and export of clean energy to Russia can be integrated. In doing so, China–Russia clean energy cooperation will be made an essential part of China–Russia strategic partnership of coordination, and the alignment between the Belt and Road Initiative and the Eurasian Economic Union.

Geopolitics and International Politics

As the development of clean energy has serious implications for Russia's oil and gas industry and their export amid a global response to climate change, Russia's geopolitical clout in Eurasia, Europe and the Middle East will be on the wane. And the United States might just seize such an opportunity to dent Russia's geopolitical influence in the Commonwealth of the Independent States (CIS) region by further expanding the EU and NATO. In this sense, Russia will have to rely more on China in geopolitics and international politics. At the same time, with the expansion of China's "Belt and Road" Initiative and the increased dependence of countries in Central Asia and the Middle East on China for oil and gas exports, China's geopolitical influence in the Eurasian region will be on the rise, which might lead the US to work with its allies to contain China.

Under such circumstances, China and Russia can strengthen their mutual reliance and form synergy, so as to counterbalance the adverse effects of the US containment. For example, as the Belt and Road initiative proposed by China and the Eurasian Economic Union championed by Russia are more aligned with each other, the two sides can hold regular climate change summits of leaders from Eurasian countries, set up permanent institutions such as the Eurasian Commission on Climate Change and its secretariat, and put forward specific targets and action roadmaps for Eurasian countries to address climate change and promote the transition to a low-carbon economy. Empowered by more cooperation with other Eurasian countries, China and Russia will play a bigger role in pushing forward the global agenda of combating climate change and driving low-carbon green growth, and increasing substantive cooperation on docking the Belt and Road and Eurasian Economic Union.

Outlook: An Era of Eurasia for Global Economic Governance

Zhonghai Li

A new era, for *global affairs* in particular, is coming. Bruno Masaes, the former Portuguese Minister of European Affairs, called it *the Era of Eurasia* (as in his book titled *the Dawn of Eurasia*), as his conclusion after his six-month trip across the Eurasian continent, a place with vicissitudes for the rise and fall of nation-states compared to other continents. Since the end of the Cold War, especially the beginning of the twenty-first century, with the rise of China's economy and the revitalization of Russia, the Eurasian continent has shown a new landscape for prosperity and development. As Masaes said, this is *a completely new picture*, where different political ideals are practiced in the same space, similar to comprehensive philosophies or religious perspectives from both the globalized world and the old times merging with each other. What surprise observers is not that the Eurasian supercontinent emerged from the Cold War as an increasingly integrated space but that it becomes the arena for so many different or even conflicting political ideas that, more importantly, have not been based on the Western model.[1]

At this moment, the formation of a multiregional system of international relations is underway around the world. Within a region, there will be overlapping regionalism as well as *interregional* and *trans-regional* international organizations. What impact will these various regionalist organizations have on the global scale? This is a major topic that needs our research. At a time when the Fourth Industrial Revolution (Industry 4.0) is in the ascendant, Eurasia still has faced obstacles and challenges on the road to greatness that exist not only in the political dimension but also in economic, social and cultural perspectives. From a global perspective, the Eurasian region has a rather low starting point for economic growth, and its unbalanced development is still prominent. Most countries in this region are underdeveloped; some countries

---

[1] Masaes [1].

Z. Li (✉)
Institute of Russian, Eastern European and Central Asian Studies, Chinese Academy of Social Sciences, Beijing, China

© China Social Sciences Press 2023
Institute of Russian, Eastern European and Central Asian Studies, CASS and Russian International Affairs Council, *Global Governance in the New Era*,
https://doi.org/10.1007/978-981-19-4332-4_18

suffer from poor economic infrastructure and small market capacity, a predicament that cannot be ruled out unless by extensive regional cooperation. In this sense, the improvement of the structure and upgrading of approaches to regional economic governance may be effective ways to expand and deepen regional economic cooperation to address the challenges in such a new round of industrial revolution. Increased research on the Eurasia regional economy and its governance, in this regard, can provide intellectual support for regional economic cooperation on this land.

Regional Economic Governance Development of Multifaceted Concepts and Multidimensional Theories

Regional governance is an important part of the contemporary global governance system. After the end of the Cold War, economic governance went on both regional and global tracks in the context of the simultaneous development of economic regionalization and globalization and developed a series of practices and theories, playing an important role in promoting postwar world economic development. After the beginning of the twenty-first century, especially after the global financial crisis in 2008, however, many countries questioned the existing structure, model and rules of global governance formed after the Cold War, particularly against the backdrop of intensified international trade disputes caused by the rise of US unilateralism. Global economic governance, therefore, has come to a crossroads, desperately requiring an answer: whether to continue bilateral or multilateral coordination under multilateralism or move toward systemic confrontation. With the continued imbalance of the world economy, the increased vulnerability of financial institutions and the impact of the COVID-19 pandemic, the world economy faces growing risks of new crises, calling for reforms on the structure of global governance to enhance its vitality and resilience. However, it is rather difficult to coordinate the confronting interests and opposing positions of major powers at this moment. Therefore, it is necessary to strengthen regional economic cooperation and improve the corresponding structure to create favorable conditions for domestic economic growth and sustainable development.

In the past 20 years, the academic circle has given different views on the positive or negative role that regional economic governance has played in global economic governance. Is the regionalized economy an obstacle (bumper on the road) or a facilitator (stepping stone) for that of the whole world? This paper will put this discussion aside. However, it is an undeniably obvious fact that despite so much criticism of it, the global structure for economic governance established after World War II is still the cornerstone of today's global economic stability. The demand by emerging economies is not to overthrow the current system and rebuild a new one but to reform the existing system for global economic governance to reflect the developmental aspirations and practical interests of the vast number of developing countries and underdeveloped countries. At the same time, the rapid development of regional economic cooperation has provided a new impetus for the economy of nation-states. The number of regional trade agreements has grown significantly over the past 20 years: according to data released by the World Trade Organization, from 1948 to 1994, there were 124 regional trade agreements signed by different countries. By December 31, 2014, the number of regional trade arrangements in force around the world had increased to 377, covering more than half of global trade, among which there were 18 customs unions and 218 free trade agreements.[2] By 2020, the number of regional trade agreements in the world reached 568, including 350 regional trade agreements in goods and 312 free trade agreements.[3]

Meanwhile, new regional organizations and cooperation mechanisms are also emerging. The most notable is the great contribution made by emerging markets to the prosperity and development of regional cooperation, such as that under the frameworks of the G20, the Eurasian Economic Union, the BRICS mechanism and the RCEP. Therefore, the previous progress, current challenges and future development of regional cooperation need to be comprehensively analyzed and theoretically examined, with perhaps new theories established in this regard. The academic circle around the world has already been conducting research and discussion on this issue. According to B. Hettne, a professor at the University of Gothenburg in Switzerland, without a comprehensive theoretical construction for regional issues, it is impossible to fully understand the ongoing process of regionalization.

The study of regional economic cooperation and governance is of course closely related to the concept of *region* and theories related to it. In the Western discourse, *regionalism, interregionalism* and *trans-regionalism* are the most frequently used terms to describe economic phenomena related to regional cooperation and governance, with the complicated research approach involving many issues with varied concepts at different dimensions. The development of theories on regional governance has experienced four stages: *early regionalism, old regionalism, new regionalism* and *comparative regionalism.* This issue has been comprehensively outlined and thoroughly analyzed by the Russian scholar Efremova (Ефремова).[4] She believes that *regionalism* is transnational cooperation based on interstate relations, following the logic of institutional construction. The forms of its cooperation range from regular ministerial consultations to the establishment of supranational institutions seeking to formulate common policies. Regionalism can be closed or open, as the former aims to address the problems and challenges posed by globalization, while the latter is for systematic integration into global agendas.

Interregional cooperation refers to institutional agreements among countries in two or more regions, which can act rather alone or as part of regional organizations or nonpolitical regional groups. The logic of interregional cooperation is based

---

[2] Дэвид Лэйн, Евразийская региональная интеграция как ответ неолиберальному проекту глобализации. Мир России. 2015. № 2.

[3] Figures on Regional Trade Agreements notified to the GATT/WTO and in force, http://rtais.wto.org/UI/publicsummarytable.aspx 2021.10.12.

[4] Ксения Александровна Ефремова, От регионализма к трансрегионализм: теоретическое осмысление новой реальности, Сравнительная политика. 2017 Т.8 № 2.

on the expansion of economic cooperation through the entrance of new regions. Geographically speaking, a typical example is the Transatlantic Trade and Investment Partnership (TTIP). Moreover, *trans-regionalism* is mainly based on political factors, which means countries with common values join forces to participate in global governance more effectively. The main mode of cooperation is to hold top-level meetings (summits) on a regular basis yet without resolutions of binding forces. The main purpose of cooperation is to seek consensus, coordinate positions and form a united front in negotiations on major issues such as global politics, international trade and financial reform. In reality, these processes are not mutually exclusive but develop in parallel.

Regional cooperation in the twenty-first century (including interregional cooperation and cross-regional cooperation) presents a trend of diversified development and multidimensional advancement. It is difficult to assess which form of cooperation is more effective. Whether and how countries participate in regional cooperation is basically a result of the calculation of interests. Andrew Hurrell's emphasis on the complex logic of regionalism is also helpful in examining regionalism. Regionalism, he argued, is a complex and dynamic process whose components are not monolithic but follow the logic with a series of constant interactions and, often, competitions, including the logic of economic, technological changes and social integration; the logic of political competition for power; the logic of security (interstate and social security); and the logic of identity and community. From the perspective of regional economic governance, the logic of cooperation among countries remains dominant. Interstate cooperation, i.e., intergovernmental cooperation refers to the construction of a series of intergovernmental agreements or a pan-regional institutional network led by nation-state governments to carry out closer interstate cooperation in multiple fields. Such institutional arrangements often serve multiple purposes, either as a means to deal with external challenges to coordinate positions in international institutional negotiations or to promote common values, address shared challenges, guarantee people's welfare and benefit countries themselves. Generally, state-led integration is one of the major goals of intergovernmental cooperation.

Since the end of the Cold War, integration by the EU has acted as both a good example and a strong stimulus: integration has become the goal for many countries on economic cooperation with others. It is generally believed that the formulation of specific policies by states to reduce or eliminate trade and investment restrictions as well as to realize mutual exchange of goods, services, capital and population can maximize national economic development, expand market capacity and seek greater economic welfare and prosperity. The development of theories on regional governance, in this regard, provides us with both directions and dimensions to study what is happening on the Eurasian continent.

Features of Economic Governance in Eurasia

After the end of the Cold War, regionalism and globalization developed rapidly and simultaneously. Many regional international organizations have been established all over the world, especially in Eurasia. The number of regional trade agreements also increased significantly with the emergence of so-called *overlapping regionalism.* There are overlapping member states among more than 60 regional international organizations. From the current point of view, such overlapping membership does not affect the cooperation among countries and regional organizations but remains conducive to the complementarity and coordination of regional cooperation. In the vast area where the Shanghai Cooperation Organization member states, observer states and dialog partners are located, international organizations with great influence include the SCO itself, the Eurasian Economic Union, the Collective Security Treaty Organization, together with the *BRICS* mechanism connected extraterritorial countries, *the Belt and Road initiative* proposed by China and *the Greater Eurasian Partnership* proposed by Russia.

Reviewing the development history of the abovementioned organizations, mechanisms and initiatives, it can be seen that regional governance on the Eurasian continent has four prominent features: first, the proactive promotion by heads of states has played a leading role in the development of regional economic governance; second, sovereign-state governments have served as the main force for economic governance in the Eurasian region; third, institutionalized integration is the key to regional governance; fourth, China and Russia have taken the lead in regional governance on the Eurasian continent. Compared with Europe, North America and Southeast Asia, the pattern and model for economic governance in the Eurasian region are still in an initial stage, without a mature, stable and well-established structure.

First, proactive promotion by heads of state has played a leading role in the development of regional economic governance. Chinese President Xi Jinping keeps attaching great importance to regional international organizational development in Eurasia and continues to promote the growth of these mechanisms with *head-of-state diplomacy.* First, he has clearly put forward the focus on global economic governance. In his keynote speech at the opening ceremony of the G20 Business 20 (B20) Summit in September 2016, President Xi Jinping pointed out that global economic governance should focus on the following priorities: jointly ensure equitable and efficient global financial governance and uphold the overall stability of the world economy; jointly foster open and transparent global trade and investment governance to cement the multilateral trading regime and unleash the potential of global cooperation in economy, trade and investment; jointly establish green and low-carbon global energy governance to promote global green development cooperation; and jointly facilitate an inclusive and interconnected global development governance to implement the UN 2030 Agenda for Sustainable Development and jointly advance the well-being of mankind.

At successive BRICS and SCO summits, leaders in the Eurasian region have put forward proposals to promote regional economic development and cooperation.

When talking about how to use the existing cooperation mechanism of the BRICS countries to realize the aspiration of connecting the Eurasian Economic Union and the Silk Road Economic Belt, Russian President Vladimir Putin criticized some countries for trying to build closed and nontransparent alliances (such as the Trans-Pacific Partnership or the Transatlantic Trade and Investment Partnership), emphasizing the commitment by BRICS partners to a nondiscriminatory and open economic space based on WTO principles. The idea of *connecting the Eurasian Economic Union with the Silk Road Economic Belt* proposed by Russia could become the basis for the Greater Eurasian Partnership involving the Eurasian Economic Union, the Shanghai Cooperation Organization and ASEAN countries. Driven by the direct promotion of state leaders, the Eurasian region has established a number of regional mechanisms for economic governance, making it an important issue for countries in this place.

Second, sovereign-state governments have served as the main force for economic governance in the Eurasian region. Different from the extensive participation by NGOs and multinational corporations in Western regional governance, sovereign-state governments play an irreplaceable role as decision-makers, organizers and promoters for regional governance in Eurasia. This is directly related to its historical traditions and cultures in Eurasian countries, as well as the power balance of politics and capital in this region. In fact, even in the heyday of Western neo-liberalism, states still played an important role in people's economic life. The American geographer Saul Cohen argues in his book that the rapid progress of the globalized world economy and the transformation from traditional communication systems into information networks spreading across the globe will not eliminate national boundaries or identity labels. Globalization does not spell the end of geography, nor does it shape a geographically *flat world*. Rather, it will generally result in a much more complicated geopolitical system.[5] Robert Gilpin, the author of *Global Political Economy*, also believes that nation-states still play the main role in economic affairs at both the domestic and international levels. Gilpin has pointed out that the benefits of globalization for a country's economy are huge, as import, export and foreign investment have improved the efficiency of a country's economy and enabled it to enter the world market to obtain capital and technology that are extremely helpful for its rapid economic development. However, he has also warned that a country should not open its economy to the world until it has sufficiently prepared for such a move.

In the 1990s, many countries in East and Southeast Asia lowered barriers to foreign capital inflows before establishing regulations and institutions that would ensure the stability of their financial systems. These missteps led to rampant financial speculation and all other kinds of irregularities, which finally resulted in the 1997 Asian financial crisis.[6] Therefore, overemphasizing economic liberalization and globalization may not be an effective and constructive suggestion. The role of the state in restricting disorderly capital competition can effectively avoid market risks. Meanwhile, Eurasian countries attach equal importance to the role of enterprises. In regard

---

[5] Cohen [2].

[6] Gilpin [3].

to the mechanism of international cooperation on manufacturing and energy production, China has emphasized the need to establish *a government-driven, enterprise-led, commercial-operated* way of cooperation, which can effectively give full play to the role of government, capital and society, therefore balancing the interests of all parties and establishing fair and efficient regional governance.

Third, multilateral economic cooperation focuses on specific projects, but institutional integration is still the goal pursued by economic governance. The Eurasian region has a vast territory, rich resources and immense development potential. However, infrastructure in many countries within this region is relatively underdeveloped, with imbalanced development, underfunded public budgets and great pressure from unemployment. Therefore, international organizations in this region all attach great importance to investing in infrastructure, particularly with regard to cooperation on large-scale projects. China's *Belt and Road initiative* and proposition for cooperation on industrial capacity are direct responses to this appeal. China advocates that the SCO should become a driving force for regional development and suggests that all countries work together to build transportation projects for interconnectivity, including railways, highways, aviation facilities, telecommunication networks, power grids and energy pipelines.

First, with the joint efforts by countries in this region, many projects have been completed and are now in successful operation, such as the China–Central Asia Natural Gas Pipeline Project, the China–Kazakhstan Oil Pipeline Project and the China–Russia Oil and Gas Pipeline Project. Meanwhile, other projects are now put on the agenda with concrete progress, such as the China–Pakistan Economic Corridor, the China–Mongolia–Russia Economic Corridor and the China–Central Asia–West Asia Economic Corridor. Second, to meet the capital needs of major regional projects, the Asian Infrastructure Investment Bank (AIIB) and the BRICS New Development Bank (NDB) have been successively established in recent years. The AIIB is a regional intergovernmental multilateral development agency in the Asian region, focusing on supporting the construction of infrastructure. Its purpose is to advance the process of infrastructure connectivity and economic integration in Asia and to strengthen cooperation between China and other Asian countries or regions. The NDB was established to mobilize resources for infrastructure construction and sustainable development projects in the BRICS countries and other emerging economies or developing countries as a complement to existing multilateral and regional financial institutions for promoting global growth and worldwide development. At the same time, Eurasian countries are still committed to realizing economic integration and have made efforts in institutional building. The most prominent proof is their effort to promote the facilitation of trade and investment through the establishment of cooperative mechanisms and their endeavor to achieve policy coordination, facility connectivity, unimpeded trade, financial integration and people-to-people bonds.

Fourth, China and Russia have taken the lead in regional governance on the Eurasian continent. The regional economic governance of any region requires one or two leading countries, while economic and political integration require a strong leader interested in and capable of promoting regional agreements as well, such as Germany in the European Union, the United States in NAFTA, Japan in APEC and Brazil in COMESA. Compared to Europe, a prominent feature of the Eurasian region is the asymmetric economic scale across the continent, ranging from China, the world's second-largest economy, to less developed countries such as Tajikistan and Kyrgyzstan. The membership of international organizations in this region also varies from one to another. For example, although the total population of the 8 SCO member states accounts for 40% of the world's total, with their GDP accounting for 20% of the global sum, China and Russia, in particular, account for the absolute majority of both people and the economy. This fact requires China and Russia to play a leading role in the regional structure for economic governance, to provide more public goods for the development of countries in the region and, at the same time, to propose a long-term vision for regional development and make tangible efforts to reach this end.

In general, there are many differences between regional governance in Eurasia and those in Europe or North America, determined by various natural geographical, history, culture and economic factors. For the most part of its history, the theoretical research on regionalism always focused on the European Union, using the EU as a yardstick to evaluate the success or failure of regional governance in other parts of the world. With the rise of *comparative regionalism*, however, the Western academic circle has also realized that their previous evaluation approach is unfair, therefore beginning to assess the achievements for economic development and models of governance by other regions in a more objective way.

Options for Economic Governance in Eurasia

Regional economic governance is a complex and comprehensive issue, and it is difficult to objectively and accurately grasp the regional development process from only one or several perspectives. As the American geographer John Agnew argued, the concept of *region* reflects both *objective differences* in the world and *ideas* about the geography of such differences, so trying to understand the whole region from any single lens of regional issues would be counterproductive.[7] If we took a look at the economic landscape of the entire Eurasian continent, the western and eastern ends of the continent are areas composed of developed countries, while the middle part of the continent, i.e., the post-Soviet region, is composed of many countries with a lower degree of economic development. The World Bank has once drawn a map of the economic size of Eurasia and described it as a *dumbbell* shape with *heavy ends* on both sides and a thin neck in the middle. The World Bank called it *the Eurasian dumbbell*, which implies that the northern and central parts of Eurasia are a vast but economically unimportant region located between the European Union and East Asia as two centers of economic power.

---

[7] Agnew [4].

It can be seen that countries in Eurasia are faced with heavy tasks for both advancing economic development and building an effective regional structure for economic governance. To meet the challenges of the twenty-first century and catch up in a dynamic tide of the fourth industrial revolution (Industry 4.0), countries in this region must not only achieve domestic development but also strengthen regional cooperation so that they, with open regionalism, can better respond to external challenges brought about by globalization. However, a regional system for economic cooperation cannot be built overnight and out of thin air. It is necessary to inherit and continue the achievements of postwar global economic governance and, at the same time, innovate regional economic cooperation according to the economic realities in this place.

It is also important to point out that although cultivated primarily in Western Europe and the United States and despite its desire to be universal, modern economics still reflects institutions and problems specific to those regions.[8] Likewise, the concept of *global economic governance* also comes from the West. If the structure, model and institutional framework for global governance are understood and designed according only to Western concepts, they must have distinctive Western characteristics, therefore, imposing inevitable discrimination against the non-Western world and impairing the interests of the vast number of developing or underdeveloped countries. Fortunately, with the rise of *comparative regionalism*, there is already a new theoretical basis for the study of regional economic development and regional governance, as well as a rethinking of the past Euro-centrism concept. We can put forward new ideas and suggestions for governance based on the realities across the Eurasian region.

First, economic governance in Eurasia should prioritize growth. Since the end of the Cold War, several relatively stable regional structures have been formed around the world. Among them, the establishment of the EU provides experience for different countries to establish regional frameworks for governance. Since then, Southeast Asian countries and American countries have successively established their own regional organizations, which have become part of the global governance structure. In the post-Soviet space, regional organizations such as the Collective Security Treaty Organization and the Eurasian Economic Union have also been established so that the regional centrifugal tendency after the disintegration of the Soviet Union has been more or less contained. These regional organizations have also become active forces on the global political and economic stage.

However, it should also be noted that regional governance in Eurasia is still at a relatively low level, with extremely imbalanced economies across the Eurasian continent. There are countries with large territories, such as Russia, populous countries, such as China and India, as well as other small and medium-sized economies with relatively scant resources and limited market capacity, whose rapid economic development may be difficult to achieve only by relying on their own resources. According to Wallenstein's *World Systems Theory*, the vast majority of countries in the Eurasia region belong to the periphery of capitalism as the source of energy and

---

[8] Reynolds [5].

raw materials as well as the sales market of products from the capitalist world. A problem that cannot be ignored is that most countries in this region are underdeveloped, with relatively low per capita GDP and poor living standards, all facing various difficulties in economic development. Therefore, this region has to address the dual tasks of economic development in both quality and quantity. Most of the economic cooperation in other parts of the world is oriented to capital profit, but the economic governance in Eurasia under the leadership of nation-state governments should properly handle the relation between profit seeking and economic development, focusing on solving basic problems for regional economic development to create favorable external economic conditions for the growth and structural reform of countries in this region. It is also highly necessary to prioritize the development of infrastructure construction, expand market capacity, build an industrial chain that meets the realities of regional resources, realize complementary advantages and promote common development.

Second, the principle of *open regionalism* should be upheld. Open regionalism is an ideal pursuit for promoting regional cooperation worldwide and an important reference for improving the global mechanism for multilateral negotiation. In the long-term history of worldwide economic development, opening up is one of the important driving forces for economic development. Open regionalism, a brand new form of regional economic cooperation formed in the process of economic integration, is different from traditional ones due to its distinct characteristics, such as openness and nondiscrimination.

The *openness* of regionalism has the following basic connotations: first, it emphasizes voluntary cooperation and is not bound by forms or systems. Openness in this regard is significantly different from that of traditional regionalist organizations such as the European Union. It does not force member states to yield their sovereignty or set up supranational institutions but constantly seeks consensus, to the maximum extent, as well as ways of informal and noninstitutionalized cooperation. Second, it advocates diversity and inclusiveness in the pursuit of interactions both within the region and between this region and the outside world. This principle acknowledges the differences in cultural traditions, social institutions, values and development models of countries, advocates adopting measures to local realities and explores the path of regional cooperation in line with regional characters and the traditions of member states. The *Shanghai Spirit* of *mutual trust, mutual benefit, equality, mutual consultations, respect for cultural diversity and pursuit of common development* proposed by the Shanghai Cooperation Organization is a powerful expression of this principle. Third, it grasps key points and fundamental aspects for wide-ranging and deep-level development. The purpose of regional cooperation lies not in form but in content. The aim of any regional cooperation is to solve specific problems of the country or the region. Therefore, open regionalism advocates reaching rational arrangements through mutually beneficial cooperation, focusing regional cooperation on the economic field, and promoting the better development of regional economic cooperation.[9]

---

[9] Zhilai [6].

The direct opposite of *open regionalism* is *closed protectionism*. From the perspective of world economic development history, some countries and regions have taken reasonable measures to protect their own markets and infant industries during a certain period of time. The theory and practice of mercantilism and protectionism advocated by Friedrich List also appeared. These policies did have a certain rationality in the period of traditional industrialization. However, with the rapid development of globalization as well as the revolution of transportation and communication technologies, the distance for both space and time among global countries has been shortened, and the ability to monopolize special resources has significantly declined, as there is no obstacle to the global allocation of resources. Therefore, the ideas are outdated for establishing regional organizations that are exclusive, closed and discriminatory against nonmember states or for establishing one's sphere of influence of its own. Closure does not necessarily bring effective protection, while orderly openness and active cooperation are feasible ways for economies with small market capacity to tide over developmental difficulties. At the same time, it should be recognized that regional economic cooperation organizations in the Eurasian region are not mutually exclusive but complementary to each other.

Third, a flexible approach to regional economic governance should be adopted. The current world is undergoing profound changes, which are based on continuous innovation and development in science and technology. These scientific and technological revolutions would first drive the industrial revolution and then spread its influence onto all fields of people's lives, which will lead to *a new stage of ground-shaking changes all over the world*. The advent of the fourth industrial revolution (Industry 4.0) requires more flexible governance methods in all fields of the world. Klaus Schwab pointed out that one character of the fourth industrial revolution, and perhaps also of the entire twenty-first century, is the unprecedented speed of change to which many states or institutions cannot adapt, posing particularly serious challenges for both policymakers and governments. This requires leaders to rethink *what we are governing* and *why we govern in this way*.[10] The white paper by the World Economic Forum *Agile Governance: Reimagining Policy-Making in the Fourth Industrial Revolution* proposes that the speed of technological development and certain characteristics of new technologies have strained many previous decision-making cycles and mechanisms. These characters include dissemination at a higher speed; crossing jurisdictional, regulatory and disciplinary boundaries; and increasingly explicit political orientation in incorporating and expressing human values and biases.[11]

For regional economic governance, it is also necessary to adopt targeted and flexible methods for governance.

First, there should be modest and realistic expectations for regional economic integration and the degree to which they are fulfilled. According to Joseph Nye's theory of neofunctionalism, to achieve integration, different countries need to meet four prerequisites: symmetry and economic equality of each unit; complementary values

---

[10] Schwab [7].

[11] Schwab [7], p. 287.

of competition; existence of pluralism; and the ability to adapt to and respond of member states.[12] He further proposed three preconditions for perception and cognition of the integration process: first, the perceptual understanding of the fairness of the distribution of benefits, because when more people in all countries feel that the distribution is fair and reasonable, the promotion of integration will have more favorable conditions; second, the awareness of external-related issues, which refers to decision-makers' perceptual awareness of external issues related to their own countries, including dependence on exports, threats posed by great powers and loss of their own status in a changing global system; third, visible or transferable low cost, that is, the extent to which it is felt that integration, especially in the initial stage, is free of cost.[13] Judging from the reality in Eurasia, this region, for the time being, does not have the prerequisites mentioned above. More importantly, although cultural diversity and differences in values are *not obstacles* to the expansion of cooperation between regional countries, they are still important *factors* for the realization of integration. The Russian scholar Vinokurov (Евгений Винокуров) also pointed out that the inclusion of members outside the Russian-speaking space into the post-Soviet economic cooperation system would rather complicate its operation; therefore, the existence of cultural barriers cannot be ignored.

Second, regional international economic cooperation should be more flexible and diverse, not only through the approach of establishing and improving regional international organizations. As mentioned above, since the end of the Cold War, especially the beginning of the twenty-first century, the signing of regional trade agreements among different countries has become the main manifestation of transnational and trans-regional economic cooperation. A regional trade agreement (RTA) is a treaty between two or more governments that defines trade rules for all signatory countries. Examples of regional trade agreements include the North American Free Trade Agreement (NAFTA), the European Union (EU) and the Asia-Pacific Economic Cooperation (APEC). Since the beginning of the twenty-first century, the number of regional trade agreements has been increasing, and their nature has also changed. There were 50 trade agreements in effect in 1990, more than 280 in 2017, and now 350 in 2021. These agreements go beyond tariffs and cover a wide range of government policies affecting trade and investment in goods and services, including regulations on competition policies, government procurement rules and intellectual property rights. Regional trade agreements involving tariffs and other border measures are *shallow agreements*, whereas agreements involving more government policies are *deep agreements* that are important institutional frameworks for regional integration. These agreements reduce trade costs and define many of the rules that govern the functioning of the economy. If properly and effectively designed, these agreements and regulations will serve to improve policies among countries, thereby increasing trade and investment and further promoting economic growth and social welfare.

Through its research, the World Bank found that deep regional trade agreements are significantly better than shallow trade agreements. First, deep agreements are

---

[12] Dougherty and Pfaltzgraff [8].

[13] Dougherty and Pfaltzgraff [8], pp. 556–557.

Outlook: An Era of Eurasia for Global Economic Governance

more likely to facilitate trade, investment and participation in global value chains than shallow agreements. The World Bank estimates that on average, deep trade agreements will increase trade in goods by more than 35 percent, trade in services by more than 15 percent and global value chain integration by more than 10 percent. Second, public goods involved in deep agreements can benefit all trading partners and bring more welfare by expanding trade and improving the policy environment. However, the design of these agreements needs to balance the interests among different member states and between member states and outsiders. Third, deep regional trade agreements could affect trade and economic relations for years to come. Active regional trade agreements currently include the Comprehensive and Progressive Agreement for Trans-Pacific Partnership (CPTPP), the EU-MERCOSUR Trade Agreement, and the Regional Comprehensive Economic Partnership (RCEP) among ASEAN and its six major trading partners, as well as the African Continental Free Trade Area (CFTA). It should be pointed out that although Brexit and the US withdrawal from the TPP are not joint (aggregate) actions but separate ones, they will still have a profound impact on the regional and global economy.

Finally, this article concludes with an excerpt from *Lao Tzu*, according to this great philosopher in ancient China, *tao,* as the most fundamental rule for everything running in this world, always means letting things happen on their original track without doing anything unnecessary: it seems that *tao* gives no contribution, but actually, it is the governing rule for all. If rulers can govern their people according to this principle, everything will develop by both self-cultivation and self-destruction. When excessive demand (abnormality) arises from within, *tao* will be needed to bring things back on track. With no such abnormality, everything will be settled, and the world will so naturally achieve stability and tranquility.

References

1. Masaes, B. 2020. *The Dawn of Eurasia: On the Trail of the New World Order*, 14. Social Sciences Academic Press.
2. Cohen, S. 2011. *Geopolitics: The Geography of International Relations*, 9. Shanghai Academy of Social Sciences Press.
3. Gilpin, R. 2006. *Global Political Economy: Understandin the International Economic Order*. Chinese edition foreword, 2-3. Shanghai Century Publishing(Group) Co., Ltd.
4. Agnew, J. 1999. Regions on the Mind Does Not Equal Regions of the Mind //. *Progress in Human Geography* 23 (1): 93.
5. Reynolds, L.G. 2013. *The Three Worlds of Economics*, 1. Commercial Press.
6. Zhilai, Q. 2008. *Accurately Understanding the "Openness" of Regionalism: Taking East Asia Regional Cooperation as an Example*, 12. World Economics and Politics.
7. Schwab, K. 2018. *The Fourth Industrial Revolution—A Roadmap for Action: Building an Innovative Society*, 281. CITIC Publishing Group Co., Ltd.
8. Dougherty, J.E., and R.L. Pfaltzgraff, Jr. 2003. *Contending Theories of International Relations: A Comprehensive Survey translated by Yan Xuetong, Chen Hanxi, etc.*, 556. World Knowledge Press.

Post-COVID-19 Sanction Policies

Ivan Timofeev

The COVID-19 pandemic has given hope for international consolidation in the face of a common threat. Alleviating numerous sanctions and economic restrictions could be one step toward unification.

UN Secretary-General Antonio Guterres,[1] UN High Commissioner for Human Rights Michelle Bachelet,[2] UN Special Rapporteur on the Right to Food Hilal Elver[3] and UN Special Rapporteur on the negative impact of the unilateral coercive measures on the enjoyment of human rights Alena Douhan[4] called for such steps. Similar proposals were made by many political leaders, including President Vladimir Putin at the 2020 G20 summit.[5] The EU authorities made declarations about the need for

---

[1] Funding the Fight against COVID-19 in the Worlds' Poorest Countries. UN Department of Global Communications. March 25, 2020. URL: https://www.un.org/en/un-coronavirus-communications-team/funding-fight-against-covid-19-world%E2%80%99s-poorest-countries.

[2] Ease Sanctions against Countries Fighting COVID-19: UN Human Rights Chief. UN News. March 24, 2020. URL: https://news.un.org/en/story/2020/03/1060092.

[3] Economic Sanctions Should Be Lifted to Prevent Hunger Crises in Countries Hit by COVID-19: UN Rights Expert. UN News. March 31, 2020. URL: https://news.un.org/en/story/2020/03/1060742.

[4] UN Rights Expert Urges Governments to Save Lives by Lifting All Economic Sanctions Amid Covid-19 Pandemic. UN Human Rights Office of the High Commissioner. April 3, 2020. URL: https://www.ohchr.org/EN/NewsEvents/Pages/DisplayNews.aspx?NewsID=25769&LangID=E.

[5] G20 Summit. The President is taking part in the Extraordinary Virtual G20 Leader's Summit. President of Russia. March 26, 2020. URL: http://en.kremlin.ru/events/president/news/63070.

I. Timofeev (✉)
Russian International Affairs Council, Moscow, Russia

© China Social Sciences Press 2023
Institute of Russian, Eastern European and Central Asian Studies, CASS and Russian International Affairs Council, *Global Governance in the New Era*, https://doi.org/10.1007/978-981-19-4332-4_19

humanitarian exceptions.[6] In the United States, during the campaign, Joe Biden spoke about this as well.[7] The U.S. administration promptly released a list of exceptions to its sanctions, many of which were in place long before the pandemic. They concern Iran, Syria, Cuba, North Korea, Venezuela and Russia.[8] A joint U.S.–Swiss relief supply channel for Iran has become operational.[9] We saw the first transactions based on INSTEX, a long-awaited channel for humanitarian transactions with Iran created by Great Britain, France and Germany back in 2019.[10] The United Kingdom made humanitarian exceptions for the Syrian oil embargo.[11]

However, declarations and humanitarian exemptions are unlikely to reverse the sanctions policy or the existing restrictions. All resolutions, decisions and laws remained in force even at the peak of the epidemic. Exemptions apply only to isolated areas.[12] The relief channels focus on the "people" of the countries under sanctions, not the "authoritarian regimes." However, the state plays the key role in fighting the epidemic or any other major challenge for that matter. It inevitably falls under the "regime" category, thus becoming cut off from many essential resources. For example, in theory, an oil embargo is bad for the "regime." In practice, the embargo makes a state less capable of fighting the epidemic. At the end of the day, firing at the "regime" means firing at the "people." We should also bear in mind that the help in fighting the epidemic provided by the countries hit by the sanctions, such as Russia, Cuba and China, to the initiators of the sanctions will not make the latter lift the sanctions afterward.

In other words, COVID-19 does little to change the way the sanctions are applied in practice. They remain an instrument of coercion and pressure that is used to attain foreign policy goals. As the epidemic subsides, the situation will return to normal with fewer humanitarian declarations or exemptions.

---

[6] Declaration by the High Representative Josep Borrell on Behalf of the EU on the UN Secretary General's Appeal for an Immediate Global Ceasefire. European Council. April 3, 2020. URL: https://www.consilium.europa.eu/en/press/press-releases/2020/04/03/declaration-by-the-high-rep resentative-josep-borrell-on-behalf-of-the-eu-on-the-un-secretary-general-s-appeal-for-an-immedi ate-global-ceasefire/.

[7] Statement from Vice-President Joe Biden on Sanctions Relief during COVID 19. Joe Biden. April 2, 2020. URL: https://medium.com/JoeBiden/statement-from-vice-president-joe-biden-on-sanctions-relief-during-covid-19-f7c2447416f0.

[8] Fact Sheet: Provision of Humanitarian Assistance and Trade to Combat COVID-19. U.S. Department of Treasury. URL: https://www.treasury.gov/resource-center/sanctions/Programs/Documents/covid19_fact-sheet_20200416.pdf.

[9] United States and Switzerland Finalize the Swiss Humanitarian Trade Agreements. U.S. Department of the Treasury. February 27, 2020. URL: https://home.treasury.gov/news/press-releases/sm919.

[10] INSTEX Successfully Concludes First Transaction. U.K. Foreign and Commonwealth Office. March 31, 2020. URL: https://www.gov.uk/government/news/instex-successfully-concludes-first-transaction.

[11] Trade Sanctions on Syria. U.K. Department of International Trade and Export Control Joint Unit. December 31, 2020. URL: https://www.gov.uk/guidance/sanctions-on-syria#crude-oil-and-petroleum-products.

[12] Blanc [1].

Today, there are many publications on how COVID-19 is going to change the world and international relations. "The world will never be the same" has become a common tagline. Unfortunately, this has nothing to do with easing the sanction policy. Moreover, the sanctions may even become tougher in a number of areas. This threat can be seen in the U.S.–China relations. Therefore, it is important to take an unbiased look at the long-term trends in using sanctions by key international players regardless of the current situation.

Over the past two decades, economic sanctions have become one of the key foreign policy instruments. The UN Security Council is their only legitimate source of sanctions.[13] However, they are widely applied unilaterally by developed states to achieve their goals in the international arena. The United States uses unilateral measures more often than other countries. Sanctions have become one of the most important EU foreign policy tools. Although China and Russia are opposed to unilateral sanctions, they are forced to respond to restrictions from third countries. China has a vast economic potential that makes it possible for it to be active in conducting its policies. Restrictive measures have become one of the key political risks for international businesses. This is especially true of using secondary sanctions and fines for violating existing restriction regimes.

At the same time, the perception of the sanctions and their place in the system of foreign policy tools, the possibilities of using them and protection against them varies significantly among the countries. National experience does not always fit in with the experience of international organizations and occasionally contradicts it. Such inconsistencies give rise to a number of conflicts and contradictory situations. The high level of legitimacy of UN Security Council resolutions is not supported by adequate tools for implementing them. Sanctioned states often use response measures against the initiating countries, but their businesses try not to violate the sanctions imposed on their country. Major initiators of sanctions can at the same time be the targets for restrictive measures imposed even by their allies. The same goes for businesses. Being part of the jurisdiction of the initiating countries does not eliminate

---

[13] Ex., Jazairi, I. "Report of the Special Rapporteur on the negative impact of unilateral coercive measures on the enjoyment of human rights", United Nations General Assembly Human Rights Council Thirty Session, 2015. Article 103 of the UN Charter reads that "in the event of a conflict between the obligations of the Members of the United Nations under the present Charter and their obligations under any other international agreement, their obligations under the present Charter shall prevail." Accordingly, sanctions introduced by the UN Security Council take precedence over international obligations of the states. Importantly, according to Article 53 of the UN Charter, the UN can utilize regional arrangements or agencies for "enforcement action under its authority." At the same time, "no enforcement action shall be taken under regional arrangements or by regional agencies without the authorization of the Security Council." In other words, Article 53 envisages that regional organizations have no right to introduce their own sanctions without approval of the UN Security Council, which should "at all times be kept fully informed of activities undertaken or in contemplation under regional arrangements or by regional agencies for the maintenance of international peace and security." (Article 54). For more detail, see Kiku D. V., "Sovremennye mezhdunarodnye mekhanizmy sanktsionnogo vozdeistviya. Politika sanktsii, tseli, strategii, instrumenty: khrestomatiya"/[ed. I.N.Timofeev, V.A.Morozov, Yu.S.Timofeeva]; Russian International Affairs Council (RIAC). Moscow, NP RSMD, 2000. P. 75. URL: https://russiancouncil.ru/upload/iblock/692/sanctions_policy_2020.pdf.

the risk of applying "sanctions for violating sanctions" in the form of fines or other measures.

The sanctions policy is a clear indicator of an unbalanced international relations system, or (using a metaphor provided in a Valdai Club report) a "crumbling world."[14] It erodes legitimacy, and the rules take on a situational dimension.

The modern world is at a crossroads. Sanctions are no longer imposed based on international rules and procedures but have instead returned to the logic of national egotism and promoting the interests of individual countries. However, they have not yet entered a stage of tough confrontation, when exchanging restrictions causes major damage to the global economy. However, such a scenario cannot be ruled out in the future. Eroding global governance instruments for economic constraints and the growing number of unilateral measures are fraught with an escalation of sanctions between major economic players. This primarily applies to the United States and China. At best, this will lead to a transformation of the international financial system, its departure from dollar domination and diversification around several economic growth centers. At worst, sanctions may escalate into a tougher form of confrontation. We know from history that sanctions were combined with the use of force on numerous occasions.

In this paper, we will look at the sanctions policy from the perspective of the UN, the United States, the EU, China and Russia. These players have different capabilities and experiences. Thus far, the use of restrictive measures by them has not resulted in major tensions. However, the risks for individual companies, industries and countries are already fairly significant. The key question is about the strategies, approaches and capabilities of the key players and how far the escalation of sanctions can take them.

The United Nations' Restrictive Measures

Today, the UN is the only international organization with the authority, legitimacy and ability to use sanctions on behalf of the international community. Strictly speaking, the concept of sanctions is not enshrined in UN documents. Usually, we are talking about restrictive measures against acts of aggression and resolving problems of peace and security. The possibility of applying such measures is included in Article 41, Chapter VII of the UN Charter. They include "a complete or partial interruption of economic relations and of rail, sea, air, postal, telegraphic, radio and other means of communication, and the severance of diplomatic relations." The decision on such measures is made by the UN Security Council and is binding for all UN member countries. In the political and media parlance, the concept of sanctions is identical to restrictive measures. There are currently 14 UN sanction regimes in force, and each one is coordinated by a separate sanction committee. Most such committees are supported in their work by expert groups and the UN Secretariat.

---

[14] Barabanov et al. [2].

Functionally, the UN sanctions seek to achieve three major goals: to force the target country to change its policy, to deter possible aggression or other actions, or to send a message to the target country that its actions are unacceptable.[15] In almost all cases, the UN sanctions concern security issues: military conflicts, civil wars, genocide, nonproliferation of weapons of mass destruction, terrorism and others. Compared with the unilateral restrictions imposed by individual countries, UN sanctions are more depoliticized; that is, they are imposed in response to a real acute problem. The decision-making mechanism in the UN Security Council virtually eliminates the possibility of making decisions based on a country's interpretation of particular actions or speculations, as is often the case with unilateral sanctions.

However, the UN mechanism has a number of shortcomings. There may be major disagreements among the Security Council members, which make working on resolutions difficult. Some UNSC members may disagree with an overly soft resolution, while others may disagree with it being overly tough. The UN staffing and financial shortages preventing the deployment of large-scale sanction programs are other problems. The total number of members of committees and expert groups as well as Secretariat staff involved in individual programs does not exceed several dozen people, if that. This may be enough for monitoring and preparing decisions but not for comprehensive monitoring of the progress of their implementation. Using restrictions is the member countries' responsibility. However, they do what they need to do with varying degrees of effectiveness depending on the available resources or political will. Given these circumstances, even the best decisions may stall at the level of implementation by a particular country. Occasionally, large countries go as far as ignore the UN Security Council resolutions, as was the case with the Iran nuclear deal. Donald Trump effectively ignored Resolution 2231 and unilaterally resumed sanctions against Iran contrary to other Security Council members' opinions.

In other words, the UN remains the single most important supranational source of sanctions, but large states are often unable to achieve their political goals using UN mechanisms. They need more efficient and effective measures that are in line with their interests. The UN limits "national egotism," which nonetheless remains a major foreign policy incentive in the modern world. Therefore, unilateral sanctions are widely used in political practice. They are imposed by a single country or a coalition in circumvention of the UN Security Council resolutions.

Unilateral sanctions include a wide range of tools, such as export and import restrictions, bans on technological cooperation or financial restrictions. Financial sanctions are the most important mechanism for exerting pressure today. Restricting banking transactions with a country, individual organizations or persons under sanctions may cause significant damage to other sectors of the economy that are connected with the outer world. Indeed, without financial mechanisms to support the transactions, they will either become unfeasible or substantially hindered. In addition, targeted sanctions have been widely used during the post-Cold War period.[16] The restrictions are imposed on individuals, organizations or sectors of the economy

---

[15] Ex., Giumelli [3].

[16] Ex., Drezner [4].

rather than the entire country. In theory, this cuts the costs for the country in general, but in practice, the most important sectors are hit, so in effect, targeted sanctions are often comparable to a full-scale blockade.

Sanctions should not be confused with trade wars. The former is initiated by governments and seeks to resolve political problems. The latter is aimed at increasing the competitive advantages of national producers, is often lobbied by businesses and use a different set of tools, such as tariffs or duties. However, today, we can see cases when the initiating country tries to achieve market advantages through sanctions. The U.S. sanctions against the Nord Stream 2 project are a case in point. The line between sanctions and a trade war is becoming increasingly blurred in US–China relations. However, even in such cases, political motives are strong and are not limited exclusively to the economy.

Adopted in circumvention of the UN Security Council, unilateral restrictive measures can be used by a coalition of states. For example, the United States often tries to enlist the support of its allies. From the UN perspective, this internationalization does not make sanctions more legitimate. Some countries occasionally seek to use the UN to internationalize their unilateral measures.[17] However, the process does not always go in the opposite direction. The UN efforts to alleviate unilateral sanctions amid the COVID-19 pandemic have yielded modest results. Even with the emergence of a global challenge, political motives for using sanctions did not recede into the background.

The United States and Sanctions: Ideology, the Dollar and the Legal Framework

For the United States, sanctions are an important part of its foreign policy toolkit. The National Security Strategy published in late December 2017 defines sanctions as an element of deterring and limiting the potential of its rivals in the international arena. Over the past 100 years, Washington has gained vast experience in imposing unilateral restrictive measures. The United States has used them more often than all other countries and international organizations combined.[18] Most sanction programs have been in place for decades. U.S. sanctions present a risk for its opponents and allies alike. In terms of the scope and extent of sanctions, the United States has gone farther than any other country. There are a few things that set the U.S. practice of restrictive measures apart.

First. The U.S. sanction policy relies on instrumental and ideological foundations. Instrumentally, it is designed to achieve specific foreign policy goals ranging from coercing a country to change its political course to blocking supplies of critical resources or technology to a target country. Sanctions are a cheaper and less risky way of exerting pressure compared with the use of military force, but they can be

---

[17] Ex., Brzoska [5].

[18] Ex., Hufbauer et al. [6].

quite damaging.[19] Additionally, they can be combined with the use of force whenever needed.

Sanctions have been used by many countries for many centuries now, but the U.S. model is somewhat different. Along with the pragmatic goals of coercing and deterring, U.S. sanctions have a regulatory (ideological) background. The concepts of democracy and human rights underlie the legitimization of many sanction programs. Accordingly, changing the political regime in the target country in the interest of democracy and supporting democratically minded opposition or protecting human rights is major ideological goals in addition to purely foreign policy goals.

The United States is positioning itself as a leader of the free world and is making its sanctions policy part of this arrangement. Promoting democracy is a priority in the U.S. foreign policy, and sanctions are one of the tools used to achieve this goal. One may agree or disagree with this statement. However, it is important to know that this is more than a front to achieve pragmatic goals for Americans. Ideology is an independent factor in their decision-making. Often, it is based on pragmatic goals but is occasionally fairly independent, especially in regard to the use of sanctions by the U.S. Congress. This means that achieving a diplomatic compromise on a particular issue with the United States can be subject to adjustment (if not devaluation) based on ideological principles.

Second. U.S. sanctions have taken on a global nature. The American leadership in the global financial system allows it to use sanctions far beyond the United States. Using the U.S. dollar for international payments opens up numerous opportunities for businesses around the world. Many third countries carry out international payments in dollars, and these transactions go through the U.S. banks' correspondent accounts. Accordingly, U.S. regulators receive information about these payments and may impose restrictions on them if they involve sanctioned countries, individuals or organizations.

Americans loosely interpret the concept of national jurisdiction and apply it to regions beyond their country's borders. For example, it encompasses the U.S. financial system with its global reach. The United States is the only country in the world that uses extraterritorial restrictions in the form of blocking or imposing fines on foreign individuals or companies that have broken the U.S. sanction regimes. In theory, foreign companies may be protected from the U.S. regulators by their respective national laws. In practice, it will translate into major costs in the form of "excommunication" from the U.S. market and, most importantly, international payments.

Today, any major bank, regardless of nationality, conducts international transactions in compliance with U.S. laws in all matters related to sanctions. In other words, U.S. role in the global economy makes it possible for it to create situations where its restrictive measures can affect both U.S. citizens and third-country nationals.[20]

---

[19] Ex., Hatipoglu and Peksen [7].

[20] Ex., Restrepo Amariles and Winkler [8].

Third. The United States has a large, well-organized and professional sanction apparatus. It is operated by several departments: the Treasury Department, the Department of Commerce and the State Department.[21] They work in close contact with the National Intelligence and the Department of Justice since criminal prosecution for violating sanctions is fairly common. The United States is far ahead of other countries and international organizations in terms of its sanction policies, as they apply to the scope, quantity and quality of human resources, as well as financial and logistical support. The legal framework for imposing restrictive measures has been put in place. The U.S. approach stands apart by its thoroughly formalized use of sanctions and a transparent inclusion of existing approaches and practices in the national law. Congress plays an active and independent part in this, making occasional and major adjustments to the executive branch's actions. The judiciary has a wealth of practical experience working with various aspects of sanctions. The analytical support also seems to be the strongest both at the level of academic research and numerous think tanks.

The research papers widely cover the sanctions' effectiveness. A view that many restrictive measures are ineffective is fairly common because they often do not result in the sought-after change in the political course of the target country or its political regime. Moreover, sanctions can produce diametrically opposite results. The political regime may well become consolidated, and economic support (explicit or clandestine) may come from the "black knights," that is, other large countries that provide assistance for political reasons or in an attempt to profit from the situation.

There is another angle to it, though. Regardless of the "black knights," sanctions cause actual harm to the target country in one way or another. Their effect builds up over time. It is multiplied by other factors, such as adverse economic circumstances. Target countries can resist U.S. pressure for years. However, it is a whole different story for international business. Faced with fines or other measures taken by the U.S. government, companies and banks try not to repeat violations and avoid sanctions risks. Paradoxically, even in countries under sanctions, megafirms avoid violating U.S. sanction regimes, especially if it is involved in international projects or operates on the U.S. market.[22]

In other words, the United States remains the world leader in terms of the frequent use and effectiveness of sanctions. The future of U.S. hegemony in this area will depend on the policies of other major players, such as the EU, China and Russia.

---

[21] Report to the Committee on Foreign Affairs, House of Representatives: Economic Sanctions. Treasury and State Have Received Increased Resources for Sanctions Implementation but Face Hiring Challenges. United States Government Accountability Office. March, 2020. URL: https://www.gao.gov/assets/710/705265.pdf.

[22] Ex., Timofeev [9].

European Union: Sanctions as an Alternative to Diplomacy and Weapons

Sanctions are almost an ideal foreign policy tool for the EU. The EU is now mature enough to pursue a consolidated and vigorous foreign policy. Soft power in the form of an attractive EU integration and partnership with the EU is no longer enough to support this level of development. Brussels' foreign policy toolkit is in need of effective enforcement mechanisms. Otherwise, its policy will be seen as mere recommendations by other countries and boil down to declarations and good intentions. However, the EU has not yet attained the capabilities of sovereign states in terms of creating its own armed forces and other hard power tools. The discussion revolving around the creation of the "European army" has been ongoing for several decades now. Currently, NATO remains the mainstay of Euro-Atlantic security, and the EU is acting as its junior partner. In addition, the EU has several major military powers among its members that are unlikely to be willing to part with their sovereignty in matters of security.

In a situation where the EU is now capable of conducting an active foreign policy but has not yet become a major military player, sanctions have become an important foreign policy tool for several reasons.

First, the EU has a powerful and diversified economy. Economic power makes it possible to use sanctions. The greater the economic weight and the role of the initiator of sanctions in the global economy, the more significant the damage to the target country will be if trade or financial restrictions are introduced.

Second, sanctions are much cheaper than military forces, with fewer costs that are inconvenient for public politicians in democratic societies. In the event of hostilities, the costs are quite specific and come in the form of losses in blood and treasure, let alone the moral side of the matter. In the case of sanctions, losses for the initiating countries are much more difficult to spot, and public opinion is less sensitive to them.

Third, sanctions are easier to approve as a consolidated political decision, especially in regard to preventive or warning measures with a minimal economic effect.

Fourth, sanctions are a convenient tool for coordinating the EU and U.S. policies. Their restrictive measures may differ, but they are symbolically important for Euro-Atlantic unity.

Fifth, sanctions are important for domestic purposes. When diplomacy fails and there is no military might, sanctions can be used to show that at least something is being done to deal with problems.

EU sanctions are imposed in more than 30 countries and sectors. Brussels is doing a good job duplicating UN sanctions and is imposing its own unilateral measures, such as restrictions on Russia for Crimea and Donbass. However, Brussels has run into two problems.

Problem No. 1: implementing the sanctions. The member countries' governments are in charge of imposing them. They can do this at various speeds and with varying efficiency and take their national interests into account while doing so. The European bureaucracy does not yet have a tool that is comparable to the corresponding departments in charge of the U.S. sanction policy in terms of power, staffing and financial capabilities. Likewise, the EU does not have similar global financial intelligence or transaction tracking tools because the euro's international role cannot yet be compared with the role of the U.S. dollar. In other words, the EU is thus far unable to transform its economic power into political opportunities. It lacks single governance mechanisms, single tools to enforce restrictions and a role that can be compared to the United States in terms of global finance and access to financial information.

Problem No. 2: vulnerability to extraterritorial sanctions of third countries, primarily the United States. Washington is actively using extraterritorial measures against foreigners to force them into compliance with the U.S.-imposed regimes. In a number of areas, the U.S. and EU regimes overlap. However, they differ in regard to other aspects. Sanctions against Iran are a case in point. In 2018, the United States unilaterally withdrew from the Joint Comprehensive Plan of Action or the Iran nuclear deal. Secondary sanctions hit a large number of European companies that managed to return to Iran after the JCPOA was concluded. To protect its companies, Brussels renewed the 1996 blocking statute. However, the EU businesses chose to leave Iran en masse threatened by crippling fines imposed by U.S. regulators.

These fears were well founded. According to the Russian International Affairs Council (RIAC), as of June 2020, the U.S. Treasury imposed fines on 43 EU companies over the past 10 years for working in various jurisdictions under sanctions (deals with Iran are the most common occurrence). This is relatively few compared to 215 companies that were fined by the U.S. Treasury, of which 142 were U.S.-based. However, of the total amount of $5.657 billion worth of fines, Europeans paid $4.677 billion, or 82.39%. If you throw Swiss companies into the equation on the side of the EU, the asymmetry will be even greater at $5.321 billion out of $5.657 billion or 94% of the fines, while 142 companies and individuals from the United States account for only $182.35 million, or 3.26%.[23] This asymmetry is due to the European business's specifics (mainly, banks with their complex structure and a large number of transactions were hit by the sanctions), as well as the European business's belated response to the very threat of secondary sanctions.

Although measures employed by U.S. regulators have had their effect, and European businesses, especially banks, are now very alert to the U.S. legal provisions and prefer not to become involved in transactions that may lead to sanctions. Moreover, the EU courts are on the side of the banks. The lawsuit filed by Boris Rotenberg, who is under U.S. sanctions, is a case in point. As a citizen of Finland, he tried to challenge, in the Helsinki District Court, the actions of four European banks that refused to service his transactions because of the risk of sanctions. The court sided with the banks.[24] This situation calls into question EU sovereignty. It turns out that European companies were forced to comply with the U.S. sanction, and they do not find

---

[23] Timofeev [10].

[24] Ibid.

convincing the protection guarantees issued by the EU. We are talking about over-lapping sanctions imposed by the United States and the EU in the case of Rotenberg, which is not applicable to Iran.

The EU sanctions policy faces dilemmas of governance and sovereignty. Both dilemmas are recognized by EU leadership. They were included, for example, in a letter by European Commission President Ursula von der Leyen to Valdis Dombrovskis, the European Commissioner for Financial Stability, Financial Services and Capital Markets Union at the time. "To support our economic sovereignty, I want you to develop proposals to ensure Europe is more resilient to extraterritorial sanctions by third countries. I want you to ensure that the sanctions imposed by the EU are properly enforced, notably throughout its financial system." The President of the European Commission transferred a significant part of the authority to use sanctions and to protect against them to the EU financial authorities, while previously the corresponding unit (Unit FPI.5) was part of the Service for Foreign Policy Instruments. Most likely, Brussels will consolidate in its hands the sanction enforcement tools. However, protecting European businesses from the U.S. remains a big question. An equally big question is the transformation of European economic power into effective sanctions. At least until the euro takes a more prominent role in global finance.

China: Sanctions that "Cannot Be Named"

China is at the heart of the sanctions policy's suspense. There are several China-related trends.

First, China is becoming increasingly active in the international arena. Beijing has significantly improved its economic and technological capabilities, which has caused considerable concern in Washington. The attempts to restrain China's growth will include exerting pressure on the country, including via sanctions.

Second, China boasts impressive economic potential and can widely use its own restrictive measures. It can impose them to respond to anti-Chinese sanctions or to achieve individual goals.

Third, the Chinese economy's influence on the global economy is increasing. Economic and trade interdependence with the United States remains strong. Therefore, the entire world will feel the pinch if Beijing and Washington choose to exchange massive sanctions.

This is not the first time China has been targeted by Western sanctions. Although restrictions have been in force against it since the PRC was established in 1947, the United States had been gradually softening them starting in the late 1960s amid the differences between China and the Soviet Union. A new surge occurred following the 1989 political events. In the 1990s, the restrictions were softened again and remained in place only in the form of bans on weapons supplies and some dual-use products. The relevant U.S. departments do not have a separate sanctions program for China (to put this into perspective, there are at least three such programs for Russia). The number of Chinese individuals and companies on the U.S. sanction regulators' lists remains low.[25]

Nevertheless, more trouble is in the offing for China. First, Chinese telecom companies were the first to come under pressure. They were hit by secondary U.S. sanctions for delivering products containing U.S. parts to Iran. That was the case with ZTE, which ended up with huge fines that were paid to U.S. regulators and restrictions on future operations. The Huawei case was even more high profile. It also began with accusations of supplies to Iran and could well have ended in fines. However, the Trump administration opted for a tougher approach. Huawei was blacklisted by the Department of Commerce. Even though the regulator promptly issued a general license allowing U.S. companies to continue to deal with Huawei, the company found itself hanging. After all, a license can be cancelled at any point or simply not be renewed. To top it all, U.S. prosecutors brought charges against Huawei and its managers. They are charged not only with conspiracy to circumvent sanctions against Iran and the DPRK but also with attempted industrial espionage[26] (these accusations and claims against China have been heard for a long time at the level of rhetoric, publications and judicial trials).

The U.S.–China differences in the communications sector escalated fairly quickly. The first state of emergency that gave the U.S. president, the right to impose sanctions was declared on April 1, 2015 (Executive Order 13694)[27] in connection with the alleged theft of the U.S. citizens' personal data by Chinese hackers. However, the Barack Obama administration chose not to make a big deal out of it. Trump, on the other hand, adopted a more aggressive stance. His Executive Order 13873[28] introduced a state of emergency in connection with communications-related threats. Although China was not explicitly mentioned in the document, the executive order directly focused on the Huawei case. Washington also made significant diplomatic efforts in an attempt to convince its allies to sever business ties with Huawei and several other Chinese IT companies. In the United States, Congress banned government imports of equipment manufactured by this Chinese company under the National Defense Authorization Acts (in 2018 for defense departments and in 2019 for civilian departments). Problems have affected other firms as well. For example, the Committee on Foreign Investment in the United States (CFIUS) blocked several Chinese companies' or related firms' attempts to acquire U.S. businesses (in one case, Trump personally blocked the purchase of the U.S. semiconductor manufacturer Qualcomm upon the CFIUS recommendation). The year 2019 saw a series of

---

[25] See Footnote 23.

[26] Chinese Telecommunications Conglomerate Huawei and Subsidiaries Charged in Racketeering Conspiracy and Conspiracy to Steal Trade Secrets. U.S. Department of Justice. February 13, 2020. URL: https://www.justice.gov/opa/pr/chinese-telecommunications-conglomerate-huawei-and-sub sidiaries-charged-racketeering.

[27] Executive Order 13694 of April 1, 2015. URL: https://www.treasury.gov/resource-center/sancti ons/Programs/Documents/cyber_eo.pdf.

[28] Executive Order 13873 of May 15, 2019. URL: https://www.federalregister.gov/documents/ 2019/05/17/2019-10538/securing-the-information-and-communications-technology-and-services-supply-chain.

Post-COVID-19 Sanction Policies   249

bills banning Chinese-made unmanned aerial vehicles (drones). The administration is working on an executive order on this matter.[29]

At the same time, pressure on China grew in the human rights area, which could be seen from the sanctions imposed in the wake of the Hong Kong protests in 2019.[30] Although these restrictions can be considered token gestures, they may expand in the future. China became the first country to have targeted blocking sanctions for defense cooperation with Russia imposed on its organizations and citizens under the CAATSA.[31] These measures also applied to the bitter trade war between the United States and China.

The COVID-19 pandemic has significantly exacerbated the anti-China sentiments in the United States. The U.S. authorities and politicians openly blame China for spreading the virus. Bills regarding sanctions against China in connection with COVID-19 have made it to Congress.[32] The number of lawsuits against China is growing. The lawsuit filed by the state of Missouri was among the most notable and may be followed by other states. COVID-19 has aggravated the already complicated relations between Beijing and Washington.[33]

All this is forcing China to revise its sanctions policy. For a long time, unilateral measures have been used very selectively and carefully. Like Russia, China operates on the premise that the UN Security Council has priority in regard to imposing restrictive measures. However, as a major power with an extensive foreign policy agenda, it inevitably uses them.

In the event of a sharp escalation by the United States, China is capable of scaling up its response. For example, Beijing may restrict exports of rare earth metals or use its position as a major U.S. lender. However, both these steps will damage China and international markets alike. In all probability, China will fine-tune its sanction policy in the near future based on new political realities, technological capabilities for monitoring economic activity at home and abroad and its role in the global economy.

The U.S. dominance in the global financial system is China's greatest challenge. China will remain vulnerable to U.S. financial sanctions until it builds an alternative system or subsystem. However, this will require enormous resources, political will and time. The risk of mutual losses may, until a certain point, hold back the rivalry between Beijing and Washington and prevent radical sanctions against each other.

---

[29] Whittaker [13].

[30] Public Law 116–76—November 27, 2019. Authenticated U.S. Government Information. November 27, 2019. URL: https://www.congress.gov/116/plaws/publ76/PLAW-116publ76.pdf.

[31] CAATSA-Russia Related Designations. U.S. Department of Treasury. October 23, 2020. URL: https://home.treasury.gov/policy-issues/financial-sanctions/recent-actions/20201023.

[32] For example, A Bill to Require Imposition of Sanctions with Respect to Censorship and Related Activities Against Citizens of the People's Republic of China. U.S. Congress. URL: https://www.cruz.senate.gov/files/documents/Letters/ROS20262.pdf.

[33] The State of Missouri v. The People's Republic of China et al. U.S District Court for the Eastern District of Missouri Southeastern Division. April 21, 2020. URL: https://www.courtlistener.com/recap/gov.uscourts.moed.179929/gov.uscourts.moed.179929.1.0_1.pdf?fbclid=IwAR1QXlx-9ok dZDq_T-tbnzQtnAG_WkYSIPXGYbQEoU0rRcLx6vi-up8mKQdo.

Russia: "Sanctions from Hell" and Potential Counter-Sanctions

Russia has an unusual role to play in global sanction politics. On the one hand, the United States, the EU and several other countries imposed fairly tough sanctions on Russia after 2014. However, its own arsenal of sanctions and their practical use are still limited. Russia's economic potential cannot be compared to that of China. Russia needs to fine-tune its policy, maximize the use of its limited resources and be strong enough to be recognized internationally.

During almost the entire twentieth century, Russia was under foreign sanctions. The country found itself in the grips of a trade and technology blockade from the time the Soviet power was first established. The process was fairly uneven. The restrictions were relaxed when the initiators critically needed the markets (the Great Depression) or allies, such as during World War II. However, with the onset of the Cold War, sanctions made it back to the arsenal of relations with Russia. The Soviet Union had a single universal response to sanctions: developing its own industry, technology, workforce and modern economy. In many ways, this challenge was successfully overcome, including by way of limited cooperation with the West. At least, the Soviet Union collapsed when the economy opened up and sanctions were lifted, not during the blockade. The Soviet Union imposed restrictions as well but did so much less frequently than the United States.[34] It acted as a "black knight" much more willingly and supported the countries under Western sanctions.

Compared to the Soviet period, sanctions against Russia in the wake of the Ukraine crisis of 2014 were imposed in wholly different circumstances. The country remains closely integrated into the global economy and financial system. Self-reliance is possible and even desirable in several strategic sectors. However, a large-scale transition to using domestic resources is impossible today, plain and simple. Nevertheless, increasing competition in international relations will dictate such a need. The United States and China prioritize their domestic production in a number of critical industries, primarily information technology and communications and are doing their best to stop being dependent on each other. It appears that Russia will have to do the same and combine maximum reliance on its limited resources with maneuvering between the power centers or forging an alliance with one of them. This is a long-term perspective, but preparations must be made now, at least in the strategic sectors that are critical to national security.

Ironically, close integration into the international division of labor and globalization itself helped Russia alleviate the impact of the sanctions. The damage to the Russian economy caused by the sanctions remains the subject of fierce debate. It is difficult to estimate this damage as a separate factor that affects growth or stagnation.[35] Without a doubt, the sanctions caused some damage or exacerbated the impact of other negative factors, such as oil price fluctuations in 2014 and 2020.

---

[34] Ex., Hufbauer [6].

[35] Timofeev [10].

Post-COVID-19 Sanction Policies 251

However, another factor needs to be considered. Blocking sanctions have not been imposed (except once as of this writing) on critically important Russian energy or financial companies. Indeed, they have been subjected to a set of sector-specific restrictions in a narrow technology segment and lending. This complicates Russian companies' operations, especially since these measures are also damaging their reputation. However, these sectors were not subjected to blocking sanctions. That is, they continue their export–import operations with their foreign partners as usual.

As mentioned earlier, massive blocking sanctions were imposed only once, on April 6, 2018, when, under pressure from Congress and amid a scandal focusing on Russia's alleged interference in the 2016 U.S. elections, a number of major Russian companies (Rusal, En+, EuroSibEnergo and others), as well as a number of business-people from the earlier Kremlin list, came under sanctions.[36] However, the premature nature of such a step was clear, since a number of blocked firms were closely integrated with the global economy and were systemic global companies. Later, some of them saw the sanctions lifted (conditional on ownership restructuring,[37] while others have been issued general licenses that allow them to conduct international activities, even though they are left hanging in the air.

In other words, the "sanctions from hell" are unlikely to be imposed in the future without a truly important reason. In this regard, Russia and China benefit from integration with the global economy. However, in the long run, this interdependence does not make them sanction risk-free. Restrictions may be imposed gradually and take time. Therefore, adaptation to them will be needed in any case.

The new international reality will inevitably make Russia think about using restrictive measures in its foreign policy arsenal. Moscow has long been reluctant to initiate sanctions. It followed a similar model to China. Russia adheres to the principle of supremacy of the UN Security Council in regard to making decisions about imposing restrictive measures. It used sanctions indirectly by way of imposing market restrictions (for example, for Georgian-made products after the 2008 conflict) or enforcing sanitary standards. Russian countersanctions imposed after 2014 were proportionate and, as a rule, came as a response to the restrictions imposed on the country. Basically, they came down to restricting market access (for example, the well-known food embargo). There are not so many retaliatory measures in Russia's arsenal due to the relative—compared to the United States or the EU—economic weakness. However, in narrow segments, Russia's restrictions are still biting. The same applies to restrictions imposed on certain countries in the post-Soviet space, primarily Ukraine.

Moscow believes that going too far with retaliatory measures is not a good choice, as it may be bad for its economy and quality of life. The federal law of July 4, 2018

---

[36] Ukraine/Russia-related Designations and Identification Update. U.S. Treasury. 2018. URL: https://www.treasury.gov/resource-center/sanctions/OFAC-Enforcement/Pages/20180406.aspx.

[37] OFAC Delists En+, Rusal, and EuroSibEnergo. U.S. Treasury. 2019. URL: https://home.treasury.gov/news/press-releases/sm592.

(No. 127-FZ)[38] passed the initiative to impose sanctions on the President and the executive branch, giving them some leeway depending on the situation. The Russian authorities were in no hurry to amend the Criminal Code and include in it criminal prosecution for compliance with the Western-imposed sanctions.[39] However, they adopted a series of measures in the event of a financial blockade: they created the Mir national payment system, the system for transmitting the Bank of Russia's financial messages and diversified national currency reserves.

Strictly speaking, Russia's full-fledged sanctions mechanism is still in the making. Until 2014, it was mainly based on the Federal Law No. 281-FZ on Special Economic Measures and Coercive Measures of December 30, 2006.[40] New circumstances called for new mechanisms. In particular, the External Restrictions Control Department was established at the Finance Ministry and has already done a great job systematizing restrictive measures.

Russia is only beginning to create a full-fledged sanctions policy mechanism. A number of steps will have to be taken to improve it. One of the most important ones is to develop legislative practice regarding sanctions in both houses of the Russian parliament. To do so, a major training effort will need to be deployed at the State Duma and the Federation Council.

At the level of the executive branch, it will be necessary to make the Finance Ministry's achievements available to other departments and create at least some basic bodies to deal with the sanctions issue. Similar small groups (at the level of directorates or departments) should be set up at the Foreign Ministry, the Ministry of Economic Development and the Ministry of Industry and Trade.

Russia needs to expand its law enforcement practice and the national sanction compliance mechanism at the level of administrative law and criminal law. Here, it will be necessary to find the middle ground between the need to effectively apply existing standards and to maintain a favorable investment climate. These tools cannot be turned into arbitrary reprisals at the discretion of the executors, but their absence devalues the restrictions regimes.

The Russian doctrine of using sanctions remains an open question. When should we impose them and against whom? How should we coordinate our actions with our allies and partners? This doctrine could be included, for example, in Russia's Foreign Policy Concept.

Finally, an extensive training and research base is needed, without which one can hardly count on adequate expertise and professional workforce that are so badly needed in Russia's foreign policy.

---

[38] Federal law of June 4, 2018 No.127-FZ. Rossiyskaya Gazeta. June 6, 2018. URL: https://rg.ru/2018/06/06/kontrsankcii-dok.html.

[39] Draft law No. 464757-7, 2018. State Duma of the Russian Federation. URL: http://asozd2c.duma.gov.ru/main.nsf/(Spravka)?OpenAgent&RN=464757-7.

[40] Federal law of December 30, 2006 No. 281-FZ. Garant Database. URL: http://base.garant.ru/12151317/.

In Place of a Conclusion. Indicator of Change

The policy of sanctions is a dramatic indicator of change in the "crumbling" modern world. National egotism, the pursuit of one's own interests and survival in the face of external pressure, has become one of the key behavior standards. UN-based global governance tools, on the contrary, are being eroded. "National" models of sanction policies are being formed.

However, it is premature to talk about sliding into "anarchy" or "war of all against all" as an irreversible process. Even the most powerful initiators of sanctions want their decisions to be legitimized by the UN Security Council. At the very least, they are trying to combine their actions with the decisions of the key global governance institution.

The interdependence and globalization of the modern world have come thus far that a sharp escalation of sanctions will entail grave consequences for both the initiating countries and the target countries. There will be a price to pay both in the case of escalation between large economies such as the United States and China and in the case of radical measures taken against Russia with its relatively small input in the global economy.

The signs of "securitization" of the economy, the attempts to become self-reliant and move away from globalization in some strategic areas can be seen already today. The question is how far this autonomy can go. How far are major powers ready to go in their competition? What is the limit of their sensitivity to economic losses as they attempt to achieve political goals or considerations of prestige? The policy of sanctions is just one side of global processes. History knows many instances when political will prevailed over economic reasons. These were the times of extremes and great losses.[41]

References

1. Blanc, J. 2020. *Coercion in the Time of the Coronavirus*. Carnegie Endowment for International Peace. https://carnegieendowment.org/2020/04/08/coercion-in-time-of-coronavirus-pub-81495
2. Barabanov, O., T. Bordachev, Y. Lissovolik, F. Luk'yanov, A. Sushentsov, and I. Timofeev. 2018. *Living in a Crumbling World Annual Report*. Valdai International Discussion Club. https://valdaiclub.com/a/reports/living-in-a-crumbling-world/
3. Giumelli, F. 2016. The purposes of targeted sanctions'. In *Targeted Sanctions. The Impacts and Effectiveness of United Nations Action*, eds. Beirsteker, T., S. Eckert, and M. Tourihno, 38–59. New York: Cambridge University Press.
4. Drezner, D. 2015. Targeted sanctions in a world of global finance. *International Interactions* 41: 755–764.
5. Brzoska, M. 2015. International sanctions before and beyond UN sanctions. *International Affairs* 91 (6): 1339–1349.

---

[41] First published by the Valdai Discussion Club. URL: https://valdaiclub.com/a/reports/post-covid-19-sanctions-policies/.

6. Hufbauer, G., J. Shott, K. Elliott, and B. Oegg. 2009. *Economic Sanctions Reconsidered*, 3rd ed. Washington DC: Peterson Institute for International Economics.
7. Hatipoglu, E., and D. Peksen. 2018. Economic sanctions and banking crises in target economies. *Defense and Peace Economics* 29 (2): 171–189.
8. Restrepo Amariles, D., and M. Winkler. 2018. U.S. Economic sanctions and the corporate compliance of foreign banks. *International Lawyer* 51 (3): 497–535.
9. Timofeev, I. 2020. Why are secondary sanctions effective? The experience of coercive measures by US authorities against US and foreign businesses. *International Trends* 3 (17): 21–35.
10. Timofeev, I. 2020. "European paradox": US sanctions policy toward EU businesses. *Contemporary Europe* 2.
11. Timofeev, I. *Asia Under Fire of US Sanctions*. Valdai International Discussion Club. https://valdaiclub.com/a/reports/asia-under-fire-of-us-sanctions/
12. Timofeev, I. 2018. *Sanctions on Russia: Escalation Trends and Counter Policies*. Russian International Affairs Council.
13. Whittaker, Z. 2020. *U.S. is Preparing to Ban Foreign-Made Drones form Government Use*. TC. https://techcrunch.com/2020/03/11/us-order-foreign-drones/

A World Crowned with "Corona": Path to Increased Cooperation or Isolation?

Natalia Romashkina

Information that Went Unnoticed

The unprecedented turn of events in the wake of the COVID-19 pandemic in 2020 has clearly demonstrated how poorly international and national mechanisms of governance and control, healthcare systems and economies were equipped to deal with pandemics. Warnings about it have repeatedly been voiced since the early days of the twenty-first century. Leading international biology and medical journals, such as *Nature*, *Nature Medicine*, *Cell*, *PNAS* and *PLOS Pathogens*, were publishing articles about the high probability of dangerous new viruses infecting humans through animals (zoonotic infections), primarily bats. Recently, these articles were interpreted in different ways and used for political purposes or in conspiracy theories. Therefore, the risk of spillover to humans could trigger a disease similar to SARS. This is why *scientists believe* we should continue to monitor the evolution of SARSr-CoV, assessing the risks of contracting such an infection. A strategy needs to be developed to prevent future disease occurrence.[1] "The constant spillover of viruses from natural hosts to humans and other animals is largely due to human activities, including modern agricultural practices and urbanization." Therefore, the most effective way to prevent viral zoonosis, as is argued by the authors of the *article* "Origin and Evolution of Pathogenic Coronaviruses," is to maintain the barriers between natural reservoirs and human society, being mindful of the 'one health' concept" (a practice that would lead to an optimal quality of life for both humans and animals).[2] In 2007, another group of scientists *warned*, "Coronaviruses are well known to undergo genetic recombination, which may lead to new genotypes and outbreaks."[3] However,

---

N. Romashkina (✉)
Russian International Affairs Council, Moscow, Russia

[1] Ibid.

[2] Cui et al. [1].

[3] Cheng et al. [2].

© China Social Sciences Press 2023
Institute of Russian, Eastern European and Central Asian Studies, CASS and Russian International Affairs Council, *Global Governance in the New Era*,
https://doi.org/10.1007/978-981-19-4332-4_20

this information went unnoticed by international and national organizations, with no preventative measures ever taken.

Even so, the likelihood of new viruses spilling over into the human population via animals continues to grow amid globalization, which has slowed down but will still increase in the years to come, albeit at a lesser pace. In addition to the more obvious dangers arising as a result of increasing economic, political and cultural ties between countries, another important condition that facilitates the emergence and spillover of new zoonotic diseases is the growing interest in tourism to exotic places, primarily to the so-called ecotourism to unusual and remote destinations, which brings humans into closer contact with wildlife. This mostly concerns Asia and Africa. Another dangerous trend that has been visible in recent years is the interest in owning exotic pets, which has led to an increase in supply from these markets as well as to a disregard for minimal sanitary norms. *Scientists have proven* that keeping wild animals as pets in conditions that are extreme and stressful for them leads to an increase in the number of viruses in their bodies.

All of this has led to profound social, psychological, economic and political consequences, and their scope will continue to grow. This accounts for the need for new approaches to expanding international scientific cooperation in biology and medicine, which until recently has mainly been carried out within the framework of the WHO, as well as in other areas. The situation is particularly troubling in countries that lack scientific potential and where the likelihood of new zoonotic infections persistently grows.

Since the threat is global, a special international legal framework for dealing with dangerous viruses should be devised to include a body of principles, norms, rules and decision-making processes that could help reduce the risk of such situations being used for malicious political purposes, serving to withstand the temptation to exploit instability to further economic interests. The rationale behind such a regime should be the realization that all countries, without exception, are vulnerable to such threats, which was clearly demonstrated during the COVID-19 pandemic. At the same time, the regime will surely be of value to its participants, since the benefits of long-term cooperation override the benefits of unilateral actions.

Information Security Threats in a World with a New Corona

The coronavirus pandemic has drawn attention to a number of information security threats that require immediate action.

Additionally, worthy of mention is the issue of global information security, which has received almost no attention although we are bombarded with information every day. This issue includes the lack of access to data and knowledge regarding basic hygiene and scientific studies in the fields of biology, virology, medicine, etc. This led to much confusion during the outbreak of the pandemic, both on the part of government institutions and on the part of the population, being the source of aggravating social, psychological, economic and political repercussions.

The pandemic has thus forced us all to try and fill the holes in our knowledge about human hygiene as well as in other important areas. International and national organizations need to step up to popularize science and remedy this lack of scientific understanding among the population. One solution could be to develop a fundamentally new policy regarding the openness and availability of information about scientific research conducted in different countries around the world, seeing how it can be used in crises. In the past, this issue was typically resolved at the state level and rather passively at that level. Now, we need to jumpstart the process, use all the available tools to accelerate mobilization and make use of scientific findings, including modern methods of storing, analyzing and transmitting information. Therefore, it may be worth creating a special international system for data collection within the framework of the new international regime that would be stored in special UN virtual archives. Regime theory suggests that countries would be motivated to submit such information with the hope of obtaining various benefits—not only in the case of emergencies but also, more importantly, to prevent them. However, the success of this endeavor will largely rest on the quantity and quality of the information gathered, as well as on the professionalism of the researchers. Should modern and impartial methods of quantitative analysis, coupled with sufficient and relevant data, be used, the project should bear fruit.

In this context, there is another challenge related to information security. It has to do with the ineffective methods of analyzing textual information, especially in comparison with the processing of structured numerical data. The type and structure of the data provided should be unified and well considered. Additionally, politics should be kept out of the process. However, this is difficult to achieve. The only way to obtain objective results is, therefore, through high-performance analytics of a whole new level, particularly with the use of artificial intelligence, which includes unstructured text information in the analysis. Thus, the ability to extract useful information from unstructured textual information may be a key challenge in the prospective UN regime.

An additional instrument that could be used for text analytics is scientific analysis, correlating and comparing data with information discussed at international and national conferences, as well as at events held by institutes and organizations. This will bring real concerns and pressing issues to the table, ones which may not be expressed in the information officially provided to the UN. Currently, artificial intelligence—in particular, machine learning—can be used to offer solutions for such issues. These are technologies for obtaining information from an unstructured source text by converting it into a set of structured data in a machine-friendly format. Typically, such methods include parsing, linguistic analysis, categorization, clustering, concept (entity) extraction, modeling relationships between entities, thematic indexing, content analysis, word frequency distribution analysis, annotation, etc. T The results should be interpreted using data mining techniques. Such information and communication technologies (ICT) are now widely used in business, science, government, security and intelligence systems.

The accelerated digital transformation of international institutions, governments, vital segments of the economy, and educational, scientific, cultural and even religious organizations has brought up a whole range of new ICT threats. The number of cyber-attacks on international organizations, government and business structures, medical facilities and online educational services during the pandemic grew exponentially. A new term, *"cyber pandemic,"* has appeared.[4] This refers to hacking, cybercrime, terrorism, interference in the internal affairs of countries and the personal lives of their citizens as well as the malicious brainwashing of people via the Internet during COVID-19.

Although these threats existed well before the pandemic, malicious use of ICT for political and criminal purposes has grown sharply during the pandemic, exacerbating all other issues of information security. Since industrial production capabilities, information technologies and the Internet of Things are closely intertwined, the competitiveness index and ICT development index of states are closely linked. Thus, the growing list of global information security threats can lead to a serious confrontation between countries in the global digital space.

As a result of the relatively low cost of malicious ICT, more countries are having access to modern instruments for cyberattacks. This opens the door to destabilization globally. In this scenario, growing isolation seems inevitable against the backdrop of increasing political confrontation and limited international cooperation during pandemics.

Threats that existed before the pandemic are becoming more dangerous, as is the case of the increased likelihood of ICT attacks on critical state infrastructure—systems and tools that play a pivotal role in the functioning of a country and whose disruption or destruction can pose a threat to national security. Even if these facilities are not directly connected to the Internet, the automated process control system (APCS) devices used for remote monitoring over secure communication lines can be hacked as a result of attacks on other facilities where the APCS operate. Isolation of the network from external systems, which was considered an effective safety measure 10–15 years ago, no longer serves the purpose. It is now seen as both costly and difficult to implement. Therefore, the threat of a large-scale complex attack on critical infrastructure is more real than ever, and the risk continues to grow rapidly. For example, there were over *one billion* attempted cyberattacks on Russian critical information infrastructure facilities in the first six months of 2020.[5] Given the unique characteristics of the ICT environment, challenges in identifying the source of the attack, the general lack of international norms in the information space and limited international communication and cooperation, a serious cyber-attack on any critical infrastructure can have global consequences. Thus, new technologies can provoke an interstate military conflict, and cyber and information wars between countries are no less destructive than traditional ones. Consequently, it is as important as ever to ensure international information security by further developing the principles and

---

[4] Virus Cyber Pandemic: Acceleration or Oblivion? Valdai Club. April 7, 2020. URL: https://valdaiclub.com/events/posts/articles/virus-cyber-pandemic-acceleration-or-oblivion/?sphrase_id=791839.

[5] The Russian Foreign Ministry recorded more than 1 billion cyberattacks on digital objects in 2020. TASS. June 29, 2020. URL: https://tass.ru/politika/8838577.

A World Crowned with "Corona": Path to Increased Cooperation ... 259

norms of conduct in the ICT environment, which Russia has been advocating for over 20 years in the UN.

Newly emerging threats underline the interconnection of biosafety, information security and international security, which is why the UN in general and the Security Council in particular need to step up their work, which is particularly relevant in the case of international cooperation.

What Should Be Done?

1. An analysis of these and other modern trends leads us to the conclusion that international cooperation in biosafety and global security—as well as in preventing future pandemics and their consequences—needs to be strengthened. The novel virus also sheds light on the need to reform the World Health Organization. However, considering the fact that the situation caused by COVID-19 was largely unprecedented and a unique event in human history, this will probably not be enough. New cooperation formats are necessary to reduce biosafety threats:

   (1) International centers for monitoring and analyzing scientific information to forecast new, potential zoonotic infections and inform the relevant government agencies and decision-makers.
   (2) Government and international support for the development of vaccines to combat new strains of potentially dangerous viruses found in exotic animals, even before their spillover to the human population (with the aim of accelerating their development or altering them in the event of a new epidemic, as in the case of influenza vaccines), and for the development of antiviral drugs.
   (3) International centers for educating and building awareness among the public.
   (4) International monitoring of exotic animals (including but not limited to bats) to assess the risk of new, dangerous virus strands emerging, including coronaviruses.
   (5) Additional international measures aimed at clamping down on illegal exotic animal trade.
   (6) Additional international measures aimed at ensuring sanitary control at trade and food service spots in exotic countries.

   These measures can be applied both at the bilateral level and at the level of existing or specially created international organizations. However, given the global scale of the threat, it is logical to consider creating a special international legal regime for dangerous viruses that would include a body of principles, norms, rules and decision-making processes. The rationale behind the creation of such a regime should be the realization that all countries, without exception, are vulnerable to such threats, which was clearly demonstrated during the COVID-19 pandemic. At the same time, the regime will surely be of value to its participants, since the benefits of long-term cooperation override the benefits of unilateral actions.

Thus, to maintain and further develop global economic, political and sociocultural cooperation between countries, a certain level of security needs to be provided, and consequently, various principles and rules need to be established. Countries with exotic flora and fauna, where the risk of zoonotic infections emerging is particularly high, will take an interest in abiding by certain rules and regulations when using their resources to generate economic benefit, such as in the case of ecotourism. As a seasoned participant in the creation and functioning of international legal regimes, Russia can adopt a proactive stance in this process.

2. The creation of a special UN structure would bring together specialists from around the globe to study the possible effects of the COVID-19 pandemic on health care, economics and politics to eliminate the most significant shortcomings and single out possible new negative consequences. This work could lead to the creation of a timetable ("road map") and an overall strategy for ensuring global security, indicating the amount of resources required to counter such threats and risks. All components of this strategy need to be explored, from prevention and protection to crisis management to remediation.

3. Given the different approaches to healthcare and biosafety standards, it would be a good idea to develop a common understanding of necessary and sufficient measures to be taken in the case of another coronavirus pandemic and the emergence of new zoonotic infections in the human population. This includes the development of a set of criteria and protocols for announcing and canceling global quarantine measures linked to zoonotic infections. Making common understanding among all countries public would serve as both an important step in ensuring global security and a critical ingredient for confidence-building measures at the international level. The first step could be a comparative scientific analysis of the legislation in different countries in the relevant areas.

4. Expanding cooperation within the G20 in the prevention of and protection against infectious zoonotic diseases.

5. Analyzing whether existing international regulatory documents include new threats to biological and global security to improve prevention and protection measures against zoonotic infections, management and control in crises and post-crisis recovery.

6. Expanding international cooperation between educational and research organizations in the relevant fields. Keeping government agencies in the loop by presenting the results of such cooperation to launch projects aimed at ensuring biological, economic, informational and global security using recent advances in modern biotechnology.

7. Developing international measures to control infectious zoonotic diseases occurring both naturally and due to the deliberate use of pathogens. The first step in this direction could be the study and harmonization of international standards and procedures for rapid notification in the event of a disease. Additionally, cooperation between health organizations needs to be expanded to exchange knowledge and experience and develop methods for monitoring symptoms and diagnoses that may point to an outbreak. These measures can form the foundation of a new

A World Crowned with "Corona": Path to Increased Cooperation … 261

international system for standardizing the detection and diagnosis of zoonotic infections using the latest scientific and technological capabilities.

8. Achieving a common understanding of information security issues within the new UN structure to prevent zoonotic pandemics. This work should seek to overcome the lack of scientific information available to the wider population, which was clearly demonstrated in the case of COVID-19, as well as boost the efforts of international and state institutions to popularize science. The principal goal should be to prevent global social, economic and political threats caused by the harmful use of ICT during the crisis. Thus, the most crucial task of the new UN structure should be to develop a system for information sharing within the international community in such conditions.

These steps could serve as the foundation for a new international legal regime for dangerous viruses, particularly zoonotic infections, including a body of principles, norms, rules and decision-making processes. They could also lead to the creation of a more sustainable global security system, the need for which was proven by the unprecedented events of 2020.

References

1. Cui, J., F. Li, and Z.L. Shi. 2018. Origin and evolution of pathogenic coronaviruses. *Nature Reviews Microbiology.* https://doi.org/10.1038/s41579-018-0118-9
2. Cheng, V.C.C., Susanna K.P. Lau, Patrick C.Y. Woo, and Kwok Yung Yuen. 2020. Severe acute respiratory syndrome coronavirus as an agent of emerging and reemerging infection. *Clinical Microbiology Reviews.* https://doi.org/10.1128/CMR.00023-07